Jumping

Joan

Joan Brooks

D1042420

MESQUITE PRESS

Jumping Joan

For information, contact:

Mesquite Press
393 Caspian Way
Imperial Beach, California 91932

ISBN 978-0-9656521-5-5

Cover photo by Jan Daniel
Book design and layout by Robert Goodman, Silvercat™, San Diego, California

printed in the United States of America

As soon as you trust yourself,

you will know how to live.

➤ Goethe

CONTENTS

PROLOGUE

I was five years old and in the first grade at Hillside Avenue Public School in Hillside, New Jersey, and our class was putting on a Mother Goose pageant. I was chosen to be "Little Jumping Joan," based on one of the poems in *Mother Goose Nursery Rhymes*. My mother made me a pretty blue and white checkered gingham dress and I took my jump rope to school, proud to be included in the pageant even though with a very minor role. I got up on the stage, reciting my little piece and trying to jump rope at the same time, and I exclaimed: "Here am I, Little Jumping Joan, when nobody's with me, I'm always alone." *Is this a preview of my future? Am I always alone? During the course of these memoirs perhaps I will find out.*

CHAPTER 1

HOME

For years when I thought of "home" for some strange reason which I am still working on, I always pictured 65 Williamson Avenue in Hillside, New Jersey as the place called "home." Hillside was once a farming area called Lyons Farms sandwiched between the large cities of Newark and Elizabeth. Later it became a bedroom community for those two cities. I lived there from birth in 1925 until I was six years old and just finished first grade. (I did move back there for a year when in third grade, but things were never the same then.) Still I often think of it with longing and a desperate loyalty. *Recently in October of 2000 I took my younger brother Herb to see the home where he had been a baby but he had no recollections of it. I had left it when I was eight years old, but still remembered exactly how to get there from any angle, as I used to roller skate to school, up Williamson Avenue to Munn and then on to Hillside Avenue School. Actually I wanted to visit the house myself to see if it were real. The two-door entrance was changed to a single front door and the "stoop" had been rebuilt, but it basically looked the same. The slate sidewalks were still there. The huge linden tree was gone. The neighborhood looked the same, if somewhat more prosperous than when we lived there. Gone, however were the grape arbor, the chicken house and chicken run. It looked like a typical middle class family home. I would love to have been there when the residents were home— just to take a peak at the rooms—the layout, the stairs, the attic and the cellar. But I did realize that "you can't go home again"*

My grandfather, Leo Severynse, a carpenter and a retired letter carrier for the U.S. Post Office, built the house. His constant walking the city streets with a heavy leather mailbag probably contributed to his slender athletic appearance. We all called him "Pop." Pop was born in Holland but immigrated to the U.S. as a baby. I never knew my maternal grandmother, Anna Van Bergen, who was part Dutch and part German. My Aunt Mildred once told me that she was descended from a German Lutheran Bishop but probably converted to Catholicism to marry Pop. She died four years before I was born, probably of the tuberculosis that was to haunt the entire family. Most of my maternal relatives lived in Long Island and Brooklyn where Pop once lived. Pop often spoke of walking over the Brooklyn Bridge. One relative, Bernard Diener, was my godfather but I don't remember him.

The two-story house had two front doors. That made us all very happy when free samples were left, as we would get two of everything. One door led to our formal parlor but we used the main door that opened on the dining room which served as the modern-day family room for eating dinner, doing homework, and playing games with my family on the large oak table. A treasured item was Robert Louis Stevenson's *Child's Garden of Verses* which Pop used to teach me how to read at an early age. An etching of the Statue of Liberty hung on the wall near the parlor. A closet held our coats and some of our toys. A large three-part bookcase had one drawer at the bottom, for my toys. I named it the Peapack drawer (the name of a town in New Jersey that I had heard in conversation.) *On my trip in the summer of 2010 to visit my brother Herb, I drove through some small towns in New Jersey. When I saw the sign for Peapack, I decided to drive through it. It seemed to be pretty much an upper class town, very neat and cared for. As I was leaving town I noticed a police car stopping at a police garage, so I asked him for directions back to the highway. Then I inquired about how Peapack got its name. He told me it came from an old Lenape Indian name that meant "where the rivers meet" or "the marriage of the waters." I took a photo of the Peapack train station, finally content that my long time curiosity was put to rest.*

A pair of solid oak sliding doors led to our formal parlor with its decorative fireplace and mantle above it with porcelain figures of Martha and George Washington. It also held a new crystal set radio where we listened to *Amos and Andy, Chandu the Magician*, the M___ Brothers, Lowell Thomas, *Death Valley Days* and other programs of the golden age of radio. *Little did I know that many years later I would be desperately looking for some recordings of the "Death Valley Days" radio programs as I was writing my book, "Desert Padre."*

Our large Victrola stood in the corner where we could play old records, such as John McCormack's Irish songs and popular tunes of the day. Next to it was an upright piano which my Aunt Mildred played from sheet music and which my Dad could play by ear. My brother Bob tells me that the radio, Victrola and piano were all gifts of Pop's New York relatives who were a little better off than we were. The parlor also served as a place for the Christmas tree, visiting relatives from Brooklyn, such as Pop's brother, Uncle Willie (a truck driver) and his wife Bella. We loved to hear Uncle Willie say things like: "Well, ya toin down Toity Toid Street, keep goin' til ya hit Foist Street, then ya come ta Moitle Avenue." We would plead: "Say something, Uncle Willie."

The kitchen was very large with an attached unheated pantry. The stairs led to the cellar, and steps to a door to the backyard. Here, mother along with her sister, my Aunt Mildred, did the cooking on the old iron stove, and did other household chores such as ironing, canning, sewing and sorting laundry while we would often play in the kitchen. Here too, mother changed baby Herbert's diapers and kept her eye on my older brother Bob and me when we were home. *More on this later.*

I remember my great love of peanut butter and the shock I received one day when I climbed to the top shelf of the kitchen cabinet and stuck my finger in the jar. What a surprise when I discovered it wasn't peanut butter but mustard! I used to stick my finger in the sugar bowl and after my finger was wet from licking, happy that I got even more on the second dip. Sugar and butter sandwiches were a favorite school lunch. Once when we had creamed codfish, which I didn't like, I was told I would have to sit there until I finished it. As my parents left the room and no one was looking, I dumped the awful codfish on my plate back into the pot on the stove and exclaimed: "I'm finished!" I remember we had to take cod liver oil in orange juice and then eggnogs. *Supposedly these were to prevent colds, but now I guess they may have been to build us up to fight the tuberculosis germ that, unknown to me, was so prevalent in our home.*

The kitchen was where I remember Pop holding me and telling me I had "Irish blue eyes and American freckles." He would say: "I'll get my sandpaper and sandpaper them off." This was deliciously scary, but did not frighten me as I was Pop's pet. When he was in his chair I would sit on his legs and would play "horsey" as he bounced me up and down. He used to give me a nickel to go up the street to buy a newspaper and said I could keep the change to buy some candy, such as a Mary Jane candy bar or a couple of ladyfingers from the Jewish bakery. The way he could sneeze "A-Russia" fascinated me. Here too every evening, Pop, with his head covered by a towel, would take his Tincture of Benzoin inhalations for his "cough."

Upstairs were three bedrooms, a bathroom and closets along a hallway. In Pop's bedroom I saw a large painting of his wife's patron saint, St. Anne. At the end of the hall a large painting of the Holy Family comforted me as I slept. Mother and Dad had their own room and my Aunt Mildred shared hers with me. Later, after Mother went to the Sanatorium I slept alone in my parents' bedroom while Dad and my brother used the attic room. I remember being told every night "Good night, sleep tight, don't let the cooties bite" to which I always added "don't forget to leave the hall light on." In spite of these large paintings and regular church attendance, the Severynse family's religious piety was more subdued and matter of fact than that of the Jolletts. *However, I do remember years later that Aunt Mildred told me she always attended rosary days on the 13ᵗʰ of each month in honor of Our Lady of Fatima.*

The third floor attic had one furnished room where my brother Bob slept and where we laid out the Lionel train tracks at Christmas time. Years later my Aunt Mildred told me that an old sea chest in the unfurnished room had been owned by one of my ancestors who had been a sea captain. *I wish I knew more about him. Perhaps he had some part to play in why I love the ocean so much.* I loved bouncing on my bottom down the shiny oak stairs or sliding down the banister until I would hit the post at the ground floor. *So many times later in life, I used to dream I was going speedily down stairs or large spaces with huge leaps—was this the remembrance of those rides down the stairs or my rush to go places even in my dreams or previews of a quantum leap in the here and now?*

Aside from childhood colds, measles, chicken pox and German measles I was a pretty healthy kid. I remember only one night when I had an upset stomach and vomited onto the hall carpet directly in front of the bathroom, and cried out "I'm sick."! *My aunt Mildred told me many years later that as a baby I almost choked when I turned over a can of baby powder and the powder had me gasping for breath.*

Pop often entertained his old Post Office buddies in the cellar on Friday afternoons with a little home-brew to take home at the end of their discussions. During the Prohibition years he would make his own Apple Jack out of apples from our backyard trees. He would never let them pay for the bottles out of fear of jeopardizing his federal pension if he ever got caught selling liquor. For us kids he would make root beer which would occasionally pop out of the bottles with a loud explosion. As a carpenter Pop had his workbench and tools there. The cellar also contained the wash tubs, a clothes wringer, the boiler, coal furnace and stove for boiling clothes.

A wooden bench swing and a couple of chairs on the porch provided a shady rest for us all at the end of the day. The four or five steps of the "stoop" were often used for playing games, such as jacks. We all loved to roll down on the steep grass-covered terrace down to the sidewalk. A giant linden tree graced the side of the house. At the back of our house the legendary "cellar door" gave all the neighborhood kids a chance to take a quick slide. *Remember the words of the old popular song: "Look down my rain barrel, slide down my cellar door, and we'll be jolly friends forever more?"*

Our small backyard boasted a crab apple tree, a sickle pear tree, a Queen Anne cherry tree and a clothesline. A tiny garden provided a space for me to admire a patch of lilies of the valley and my parents gave me a few nasturtium seeds big enough for a child to plant. We also had a tiny vegetable patch. The sidewalk from the house to the back of the property on Bailey Avenue was covered with a Concord grape arbor with tulips and daffodils lining the sidewalk. The neighbor children liked to pick the grapes as they used the unfenced sidewalk as a shortcut to Williamson Avenue on their way to school. Although I don't remember Pop ever yelling at me, I do remember him shouting at the kids, "You kids, stop stealing our grapes!"

The chicken house in the backyard held cubicles for about 20 Rhode Island Red hens. The chicken run was surrounded by chicken wire and across from it was a small shed used to incubate the baby chicks. The chickens were Pop's concern and he always carried out the "swill" for the chickens, collected the eggs and killed the chickens when needed for a meal. As our neighbor, Mr. Trevaskis, also had chickens, but black ones, Pop made it clear to him that if his chickens got into our yard, they would be our Sunday dinners. Ours never strayed from home because they were never allowed out of the fenced enclosures.

My Dad, Raymond Jollett, was born from a farm family in Honesdale, Pennsylvania of a mother of Irish descent (Reynolds and McManus) and a father who was presumed to be French (by his name) but had been raised in an orphanage so no one really knew his heritage. I have seen a photo of Grandpa Jollett with my brother Bob when he was two years old taken in 1924 in Madison, so he must have died shortly after as I don't remember him when I moved to Madison in 1932. My younger brother Herb on hearing he was dead inquired: "Who dead him?" but I don't remember hearing the answer on the cause of his death. The Jolletts had eight children, four boys and four girls. Later the Jollett family moved to New Brunswick, New Jersey and then to Elizabeth where the family lived on Lower Road next to the Evergreen cemetery where my grandfather worked as a stonecutter.

Dad had only an eighth grade education and as the oldest he worked at various low paying jobs. He was inducted into the Army in World War I and as a sergeant in the Quartermaster Corps he was in charge of a military commissary. After the Armistice he was stationed in France during the Occupation. He noticed that those with a hankering for alcohol often came to the store to buy extract of vanilla and other alcohol containing items, such as cough syrups with an alcohol base. My Dad always appreciated a cold beer but was not an alcoholic. While in France he learned to speak and write French (probably from some young ladies he had met there.) He also produced, directed and starred in homemade minstrel shows and skits for his army buddies in the war.

When Dad returned from the war he soon married my mother, Petronella Severynse, whom he had met before the War at a social event at St. Catherine's Church in Hillside. Mother had once worked in Newark as a stenographer. She was born in Brooklyn and raised in the Bronx and then moved to Lyons Farms with her father. Dad was about 30 and mother about 26 when they married and first lived in Elizabeth on Anna Street in a house shared with my mother's relatives. Later they moved to Hillside to live with my mother's father (Pop) who owned the house, and my mother's younger unmarried sister, Aunt Mildred. I'm not sure of the dates of these moves.

My older brother, Bob, was born in 1922; I was born in 1925 and my younger brother Herb was born in 1929. My birth certificate reads that I was born at St. Elizabeth's Hospital in Elizabeth. I was baptized in Pop's church, St. Charles Borromeo in Newark. My parents wanted to call me Bernice Joan, but the priest said Bernice was not a Saint's name, so I was baptized with only the name of Joan, which pleased me as I later came to love and admire St. Joan of Arc.

Dad worked as a bookkeeper at the Jersey Central Railroad in Jersey City and it was always a treat to skip down the street to the trolley stop to meet him at the end of the day. Dad was great at comedy and sometimes at meal times would imitate almost any ethnic accent with jokes that today would be "politically incorrect." He was not above teasing the Severynse relatives who had worked diligently to prepare a holiday dinner by leaning back, patting his stomach and exclaiming "Thank the Lord and pray the next may be a meal." Or on being served rice pudding with raisins he might demand: "Who put the flies in this rice pudding?" Dad had a long work day so I saw less of him than of Pop.

He used to belong to the Knights of Columbus and an organization called the Star Wheelmen that was originally founded for fans of bicycle riding. I never saw my Dad ride a bicycle but I guess he enjoyed meeting with his buddies over beer and pretzels at a club meeting. Once I remember that he let me go with him to a place that served all the corn on the cob you could eat if you bought a glass of beer.

Although the Depression had started, we were still not too hard-hit. Occasionally, hoboes would come to the back door for a handout and my mother would fix them a sandwich. Pop owned the house and had his Post Office federal pension, so things were not as bad as for some other folks who had lost their jobs. I don't remember us seeing ourselves as "poor." However, my Dad's salary was very modest and the family consisted of four adults and three children, so money had to be spent wisely. On Sundays we would go out for a ride in Pop's '29 green Chevrolet to the "country" and buy fruit and vegetables sold on stands in front of people's homes. My mother did some canning and also made some of our clothes. Having our own chickens and eggs and some fruit, helped a lot to keep expenses down. Mother watched our expenditures very carefully. In retrospect I think Mother was stronger than Dad. I'm sure it was hard for him to depend on Pop for the house and also the car, so he couldn't feel free to assert himself too much. By the time he got home from Jersey City he must have been pretty tired too, although he did help with yard work whenever he could.

I went to Hillside Avenue School for kindergarten when I turned five in March and then on to first grade in September, often roller-skating to school. I complained that all we did in Kindergarten was play in the sandboxes, and because Pop had taught me how to read, I felt a little disappointed. I did not excel in things like making little paper Easter baskets or paper doilies.

Aside from roller skating, we kids, both boys and girls in the neighborhood, played games such as hide and seek, tag, ring-alevio, captains and giant steps ("may I".) I played jacks with other girls on the front porch, jumped rope and played Hopscotch on the sidewalk. Some of the older kids mounted wooden crates on old roller skates that made a great noise on our concrete-paved street where I rode my tricycle. Some of us would go to the local dump looking for "treasures." We were amazed that anyone could throw out a beautiful chipped china cup or a doll with only one arm missing. Except for rainy days, play was mostly outdoors. Indoor activities were Tiddly Winks, (popping a small disk into a small cup by using one of the disks,) card games, checkers, Parchesi, (an Indian board game,) Tinker toys, (interconnecting small wooden rods for construction projects) and various paper dolls. I had a series of dolls at different times—a rubber baby-doll with bathinet, a Raggedy Ann, a Patsy doll with her own clothes, and a beautiful Effanbee doll, Mary Jane, that had long chestnut curls, movable eyes and a cup-like record mechanism in her side that played nursery rhymes. My brother Bob's small Victrola played the same records. He teased me by setting my record with the song "Rockabye Baby" so it sang, "Rock-a, rock-a, rock-a" and he would say: "What a dumb doll." I also had a doll house. Most of these were Christmas or birthday presents from Pop or Mildred, because Mother and Dad gave me clothes and smaller toys.

I was very curious, always asking questions, "What's that for?" My Aunt Mildred's answer, if she didn't know the real answer, was: "Cat's fur to make kittens' britches." Once I was home from school sick, but not too sick to not want to be active. When she tired of answering my persistent questions, she promised me a nickel if I could keep quiet for an hour. I agreed to do so. When the second hour arrived, she offered me another nickel. "No thanks," I said. That was really too much silence for my liking, although I knew a nickel would buy quite a lot of candy. My Aunt Mildred told me many years later that my mother almost delivered me in the taxi before she could get to the hospital. So I guess I was born in a hurry and have been on the go ever since.

On rainy days or when alone, I played with a large tin of old buttons and marched them up and down the carpet in various formations. After it rained, I always enjoyed making mud pies in the gutters or sailing little boats. I used to take my little umbrella and hold it up in the wind, convinced that if I just could think light enough and make a big leap I would be able to fly. Sometimes I played marbles with the boys or tried to help them with their roadside stands where they sold homemade butterscotch candy, but they didn't want "girls."

Every Saturday it was a neighborhood ritual for all the kids to go to the matinee with double feature, cartoon, newsreel, serial and coming attractions. I'm sure most parents breathed a sigh of relief when Saturday afternoon came and the kids would be out of the house. It was worth the ten cents admission. Some movies I remember from that time were *King Kong, Dracula* and *Rebecca of Sunnybrook Farm* and of course Shirley Temple, Our Gang Comedy and many cowboy movies. Dad took us to the Barnum and Bailey Circus in Newark, a very special treat. He also took us to church bazaars at St. Catherine's. I remember St. Catherine's Church with its cool flagstone bare floor and the buttons on the back of the seat where men put their hats.

In the summer Dad drove us to "the shore" where we jumped in the waves holding on to the ropes, walking on the boardwalk eating salt water taffy or cotton candy and playing in the sand. We usually went to Bradley Beach, Point Pleasant, Asbury Park or Ocean Grove, a town founded by fundamentalist Christians, where signs were posted "Only Gentiles Allowed." Prejudice against Jews was quite common in many aspects of society during my childhood, so this sign was only a more open expression of it.

I especially remember our Christmas trees. Most people use garlands of popcorn as tree decorations, but we used the sugared (not sticky but dry) pink and white popcorn to pin a single popcorn on the nubby ends of the branches. Of course we would eat a few as we went along and all that were left at the end of the season. The ornaments were mostly very delicate ones made in Germany, so we weren't allowed to handle them. *Maybe my parents invented or adopted the custom of the popcorn "snow" to give us something to share in the Christmas season as we couldn't touch the ornaments.*

A boy my age, Buddy Trevarrow, lived across the street. The taunting refrain was "Buddy loves Jo-oan, Buddy loves Jo-oan." One day my older brother Bob and some of his friends decided we should get "married." *At that time the circus used to have two adult midgets that got married and every kid was interested in having a "Tom Thumb Wedding."* They outfitted me with a wedding veil made from an old lace curtain and everything went well until Buddy was told he had to kiss me. That abruptly ended the wedding. I don't remember being too broken hearted. We were just friends and teasing was taken in stride by most of us in the neighborhood. It was a carefree wonderful life with fun and friends every day with no thought of the morrow. I would wake up early each day eager to see what lay ahead. Soon this would all change.

When second grade came around my Dad moved us kids to his mother's home in Madison, about 14 miles from Hillside. Mother had come down with tuberculosis and was hospitalized at Bonnie Burn Sanatorium in Scotch Plains where she never left. We were never allowed to visit her. About the same time my Aunt Mildred went to Glen Gardner Sanatorium, an institution for those with less advanced tuberculosis. *I don't remember my mother being sick but my Aunt Mildred told me many years later that she had been doing poorly since Herbert's birth two years before.* Pop also had t.b. but stayed at home—the reason for his cough and the Tincture of Benzoin inhalations. As my father worked, it was logical we would have to move as there was no one to take care of us kids during the day. It was a sad day in my life. *Later my brother Bob told me that mother would have preferred that we go to Brooklyn to live with her brother Len, and his wife, Aunt Lil, and four children, but I guess my Dad made the final decision.*

Tuberculosis had already taken Pop's wife, my grandmother, before I knew her, and their two sons, Frank and Edward, both handsome young men who died before I knew them. *As I think back now on the whole family situation, I can hardly imagine what Pop's thoughts were when his two daughters might also be taken away by this dread disease. He may have revealed these thoughts to others but never shared any with me, as I was still quite young.* His only other child was my uncle Len who lived in Brooklyn, who had been injured in World War I, but managed to survive many years with no noticeable disability. Apparently, my Dad and Herb never contracted the disease, but Bob and I both turned out to be tuberculin positive and needed to be monitored, although we did not have active tuberculosis.

CHAPTER 2

GRANDMA'S HOUSE

Life in Madison with Grandma was quite different than Hillside. Actually we lived at 39 Broadway in a fairly new development called Brooklake Park which was part of Florham Park, but our mail was always addressed to Madison. All stores, churches, library, train station and bus service were about a mile or two away. We really lived in a suburb as there were no public facilities or stores nearby except for Viana's, a tiny grocery store down the street. As Grandpa Jollett had died some years before, Grandma was the head of the household. She was a taciturn, hard working lady, sometimes sullen, who often made disparaging remarks about people in the news or the neighbors, such as "My lands, did you see how short her dress was," etc. She made it a daily practice to sit in her armchair and say her Rosary or read her prayer book. She practically never ate with us in the dining room, but lived mostly on boiled eggs, tea and toast. She would sometimes tell Herbert to get a twig from the apple tree so she could give him a switch on his legs if he had done something naughty. I don't remember any physical punishment, but she set the tone of behavior.

She did try to look pleased when we gave her our homemade presents at Christmas, such as an old jam jar with cut out pictures of flowers from the seed catalogs and then shellacked to be used as a vase. Later she wrote me occasional letters when I was in boarding school. They were simply written but just one long sentence. I guess her Irish Catholic heritage and farm upbringing made it hard for her to show her affection. When I went off to boarding school she might give me a little goodbye peck on the cheek. I don't remember her as a warm, cuddly grandmother. *(Grandma died several years later when I was out of the country.)*

Also still at home were my four adult maiden aunts—Marie, Anna, Loretta and Marguerite; my Uncle Gene, also single; my Dad and we three kids. My Uncle Edmund had died in France in World War I. *Recently I checked the Internet and found he was buried in the Meuse-Argonne Cemetery in France just before the Armistice. Bob told me recently that Grandpa Jollett received money from the U.S. government after Edmund's death. He used the money to buy the house in Madison.* My Uncle Clarence lived in Newark but I only saw him a couple of times. He was married but they had no children. I think he had an alcohol problem.

When we were all home, the household consisted of ten persons. My aunts all preferred we call them just by their names without the

"Aunt." I guess the "Aunt" made them feel too old. All of my Dad's side of the family had dark hair and dark eyes that my two brothers inherited, whereas I had the Severynse light brown hair and blue eyes. Marie was short and stocky and worked as secretary to the parish priests at St. Vincent's Church in Madison; Anna was slender and Loretta was short and lively and had suffered from spinal tuberculosis as a child and had to wear a back brace. Anna and Loretta both worked in Newark at the Star Ledger newspaper as comptometer (an early calculator machine) operators; and Marguerite, the youngest, who had just graduated from the Catholic Bailey High School in Morristown, worked for the Bell Telephone Company in Newark in the Classified Ads section. The last three walked every day about a mile to the Madison Lackawanna Railway station and then commuted to Newark, about 15 miles down the line. At the time I knew them, none of them had a boy friend. They all had a good high school education at Catholic high schools and fortunately never lost their jobs during the Depression.

All four of them were nice to me and I don't remember any really unpleasant moments, except sometimes from Aunt Marie. As the oldest and the more assertive, she was the disciplinarian who would ask "were you smoking?" if I happened to arrive home after traveling in the smoker on the train from boarding school or college; or she would wonder "were you wearing lipstick?" She supervised the purchase of my school clothes. A red dress was not considered ladylike, but I do remember finally getting a beautiful cherry-red wool dress and also a sophisticated black dress that I liked. *A small expression of adolescent rebellion?* Anything sleeveless or low-cut was not allowed, mostly because it was frowned upon by our parish priests as not appropriate for wearing to Sunday Mass. Marie liked it when I would play with her hair by putting it up in bobby pins, braids and curls. She said it relaxed her. She had a beautiful contralto voice and was often asked to sing at church weddings—one favorite was the very sentimental "Lovely Lady Dressed in Blue, Teach Me How to Pray." She also sang at the Christmas services and set up the Nativity scene.

Loretta was the jolliest of the four. Not surprisingly, she was the only one of my aunts who got married. She met Bill Milligan through friends at her office and got married in 1942 but I was then away at college, so I did not attend their wedding. The youngest, my Aunt Marguerite, entered the Sisters of St. Joseph much later as Sister Raphael and taught the blind in Jersey City. Of the four sisters she was the last to die. Anna was proud of her classes in Elocution and read a lot. I remember Anna couldn't eat anything with onions, so she would have her own special potato salad, etc. I learned later it was because she had previously eaten a lot of onions and probably just too many. *When she was nearing ninety and in a nursing home and quite sick, I called her once and after a few words of concern on my part, she said, "I love you." Her words really touched me. That was the first time anyone in my family had ever said those three important words. By the same token, I had never said, "I love you" to any of my family either. During the Depression and World War II personal disclosures and open expressions of emotions were not the cultural norm. These became more common during the more open "sixties" or later in the age of "Oprah." She died about a week later in 1995.*

My Uncle Gene, a bachelor and a former merchant marine, worked as a laborer at the local plant nursery. He was a sullen, quiet type with a short temper, but kept to himself. Everyone kind of tried to stay out of his way. We always had to make sure too, that we didn't drink all the milk, as he would get angry if there was none left for him, so one glass each was our limit for the day. *I found myself years later hesitant to drink more than one glass, when I realized I could certainly afford to have two glasses if I wanted to. I guess Uncle Gene's ghost was still hovering.* Uncle Gene usually ate in the kitchen by himself whereas the rest of the family ate in the dining room. He died some years later in an institution for chronic alcoholics. Grandma did all of the cooking.

The house consisted of two stories, but very different from what I had known in Hillside. On the ground floor was a small living room with a baby grand piano that my Aunt Marie played. A painting of Saint Cecilia, patroness of musicians, hung on the wall behind it and a statue of the Infant of Prague was on a stand. My Aunt Marie made beautiful clothes for the statue. She often made novenas to the Infant of Prague, but was always in a hurry for a positive answer to her prayers, so she made novenas of nine hours instead of nine days.

There was a pleasant screened-in side porch where we would sit on warm summer evenings and eat ice cream that my Aunt Marie bought at Viana's store. Later my brother Herb was usually the one to take the little red wagon to pick up groceries there. My grandmother would call in her order and "charge it." *I think the only reason we had a phone is because Aunt Marguerite worked for the phone company.* We often went barefoot in the summer and hopped down the hot sidewalk with some sidestepping into the empty lots to cool off our burning feet on our way to the store. The porch was not used in the winter, as it was too impractical to keep heated. The dining room held a large dining table where we ate, and a china closet and sideboard for tablecloths and silver. A painting of the Last Supper hung over the sideboard. I was the one who set the table for dinner.

The kitchen provided space for only one person, or at best, two, to eat at a time. For this reason Grandma didn't want anyone hanging around in the kitchen or helping with the cooking. Her cooking was quite plain but adequate. During the War years she put up stoically with ration coupons and limited supplies of sugar, coffee, butter, meat etc. Once my brother Herb reported that they didn't have any potatoes at the store and she replied in true Irish form, "well there's no use eating."

My only duties in the kitchen were to wash dishes after meals. I usually washed and Bob, or Herbert when he got older, dried. As we only lit the hot water heater on Saturday for our weekly baths, we boiled a kettle of water and washed dishes in a dishpan, using bits of old soap in a little metal cage with a handle that we shook in the water. Later, I envied other girls in college who talked about helping their mothers make cookies, fudge, or even preparing some meals. I considered it a good day if Grandma handed me the peach peels and I would sit on the back kitchen steps and eat them. I never learned to make anything except how to fry an egg. My brother Bob called them "vulcanized eggs."

Upstairs were three small bedrooms—one for my Dad, Herb and Bob, one for Grandma and Marie and the other where Anna and Loretta shared the double bed and Marguerite and I slept on the cot which had to be pulled out and made up every night. I remember peeling the wallpaper off the wall close to the cot. It was very cramped quarters with only one dresser for all our underclothes. A small closet kept all of our dresses and coats. There was absolutely no place to keep a young girl's treasures or keepsakes. *I think that is why I am now such a collector of "my stuff."* Uncle Gene slept on the sofa bed in the living room.

The cellar was a more comfortable place, especially in the summer. It had a packed dirt floor and cement in some places, so it was cooler. An elevated coal bin was in one corner; the washtubs, boiler and stove in another. We kept our old Easter baskets near the coal bin section. When summer rolled around we would get a hankering for some candy so rifled through the Easter basket grass to see if we had missed a jelly bean left there at a time when candy was plentiful. Christmas and Easter were the only times we had candy and maybe some candy corn at Halloween. I don't remember ever having spending money to buy candy.

One interesting place was the cupboard that stored things that were not in everyday use. When Herbert got older we used the ironing board as a counter to play store and we would "buy" and "sell" a box of toothpicks, a flat piece of wax to clean the iron, an old jar, and numerous other household items. The other bright spot was a small bookshelf. Unbeknownst to my aunts, I sat in the old beach chair and spent some time reading *Dracula*. It got a little too realistic though one day, when a bird got caught in our furnace (not functioning in summer) and was flapping around desperately inside the furnace. It really scared me. Birds were nice in the trees, but scary in the furnace! I hollered and helped open the side door to the outside while my Aunt Loretta opened the furnace door and liberated the poor distressed bird. I was relieved to find out that it wasn't a bat!

Sometimes I would accompany Bob when he went to the nearby woods to chop wood to start the fires for our coal furnace and I would sit on the logs and enjoy the woodsy atmosphere, even spotting a deer once in a while. Other times we would go to the local golf course, Braeburn Country Club, and pick mushrooms in the early morning. Uncle Gene sometimes did caddy work there so knew where to find them. We brought them home where my grandmother fried them in butter for breakfast. Other times we picked wild strawberries in the meadow near our house, or blackberries in the woods. These went into delicious pies.

The backyard had a nice lawn and a circular goldfish pond with a birdbath in the center. My Aunt Marie constructed it herself with cement and stones. On the sides of the lot were beds with gladioli, irises, cosmos, dahlias, and bachelor buttons. I remember once going out in the evening by myself and looking at the irises and wishing I could "possess" them in some way, not just smell them and enjoy their colors and shapes. Cannas, peonies and zinnias were planted in a separate circular bed near the house. I loved to bury my face in the silky peonies. Their smell always reminds me of the feast of Corpus Christi as there were so many vases of them in church on that day. We also had an apple tree near the house where the birds would all fight in the evening to get their favorite branch to perch on and where they woke us up in the early morning by their chattering.

Petunias grew in the window boxes and around the fishpond. Every time I smell petunias I remember them. At ground level were several hydrangea bushes and some on the front lawn. One year when destructive Japanese beetles had invaded the area, my brother Herb would go out and collect beetles in a jar, mostly from the hydrangea bushes, and bring them to the movie house. One full jar gave him a free pass to the movies. He would say, "Well, got to go out and pick beetles." The whole yard was surrounded on three sides by a hedge that my Aunt Marie cut regularly. She also was the one to mow the lawn and do the gardening. Strangely, I don't remember seeing cut flowers in vases in the house and I never was asked to help with planting or weeding, (of course I was away at school most of the time, so I guess that was understandable.)

The house in Madison was comfortable enough and the garden beautiful, but it seemed so "unlived in." And of course, I was still desperately attached to my "real" home in Hillside and steadfastly unwilling to consider Madison my home. I used to go across the street to play with my girl friend, Imogene. There were so many interesting objects around—knickknacks, books, magazines etc., and she had her own room. *I don't remember having any of my Hillside dolls or the dollhouse or other toys. I now wonder why no one had brought them from Hillside when we moved. Maybe because my Dad thought this was just a temporary arrangement. In fact we did move back the next year when I was in third grade, but later moved permanently to Madison and I never knew what happened to those toys.*

Sometimes Imogene would come over and we would sit on the side porch and draw pictures in a little book that had blank pages. We also played a game of describing a character, such as "Helen" and then argue over whether she should have had red hair or brown. I favored brown, she red. Of course, the names of the current movie stars colored the descriptions in our imaginations. There were few other children in the neighborhood—nothing like the always busy game-days and roller-skating we had in Hillside. I only spent summers and a few Christmas vacations in Madison so never developed any lasting or close friendships with the girls or boys in the neighborhood or any from local schools.

My brother Bob and I both attended St. Vincent's parish school, walking about a mile each day both ways, short-cutting through a pretty meadow. I still remember the daisies, buttercups, (holding the buttercup under your chin to see if it reflected back—if it did, you liked butter,) black-eyed Susans, Queen Anne's lace, butter-and-eggs and tiny wild strawberries. Nature in all its forms appealed to me.

Many Italian children attended the school as the town had many first generation Italian parents. I still remember unfavorably one Jenny R. when I was in second grade, as I suspected she stole my blue pencil with a spiral design. Prejudice against different ethnic groups was quite common at the time. Unfavorable remarks about the Dagos, Guineas, Wops, Kikes, Polocks, and Niggers etc. were common and all were expressed without apologies. Of course, there were always the "exceptions," such as an Italian member of the church Sodality of Our Lady; or the Italian florist who "really was pretty decent;" or the cab driver, Mr. White (black), who was always very respectful and who drove us all to church on Sundays as my grandmother couldn't walk that far and we didn't have a car; or some of my Aunt Anna's co-workers, such as Adolph Finkelstein, who was Jewish and very "nice." *I don't consider myself prejudiced but occasionally the old stereotypes flash into my memory.*

In 2nd grade at St. Vincent's we had Catechism classes every day. We used the Benziger Brothers' *Bible History* that had black and white drawings of all the popular stories. David killing Goliath, Moses and the Ten Commandments, and Noah and the Ark come frequently to mind. *Contrary to what many non-Catholics think, the Bible* was *taught to Catholics.*

In the spring my preparation for my First Communion began, but my focus was more on how I had to go to Confession first, be fasting, walk to the Communion rail with my hands folded, stick out my tongue to receive the Host, swallow the Host whole, go back to my pew and bow my head. Wearing a pretty new white First Communion dress was also on my mind. Somehow I tried to think about the fact that I had Jesus inside me and prayed that I might be a good girl. After Communion the whole congregation recited the Anima Christi (Soul of Christ) prayer which by chance happened to be inscribed on a plaque on the church wall close to where the Jollett family pew was located. I received my First Communion white prayer book with a little latch on it containing the Mass Prayers and other daily prayers, which I used for some time after. I went to Confession every week after that with preparation help from my second grade teacher. I first saw the statue of St. Gabriel of Our Lady of Sorrows at St. Vincent's Church. He was much loved by the Italian parishioners.

Mass was said or sung in Latin, with the priest with his back to the congregation and only the altar boys made the Latin responses. Some priests mumbled the prayers quickly so Mass was soon over. Others were more reverent as we followed the translation in our prayer books. The choir was up in the back of the church where they sang mostly English hymns except for Benediction when we all sang "O Salutaris Hostia" and "Tantum Ergo" in Latin. Common English hymns were: "Mother Dearest, Mother Fairest;" "To Jesus Heart All Burning;" "Holy God We Praise Thy Name;" "O Sacrament Most Holy" and "O Lord I am not Worthy." Occasionally on major feast days the choir sang two-part Latin Palestrina hymns with little participation by the congregation.

The Jollett family was imbued with a brand of Irish Catholicism (Grandma was of Irish descent) that dated from the post-Reformation period and post-famine time in Ireland. This was more Rome centered and unrelated to the Celtic Christianity of previous centuries dating back to St. Patrick's time. After Catholic Emancipation the number of priests increased and many were sent to Europe for training. They brought back from their education in Europe a different regime of pious practices, such as devotion to the Sacred Heart with its focus on reparation and penance; Forty Hours; Benediction of the Blessed Sacrament; May devotions; the Rosary often said while the priest was saying Mass; First Fridays and Novenas of various kinds. I heartily accepted all these Catholic customs without questioning. *At that time the Church was pretty much united. There was not the division we now see with conservative Catholics and liberal Catholics. You were either a Catholic that practiced your religion or a "fallen away Catholic."*

I remember that I went to Communion on First Fridays and as I was fasting, I went after Mass to the Lackawanna Restaurant and had a hard roll and a glass of milk as no time to walk back home. We never ate at a local restaurant so this was a special treat. Religious art was mostly sentimental, portraying Jesus and the saints as holy and to be venerated and prayed to but not as human persons easily imitated. Holy pictures, scapulars, medals and statues proliferated. Some practiced devotion to the Holy Souls in Purgatory. On Good Friday we always listened to the Seven Last Words of Jesus sermon from twelve to three and of course, dressed up at Easter in our very best outfits.

When a thunderstorm occurred at night I was told to get up and sit down in the living room and say the Rosary. For evening prayers I was taught to say the Our Father, Hail Mary, Apostles Creed, I Confess, the Acts of Faith, Hope, Charity and Contrition, followed by the petitions to Jesus, Mary and Joseph for a happy death and then blessings of all members of the family. *I still use some of these prayers but not as consistently as I did then.*

At church the Jolletts bought the weekly Catholic newspaper, *Our Sunday Visitor,* the two Catholic magazines, *Commonweal* (by lay Catholics) and *America* (by the Jesuits.) They also subscribed to the monthly *Messenger of the Sacred Heart*. Catholics in good standing and in the public eye were always proudly mentioned especially singers, actors, politicians, writers, etc. Many articles in all of these focused on the dangers and evils of Communism, the Church's strict moral code and stories of the Saints. I read these in my time in Madison in the second grade and during Christmas and summer vacations. They formed many of my opinions.

CHAPTER 3

MY GREAT LOSS

I was happy that after a year of living with my grandmother, four maiden aunts, my uncle, my Dad and my brothers in Madison, we (my Dad, Bob and I) moved back to my beloved home in Hillside after my Aunt Mildred returned from Glen Gardner Sanatorium. She was still getting periodic pneumothorax treatments (putting air into the space next to the lung to rest it,) but able to do the household tasks and look after me and Bob. Herb remained in Madison. *I do not know why these decisions were made.* My brother Bob and I went to St. Catherine's School in Hillside, I in third grade and he in the fifth. We walked to school unless it was raining when we received money for carfare. It could be pleasant as we would sometimes wait for the freight train and look at the different kinds of cars and count them. Naturally we had an excuse for being late, "We had to wait for the train to go by."

I liked the Dominican Sisters at St. Catherine's and one aspect that remained in my memory was the Holy Childhood posters of "ladders" we made to help save the "pagan babies." Each nickel we gave moved us one more rung up the ladder. The different classes vied with each other to reach the top. We had very little money but often tried to contribute a nickel if we could. The missions were important to me. A seed had been planted.

At St. Catherine's the Catholic reader books told stories about saints, such as St. Tarcisius, a young boy who was martyred in the early Christian persecutions and St. Sebastian who was killed by arrows. Most of the Sisters were of Irish descent and passed on some of their pious traditions and of course, St. Patrick's Day.

Pop was sick and doing his nightly inhalations for his "cough," but kept doing his chores and caring for the chickens, etc. Mother was still in Bonnie Burn Sanatorium.

In March, just after my eighth birthday, we were practicing for the St. Patrick's Day play at school, singing "Oh, we've...just about concluded...that we'll organize right here" and I was called out as my Dad came to take us home. In the car he told us that mother had just died. All I remember is that Bob and I sat in the back seat, each of us looking out the window on our own side. *Did I cry? I don't know and still today that whole time or what my father said is an enormous blank space in my memory.* I do vaguely remember going to the funeral home but not to the cemetery. *In a letter Bob wrote me many years later he mentioned how devastating mother's death had been for my Dad. She had been his "dream girl" and found it very hard to take. This explained a lot of events that followed later, but I was not aware of this at the time. More later.*

Then in June I was told one morning that Pop, whose tuberculosis had gotten worse, had "coughed up his lungs" during the night. He was laid out in our parlor. I do remember at Pop's funeral that my Aunt Mildred wore a black suit and appeared overwhelmed. She still cared for us the rest of that school year. All of our lives would be changed forever after Mother and Pop's deaths.

CHAPTER 4

BONNIE BURN SANATORIUM

Whatever the circumstances after Pop's death, possibly the fact that the house was inherited by my Aunt Mildred, my Dad decided (or was encouraged by the Health Department to do so as Bob and I were both tuberculin positive) to send Bob and me to Bonnie Burn Preventorium in Scotch Plains. *Perhaps it may have even been a suggestion of my mother's as she must have been aware of the program that was close to where she was.* Herb stayed in Madison. The Preventorium was an adjunct to the Sanatorium where my mother had spent over two years. Dad had pointed out to me the room where she had been hospitalized—the second window from the end of the building—a spot I would look at longingly.

It was somewhat like a Girl/Boy Scouts Camp with outdoor activities. The girls were housed in separate quarters from the boys. We wore khaki colored shorts and tops or one-piece rompers that were not given to us to keep but left unironed in the linen closet and we got more or less our size outfit. At that time, fresh air and lots of good high-protein foods were all that could be done for tuberculosis. Here I had my first encounter with a "colored" girl. *It's strange but her name, Dorothy Troop, is the only name I remember now of all the girls there.* They took our temperatures every evening in the large dormitory. Those that had a tendency to wet their beds were wakened up in the middle of the night by the night nurse with a loud "Tea-Timers up!" They had to use the potty-chair in the middle of the dormitory while the rest of us would just roll over and go back to sleep.

Two Irish Catholic nurses—Miss Daly and Mrs. McCauley, more or less looked after those of us who were Catholic. We attended an occasional Mass on Sundays in the dining hall. I still remember though, saying prayers with all of the children assembled and resolutely refraining from saying the "Protestant" ending of the Lord's Prayer—"For thine is the kingdom and the power and the glory, now and forever." *It's ironic, that nowadays we have added this to our Catholic version of the "Our Father." What the Jewish children, if any, did, I can't even guess.*

I got a strange pemphigus-like rash with large blisters on my hands that had to be treated with zinc oxide and/or boric acid ointment. No one else had it and I never got it again. *My present day interpretation is that it may have been an unconscious desire to be touched, but I don't know what caused it.* Eventually it disappeared.

We did not get home for Christmas and I remember getting a pair of flannel pajamas from my Dad—a far cry from the numerous toys and clothes I used to get for Christmas. I had a very good teacher in the fourth grade. I had to sit sometimes with one of the boys in the class to help him with his long divisions. I only remember that he wore high top shoes and his feet really smelled bad. On special occasions, and at the end of the school year, we would sing "Bonnie Burn, dear Bonnie Burn" to the tune of "Oh Tannenbaum"—"The Watchung Hills surround thy grounds, Bonnie Burn dear Bonnie Burn. . . . to doctors, nurses, teachers too, it grieves our hearts to say adieu, Bonnie Burn, dear Bonnie Burn." *Apparently the fresh air and good food worked as neither my brother Bob nor I ever developed tuberculosis, although we always remained tuberculin positive and had to have X-rays taken periodically. Recently I called Scotch Plains, New Jersey and Bonnie Burn was only a memory for some of the older residents. Other developments have taken its place.* After the year at Bonnie Burn I wondered where I would next attend school.

CHAPTER 5

ST. MARY'S ACADEMY

The following year Dad decided to move us back to Madison. My Aunt Mildred had sold the house in Hillside and moved to a house on Munn Avenue she rented from an older lady and her adult daughter who had polio. Mildred had a small room with kitchen and bathroom privileges. After a discussion between my aunts and my Dad and grandmother, they decided that a Catholic boarding school would be the best for us. I still don't know what motivated their decision as we had a very good Catholic parish school in Madison. Did they feel that the house was too small for so many? Did my Dad feel he had to do something or did no one want us around? Discussions were always held when we kids were in bed so I had no way of knowing what the pros and cons were. Much time was spent going through the *Sacred Heart Messenger* magazine ads for Catholic boarding schools and they picked the cheapest one in Champlain, New York—St. Mary's Academy—a couple of miles from the Canadian border. I got the impression that the decision was mostly my Aunt Marie's but don't know who actually paid for the board and room for us three kids. In the beginning it was probably my Dad, but later I guess my aunts all had to chip in.

In the first few years Dad drove us three kids up Highway 9 through the Adirondacks to Champlain. Later I always had to take the train. It was decided that I should skip fifth grade and go directly into sixth grade as I had apparently learned a lot in Bonnie Burn. *I'm not sure that was a good decision as I was so much younger than most of the other students, being nine years old and in the sixth grade. I had to sit on a geography book, a history book and a dictionary to be able to see the teacher.* The class combined sixth, seventh and eighth grades in one room, so I listened and learned whatever was being taught. I only had to catch up a little on arithmetic. I would get very fidgety, especially if I was listening to something I had already heard before. The teacher, Sister St. Ignatius, was quite strict, but must have had a sixth sense of my needs. When she saw me squirming in my seat, she quietly told me to take about a ten minute break in the playground. Recess was supposedly no longer needed for these grades. So I would go out to the playground, take a ride on the swings, pick and eat a few choke cherries from the trees growing nearby, take a little walk and then return to the classroom. This was done in such a matter-of-fact way that I don't remember being embarrassed or singled out. Actually, I don't think I missed my classroom material, but I was able to get back to my studies with renewed interest. *In today's world I would probably have been put on Ritalin as a hyperactive child. Now, in my later years (or is it second childhood?) I am still on the go. Traveling to far away places or even closer places is always a pleasure.*

St. Mary's was not only an Academy or boarding school but a parish school as well, so there were many local boys and girls. I was the only boarder in my class. Many of the boys were just waiting to be sixteen so they could leave school and work on their parents' farms, and the girls would marry. Very few were interested in college. As Sister St. Ignatius would say of them, "you're just warming the benches." The academic standards were excellent however, as St. Mary's Academy followed the New York State Board of Regents curriculum and exams at the end of each school year. We prided ourselves on knowing that our school always did better than the local public school. We also followed guidelines from Catholic University of America in Washington, D.C. and in high school took their exams. In addition we took our regular school exams in each subject. There was nothing else to do so studying became a priority. The school day ran from 8a.m. to 4 p.m.

Extracurricular activities however, were at a minimum. I remember playing tennis a couple of times with some of the younger Sisters. My tennis racket was a gift of Aunt Mildred. The girls and boys who were boarders never had recreation together. I only saw my brother Bob on occasions when I needed some spending money as he was in charge of that. Before I could get money to buy a new composition book he would check to see if there were any blank half pages which had to be filled before getting a new one. We did have a girls' volley ball team, but I was never much good at sports. School dances were unknown and dates were impossible.

Friday afternoons (if we had been good all week) were devoted to some more entertaining reading, such as the Horatio Alger books, like *Ragged Dick* or *The Errand Boy*. We also read *Anne of Green Gables*, or the Civil War novels featuring two teenagers, Bob and Jim. Bob, from an aristocratic Virginia family and Jim, a hillbilly from West Virginia were scouts on the Union side and according to the books, helped win almost every battle during the war. Of course, there were conflicts with some of Bob's family being Rebels and class distinctions when it came to Jim socializing with the elite. Now I realize that this series helped us all a lot in remembering all the battles of the Civil War and providing us with many examples of what is now called "family values."

The small library had a few sections devoted to fiction. I started from the A's and worked my way down to the Z's. I read dusty historical novels and classics that had not been touched in years. Some of them turned out to be very interesting. Among my favorites were detective novels, "The Saint" stories by Leslie Charteris, S.S. Van Dyne mysteries, and a book called *Cleek, the Man of Forty Faces*. I was never without a book in my hands. I would read while waiting in line, going up the stairs to the dormitory and whenever there was a spare moment. I would dress quickly in the morning and start reading. I did the same at bedtime before the lights went out.

In high school the local parish priest, Father Duford, a distinguished looking middle aged priest, gave us a class on Etiquette once a week, so we could act in a socially acceptable manner—how to eat our soup, use our knife and fork and make introductions, etc. At that time there were no teachers' aides or helpers. The students vied with each other for the "privilege" of cleaning the blackboards and the erasers.

We spent about an hour in the evening in the recreation room where we could play board games, cards or read. As I could read well and fast, the younger kids often asked me to read aloud from books from the library. Historical novels such as *Richard Carvel, Lorna Doone* and *Richard Meredith* were popular. The Foreign Legion novel, *Beau Geste*, was a special favorite and I remember using the code word "Sergeant Lajaune" when talking about how "mean" and strict one of the Sisters was. I loved the sentimental romances by Grace Livingston Hill, especially one called *Crimson Roses*. I enjoyed those that featured the hero falling in love with a rather plain or poor young woman with the stereotype of the hard-working sales-girl or the serious librarian. These themes hit home to me as I was considered "homely" by the other students. I was adept at making up haunted house stories on the spot. Of course, the Sisters recommended that we read the lives of the Saints and other pious stories.

If the entire group had misbehaved in some way, our punishment was to spend about 15 minutes in silence at recreation time. At the end, Sister would ask: "those that didn't talk raise your hands." Once I raised my hand as I hadn't talked and Sister said: "no, but you laughed." I felt you just couldn't win.

Our outdoor activities were mostly walks where we had to march two by two and not talk too loud. At least we got to see some of the town. However, in upstate New York winters were quite cold and I remember really freezing and hugging the radiators when we arrived back at the rec. room. Other times we visited farms and orchards owned by parents of some of the day students. *My dislike for butter-milk, yogurt and cottage cheese came from those trips when they had us drinking fresh warm milk from the cows—yuck!* However, the orchards were great as we got to pick apples and eat them right there. I also remember picking wild roses on some of the back dirt roads. These I laid on the shelf of my bedside stand where I made a small shrine to the Virgin Mary with a holy card of Our Lady of Sorrows (the Pieta.) I saved my pennies to buy a couple of holy cards which I treasured. I remember one of my favorites was that of Mary as the Morning Star.

We skated on the frozen Chazy River, just down the hill and across the street, playing "crack the whip." My Aunt Mildred had given me a pair of ice skates for Christmas. Every spring we waited for the ice to break up in the river and watch for the possible flood when the dam overflowed. We went fishing in it in the summer and as we didn't have bathing suits we would "fall in" and then exclaim "I'm already wet, can I stay in?" At these times the Sisters were pretty lenient, probably remembering their own childhood outings.

I spent one summer, (probably between seventh and eighth grade) at the school. Being the only girl boarder there at the time, I had the dormitory to myself. I was occasionally treated with an unusual sight of one of the Sisters washing her long hair in the sink in the girls' dormitory. Several boys stayed in the summer, so I joined them in climbing trees and going to Lake Champlain for picnics etc. I got away with more than the boys did as no one was really checking on everything I did. I do remember though, that at Isle La Motte on Lake Champlain, the Sisters had the boys swim in one area and the *girl* in the other. As I had no bathing suit, I wore my most modest cotton slip and panties.

We had annual class picnics that were just great. We'd all pile into a cattle truck, owned by one of the students' parents and drive all the way to Ausable Chasm, Fort Ticonderoga, or Lake George. We sat packed on wooden benches and waved and shouted at every car, every farmer in his field, and every cow along the way. We even had a parent who was a warden at the Dannemora State Prison, so we took a tour of the prison. We were taken aback when we saw these good looking guys dressed in overalls baking bread, folding laundry etc. As boarders we envied the inmates as they had movies every week. In all the time I was in boarding school we saw one movie,

The Count of Monte Cristo. It was in two installments a week apart, so we all behaved like little saints so we wouldn't be punished by not being able to see the ending.

Champlain was only two miles from the Canadian border, so we sometimes had the opportunity of going to a maple sugaring party in Canada. We watched the tapping of the trees and the huge vats where the sap was boiled and later made into maple sugar cakes. The treat was to find a last patch of snow so we could pour the hot syrup on it to make delicious candy.

As boarders we lived in a convent-like atmosphere. Most of the Sisters were French Canadians who all knew and spoke French. Some of the Sisters in the kitchen and the infirmarian, Sister Beatrice, did not even speak English. Most of the students knew French and I took some teasing for my New Jersey accent with its broad "a's", but I would return the teasing with "but at least I don't say 'look at her 'igh 'eels'!" At first my French was rudimentary and I said the "Hail Mary" as best I could, thus: "Zheva sally mally Pentecost, sissy had a teddy-boo, zebenee ontray tulay fam ay zhezu lefree de voz on try beni. Sent Maddy maddy diu pray for the bishop metna ay ler de nut ra mor swatsit, swatsit." The French "Hail Mary" prayer really goes like this: "Je vous salut Marie, pleine de grace, le Seigneur êtes avec vous. Vous êtes beni entre tous les femmes et Jésus le fruit de vos entrailles est beni. Saint Marie, mère de Dieu, priez pour nous pecheurs, maintenant et a l'heure de notre mort. Ainsi soit il." Eventually I learned all the prayers and many French hymns and songs.

One year I came down with scarlet fever (no one else got it) and I was quarantined in the Sisters' Infirmary for two weeks. That's where I had to learn French. Sister Beatrice gave me comic books (which if I had been well, I would never have seen) and newspapers to read as they could be destroyed after use. They also gave me some paper and study questions so I could keep up with school lessons a little. I would look out the window, count the squares in the linoleum floor and the old fashioned ceiling and generally tried to entertain myself.

At evening prayers in the chapel I was assigned the task of reciting the examination of conscience. What I do remember of it went somewhat like this: "Let us examine our conscience on our duties to God, our neighbor and ourselves. Did I arise at the first call this morning and give my heart to God? Did I dress myself promptly and modestly? How did I say my morning prayers, night prayers and all my prayers during the day? Did I attend Mass with modesty and devotion? Was I guilty of pride, envy, gluttony, anger, and sloth? Was I honest? Did I attend to my studies carefully? Did I keep silence in the halls, in the refectory, in the dormitory, and going up and down stairs? Did I obey my teachers?" There may have been a few more items which escape my memory. It was hard to keep my composure as when I would get to the part about gluttony, someone would whisper, "How can we—we don't get enough to eat?" or other distracting comments. We did have to keep silence in going up and downstairs and I remember at night sometimes having to sing "Good Night Sweet Jesus, guard us in sleep" which gave us something to do besides talk as we ascended the stairs to the dormitory.

Sister Rita had been the high school English teacher for a while and spoke often about wanting to go to her community's missions in Basutoland (now Lesotho). This intrigued me and added fertilizer to the seed planted at St. Catherine's with its Holy Childhood ladders and increased my interest in the foreign missions. She did get sent to the missions and we eagerly listened to her enthusiastic letters. On the negative side were the stories of the North American Jesuit martyrs that were read to us with all the gory details of their torture and martyrdom by the Indians. It didn't help me form my opinion about Indians.

We ate at long "refectory" tables and as in a convent, ate our breakfast in silence with someone reading from a pious book, such as *Little Lady Bountiful* or *Elsie Dinsmore* and other "edifying" stories of saints, such as *Little Nell of Holy God*. As "little girls" we had to wear black smocks so we wouldn't soil our regulation middies and skirts. The smocks saved the day once when someone was passing the oatmeal dish over Teresa DeSimone's head and then she sat up straighter and the whole plate of oatmeal landed in her hair, on her glasses and down the smock. The smocks had handy pockets in them where we could stash some item we didn't want to eat or save it for eating later. It became messy if the item was lumpy oatmeal or pieces of fat from the stew. Bread soup was always a treat—to this day I'd love to know how they made it so tasty as it had nothing else but bread in it. It was not so tasty when the cook put in pearl tapioca that looked like fish eyes, big transparent blobs—that were kind of difficult to fish out from the soup and get into the smock pocket without being seen. When I got to be a "big girl" and got caught talking out of turn, the routine punishment was to have to sit at the "little girls" table. I'd get around this by making them believe that it was their privilege to have a big girl sitting with them. As a good reader, I often was asked to do the prescribed reading.

Saturday mornings were devoted to a couple of hours of "Manual Training" which meant doing some embroidery work or other sewing craft. Once I was so lackadaisical in my embroidering that I noticed when I went to get up that I had sewn the stitches to my skirt. I did manage to make a few gifts for Grandma, a pillow cover or an apron. I was only too happy to have as an excuse that I had to help my teacher, Sister St. Ignatius, who was also in charge of cleaning the chapel and the care of the sacristy. The floors were of beautiful polished hardwood, and after scrubbing, I had to wax them on my hands and knees and then I tied old wool sweaters around my feet and "skated" up and down the aisles and pews to polish the floor to a brilliant shine. It was hard work but it beat having to go to Manual Training. I always tried to dawdle long enough to arrive almost at the end of the class. *Many years later I did attempt crocheting an afghan while living in Boulder. It actually took me about 10 years to finish it—still dawdling!* While cleaning in the chapel I remember what a privilege to be so close to the tabernacle, as I could talk directly to Jesus.

On Sundays we wore our special uniform. Instead of middy blouse, skirt and tie we wore a black wool serge long-sleeved dress. With it went a stiff celluloid white collar, not unlike the kind the priests wore, but open in front. It had a collar button in front and in back, with a sateen black ribbon tied to the collar. We older girls often had to help the little girls with getting them buttoned and tied. Stockings were always black "lisle." On occasional holidays we could wear a "colored" dress with brown stockings. As I needed one,

I remember going once with one of the Sisters down to the local dry goods store and ended up with an ugly orange, long-sleeved, knit dress that really made me look even more homely and skinny, but of course, it was "modest."

Mass was sometimes said in the convent chapel but often at the local parish church as we had to sing for High Mass. The French Canadian parishioners frequently requested High Mass for the Dead and we were asked to sing the Requiem Mass. My love for Gregorian chant began up in the choir loft. Although not a great singer, I could hold a tune. The times I stayed for Christmas vacation were also special as I loved the beautifully decorated church and the Nativity scene. The singing of carols warmed my heart, as the radiators rattled and banged trying to warm up the cold church. Upstate New York is noted for its cold winters and I found them trying. I did miss our wonderful Hillside Christmases, but joined in whatever the Sisters could provide us with good holiday cheer. They taught us how to "pull" molasses taffy and we helped decorate the Christmas tree.

In English Literature class I was moved by Francis Thompson's poem "The Hound of Heaven" where God is the "Hound" seeking a soul who was searching for Him everywhere without peace. This theme of searching for God has followed me for the rest of my life regardless of the religious fads of the day. Often I had a problem with sermons about God as a loving and caring Father of us all, when my only image of a father was of Dad who loved me but failed to always be there for me when I needed him.

Many of the girls were orphans or their parents had separated so it was not common to be asked about my parents. I usually lied about my mother's dying of tuberculosis. I used to say "she died of pneumonia or something" and then quickly change to another subject. At that time, tuberculosis still carried a stigma. I also shied away from the sentimental pitying that often accompanied well-meaning sympathy, even though deep down inside I craved a sympathetic ear. However, I was spared many of the problems of girls in public schools in their home towns who were orphaned or lost a mother and felt left out of a lot of events that included their mothers, or were shunned by the other girls.

A Truant, and Another Loss

Things went along fairly well until my eighth grade Christmas vacation. I went back to Madison, but did not return to St. Mary's. Bob, after his sophomore year, had now gone to the Seminary of the Missionaries of the Sacred Heart to study for the priesthood. He had met the priests of that order at a parish mission in Champlain and was at a Seminary in upstate New York. Bob belonged to the Canadian Province but was stationed later at a T.B. Sanatorium in Saranac Lake, then as a chaplain in a Rhode Island State Prison, as an assistant pastor in various parishes, but never assigned to the foreign missions. As his community needed a bilingual librarian, he studied library science and then was assigned as librarian in the seminaries etc. He later became a Canadian citizen and has worked mostly in Quebec and other areas of French Canada.

Herb went to the parish school at St. Vincent's in Madison. I was not sent to school anywhere. As far as I can piece together, Dad had lost his job when the Jersey Central Railroad had financial problems and he was living in Elizabeth in a boarding house in a poor neighborhood, and working for the WPA (Roosevelt's Work Progress Administration) and obviously not making much money. There must have been some kind of impasse, but I don't know what actually transpired. I was a truant for the next six months, so on weekdays I had to stay in the house. As I had not attended any local schools, the truant officers weren't aware that I wasn't in school. On weekends I took out books from the library so spent a lot of time reading mostly fairy tales and detective stories and helping with the housework—making the beds, dusting, hanging out the laundry, ironing, setting the table, and washing dishes. I always loved school so it was a difficult time for me.

Somehow, my aunts decided to return me to St. Mary's where I went back in September, finished the eighth grade by January and then finished the first year of high school by June of the same year. The sisters were very helpful in getting me up to date to take exams etc, so I was back with my original classmates. I never had the usual eighth grade graduation.

I soon received the Sacrament of Confirmation and noticed on the bottom of the certificate was the word "guardian" with my Aunt Marie's name in the blank. *I now wonder if there ever was a legal process for that change of guardianship or did the Sisters just go along with whoever was paying the bills. Bob once wrote later that my aunts resented that my Dad had "dumped" us kids on them. I always sensed this, although nothing was said and they didn't take it out on me. We seldom talked about my Dad after that. However, I was desperately loyal to Dad and never could work up a spontaneous love and gratitude for my grandmother and aunts for the sacrifices and hardship they endured to keep me in school.*

From that time on, my Dad lived in Elizabeth in various places and I only saw him for maybe a week or so in the summer vacations. I would take the bus alone from Madison to Springfield and transfer to Elizabeth. Once he lived in an apartment on Delaware Street with a young couple. Later he moved to rooming houses that provided a tiny single room with the bathroom down the hall. These were on Flora Street, then on E. Grand St. and later on Magnolia Avenue where he met Bella Newman, a divorced lady about his age. She had a larger apartment with a kitchen as she had two of her children with her. One was her son, Sonny, about my age (14 or 15). We used to play pinochle and other card games with Dad and Bella, Sonny or his older sister, Mickie. Sonny and I used to lock feet under the card table and took walks together. He would often sing his old favorite "I'll Be Down to Get You in a Taxi, Honey." I was thrilled when back in boarding school I got a letter from Sonny, written in pencil, saying how much he missed me. Two weeks was a short time to build up a relationship, so nothing came of it. Sonny soon moved to live with his father out of state, so I didn't see him again. When I visited Dad in the summer I would stay with Bella, as Dad's room was very tiny with just his cot and a hot plate and no room for another bed or couch.

When World War II started my Dad got a defense job as an assemblyman at General Motors in Linden, New Jersey so his financial situation was much better, but he never sent money, nor did he offer to help my aunts with my school expenses. About my second year in college my Dad wrote to tell me that he and Bella had been married by the Justice of the Peace. This was a big blow to me, as I had been taught that Catholics had to marry in the Church and certainly not to a divorced woman. I was never able to think of her even as my stepmother. The church's stand on divorce kept me from getting closer to her. She was a nice woman and liked me, but I held back. Also, somehow I felt it would be disloyal to my own mother to let her into my heart. I never sent her a Mother's Day card or acknowledged her concern. Of course, a week every year was not long enough to really get to know her or bond with her in any real way. She lived many years after my Dad died in 1949 and Bob used to visit her occasionally when she lived in Atlantic Highlands on the Jersey shore. As I was later out of the country, I never saw her again. When I returned to the United States she did write me one letter. My brother Bob kept in contact with her.

If there were empty places in my heart, at least I had a few friends to fill some of the vacancies. At St. Mary's I met three Brazilian girls, Otilia, Zelia and Lucy Pereira. Their father, who was a jeweler, had to leave the country when the Brazilian President, Washington Luis, was exiled. Their mother had died and their favorite aunt was still in Rio de Janeiro. They used to brag about how she got prizes for dancing for 24 hours during Carnival. It was great to see how they quickly learned English. Once, Lucy was looking through the window to the music room while a student was practicing piano, and was told to leave. She squinted up her face in a question until the student used the vernacular "Scram" and she quickly left. I used to help Lucy (the youngest) write her letters to her "Papae"—pronounced Popeye with the accent on the "eye". She could speak Portuguese but had not learned to write it. She didn't want Papae to know she couldn't write Portuguese. She would dictate it to me and I would write it. I didn't always know what I was writing, but she seemed satisfied. They taught me to sing the Brazilian national anthem and the St. John's Day (John the Baptist) popular song, "Chego agora da fuguera e noite do San João," (the night of the bonfires of Saint John have arrived,) referring to the bonfires that were lit on that day and the fire that burned in the heart of a lover. I also picked up from them the vulgar expression "pesto do diablo," (pest of the devil) but they cautioned me not to use it. Their biggest treat was to have their Papae send them a tin of guava jelly (guayabada) and Brazilian cheese, which they shared with me.

The oldest, Otilia, was my special friend. One summer she invited me to the family's apartment on 52nd St. in New York City where the guest of honor was none other than the exiled President, Washington Luis. As he was the honored guest, not me, they had to speak in Portuguese. I would listen and try to figure out what they were saying. When I joined the conversation with an English comment they were surprised. I had a facility for languages that helped me a great deal later in my work. I still have a rose petal that Otilia inscribed with a little poem "To my dear Joan. Se eu fom uma rosa, dar-te-ia um botão, mas como seu tu amiga, dou-te o meu coração. Tiloca. December 31, 1939." ("If I were a rose, I would give you a bud, but as you are my friend, I give you my heart.") Her nickname was "Tiloca" pronounced "Chilocca" and when she heard about a flower called portulaca she exclaimed, "See, I'm poor, even as a flower." They used to spend time at the Brazilian embassy and knew Carmen Miranda (the famous Brazilian singer who was always seen dancing with a large basket of fruit on her head,) who was at the local nightclubs. I lost track of them after graduation but think they had moved back to Brazil when the political climate had improved for them. In the class prophecy I was appointed ambassador to Brazil. *Not really, but close enough.*

Another girl who befriended me was Marjorie Riel, a plain motherly person who once, while in the bathroom from the next stall, explained as best she could about what happens when I would get my period. When one of the Sisters later discovered my soiled underwear she asked me if my aunt had talked to me about menstruation. Of course, I lied and said she had, but then she had to set me up with Kotex, a belt and pins and how to discreetly dispose of the pads in a locked sanitary can. Only the big girls had access to the key as it was hung on a high hook in the bathroom. Later when my Aunt Marie asked me if I knew about periods, I told her that I did. Nothing was ever said again about the matter or anything related to sex, so my knowledge about sex was pretty minimal. In Madison we (four aunts and me) put our used pads in a hanging laundry bag in the closet and when more or less full, one of my aunts would take the bag to the furnace to burn the contents. High school biology helped a little in my understanding of reproduction, but not much about sex and intimacy.

I vaguely remember one play called *The Poor Little Rich Girl* and I played the part of the poor ragged Irish girl, crying piteously as she went from one end of the stage to the other with clasped hands. In another one whose name I forget, I played the part of a jolly Negro maid who was generously endowed (me stuffed with a pillow) and came in with a plate full of doughnuts (we all liked plays that included food in the props.)

In our class yearbook *Sesame* my photo showed me in my white middy blouse, blue tie and jacket with the caption "studious, loquacious, quick-tempered. President '41, brains of the class." All of these were apt adjectives but the "brains of the class" byline was a bit disheartening, as it meant to me the same as it means to today's teenager being called a "nerd." The other girls' captions had little sly references to their current boy friends. I was the only boarder, so boy friends were out. I was considered "homely." In fact, one of my Brazilian friends was remarking about a girl from another school and she said, quite innocently, "She's even more homely than you are." Wearing wire-rimmed glasses since age eleven and having straight hair didn't help either.

The class history noted, speaking of our freshman year, "In January we were joined by Joan Jollett, the mental genius from New Jersey." We started out as twenty, but ended up as only seven in our senior year as a new High School had been built in Alburgh, Vermont and the Vermont students no longer needed to come by train to Champlain. We lost a few more students to other schools and were left with no "boy students." The class Prophecy noted thus: "The stars of '41. What have we here—a star that foretells a future of brilliancy and honor and who is it? Yes, the great Joan Jollett, the famous reporter traveling throughout the country making American newspapers the most interesting reading of the world." I guess what suggested that was my writing for the school paper, *The Blue and White*. I only remember writing one whimsical article about "noiseless chewing gum" inspired by the new "noiseless" typewriters and my attempt to find a solution for most of the students who were caught chewing gum. *What did they know that I didn't know? It was many years later that I started writing.* The Class Will bequeathed various gifts to the juniors, "We bequeath to Francis White, Joan's ability of mastering languages. Your troubles should be finished with this help, Francis." *Francis used his inheritance quite well. When St. Mary's had its 90th anniversary, I discovered in the literature that he later became a priest. I hope he got A's in his Latin classes.*

As valedictorian for my class I gave the usual commencement speech. I had just turned sixteen in March of 1941. I never got a graduation ring, as we couldn't afford it. *When I hear stories of other people my age, I realize how much I missed—no proms or dances, no dates, no football games to cheer for although we did have inter-school boys basketball games, and no boyfriends although the school was co-ed. We didn't even have access to radios, newspapers or magazines and certainly no movies (with the exception of the "Count of Monte Cristo.") I guess I did lead a rather sheltered life.*

CHAPTER 6

TRINITY COLLEGE

The next decision to be made by my aunts was where I should attend college. Being only sixteen, getting a job was not an option and they thought I should have a college education. Again, economics was the deciding factor. They picked Trinity College, a woman's college run by the Sisters of Mercy in Burlington, Vermont. I was able to get a tuition scholarship if I kept up good grades. I was offered room and board if I worked in the kitchen. As a boarder I shared a room on the third floor of St. Joseph's Villa with another student, Claire Morrisette, from Danielson, Connecticut. The Villa was an old home or boarding house converted into a student residence. Other students who were able to pay more were in the more modern college building which also housed the classrooms, labs, auditorium, gymnasium and chapel. Trinity was a small college, founded in 1925 so we got to know everyone. Here too were day students as well as boarders. Our class in our freshman year was composed of only 28 students, memorialized by our class song to the tune of Glenn Miller's "Moonlight Cocktail"—"Twenty-eight beautiful freshmen beyond compare..."

I was somewhat influenced by my friend Imogene in Madison who had gotten a part time job with the pharmaceutical company, Ciba's, in Summit, New Jersey. I signed up for the Bachelor of Science program thinking that someday I might get a job there too. However, I did have a pretty rounded-out liberal education. Education classes were the easy courses where I always had a book in my lap to read during class. Not so easy were the French and Spanish classes as we had an excellent teacher Sister Cyril, who demanded and expected a lot of serious work. My high school French helped a lot, but Spanish was new. A "B" from Sister Cyril was better than an "A" from Miss Collins in Education. Chemistry and Physiology also required time to do experiments correctly and accurately. Our English teacher was a man, Dr. Beers, who just loved Tennyson so we learned to regurgitate Tennyson for him on the exams.

For Music Appreciation I was fortunate in that my second year roommate was Gennie McKnight who was one of two music majors. She could coach me in recognizing different works and told me what to listen to on the radio (operas, symphonies etc) so we could report on them in Music Appreciation class. Often, however, some of us would listen to the introduction and the first piece and then switch over to our favorite swing band or the Hit Parade.

I also belonged to the Literary Club and the Drama Club. I played the part of a French peasant in one, *The Child of Flanders*, complete with beret, smock, mustache and a French accent. For the Gilbert and Sullivan operetta, *Iolanthe*, I was on the makeup committee. I joined the orchestra and was asked to be the "percussion section" which consisted of Xylophone, triangle and cymbals. However, the pieces did not call for many parts for these instruments and I had to count "one and two and three and four and" until my turn came. Once it came on the fifty fourth measure of "Song without Words" and I had lost count, so was waiting for a nod from Miss Hunt to play my three strokes on the triangle. "Where was the percussion section?" she later asked. The next year she asked me to be in the Chorus, but I said I preferred the orchestra, but she replied, "I don't think so."

On December 7, 1941 we were eating our Sunday evening meal of potato salad and bologna sandwiches, and listening to Monsignor Fulton Sheen on the radio, when the program was interrupted by an announcement by President Roosevelt that the Japanese had bombed Pearl Harbor: "A day that will live in infamy." World War II affected much of our lives for the next four years. Several students had brothers, other relatives and boy friends that had to go off to war and it became common to see letters postmarked from overseas and V-mail was common. Food was rationed, although at a boarding school it was not so severe as for our families; gasoline was rationed, but didn't have much immediate effect on us students as we walked just about everywhere since none of us had a car. If the weather was severe, we took a bus to get downtown.

Burlington was a small town with one traffic light. However, its facilities were stretched with the many servicemen in the nearby area. We had the Field Artillery in Essex Junction, the Paratroopers nearby, the Air Force Cadets at the University of Vermont and the Navy Midshipmen at Middlebury College. The big bands played songs that reminded us that we were in a war—"The White Cliffs of Dover," "Don't Sit under the Apple Tree," etc. Uniforms were every-where and we learned to recognize the various military insignia as we tried to find a seat in our downtown hangout, Upton's Drug Store.

It was common in the movie houses to have to stand for the whole show or wait in a long line to get a lane in the bowling alley. We became patriotic and diligently "knitted for Britain," learned the various types of airplanes—the P-38's, the B-17's etc. We volunteered at the USO downtown and made sandwiches for "the boys," and got a chance to dance with some of them. The Sisters allowed us to date them except for the Paratroopers. They considered them just a little too "tough" for us young ladies. Many of the movies were war stories, such as *I Wanted Wings, Guadalcanal Diary,* and the classic *Casablanca.* If anyone wasted something or there was a shortage, the watchword was always: "There's a war on, moron." This is when we had to give up our new Nylon stockings (just recently introduced to replace silk stockings from Japan.) The Nylon was needed to make parachutes. We soon learned we could paint our legs with leg makeup and use an eyebrow pencil to make a nice seam up the back. The Sisters probably knew that we did this, but went along without much protest. To conserve the stockings we had, we used nail polish to stop the runs in our stockings. The college dress code included that we wear stockings even when we wore knee socks over them. Even the garbage trucks went patriotic—the truck now sported the sign on its side: "Used Vitamin Convoy Service." Radio commercials adapted as well—"Lucky Strike Means Fine Tobacco" became "Lucky Strike Green Has Gone to War."

During one summer vacation in Madison, St. Vincent's Church sponsored a dance in the parish hall for the U.S. sailors and as it was sponsored by the church, Aunt Marie allowed me to attend. I danced with a very good looking guy, but when he asked me for my phone number, I didn't give it to him as I knew Aunt Marie wouldn't like the idea of me dating a non-Catholic.

My first year roommate, Claire, had decided to go to School as a Nursing Cadet student so she didn't return. However, I spent the next summer with her at her home in Danielson, Connecticut. Her father had just died and her mother was having a difficult time running the family drugstore. They had one pharmacist, but it was hard to get any help, as most people were either in the armed forces or working at a defense plant that paid a lot more than a drugstore. So, I took a bus from Madison and arrived at her home in Connecticut, near the Rhode Island border. Every day I went with Claire to the drugstore and helped make sandwiches, serve up sundaes and sodas and generally helped out. It was good experience for me. I didn't get paid, but could eat at the drugstore or occasionally be treated to New England fish and chips at a local seafood restaurant. We did take a few trips to Mystic on the seacoast and other places in nearby Rhode Island. Here I had my first experience with sexual harassment. The pharmacist would tease me a lot. He'd offer me a piece of chocolate from an opened box of gift chocolates and then laugh as I tried to pick one out of the box of fake chocolates. He went too far though when he asked me "are those mosquito bites?" referring to my budding breasts. I weathered that incident and don't remember any more after that. Claire's little brother was also around when he wasn't out playing ball with his friends. He kept me up-to-date on the identity of the airplanes overhead. I corresponded with Claire for a while after that but lost track of her eventually. She was a very mature young girl and a pleasant roommate.

My roommate for the next three years was Gennie McKnight, the music major. We both earned our board in the kitchen—she washing dishes and I drying. Gennie was an avid smoker, so she quickly managed to finish her chore while I was still drying. She would run over across the street to our hangout, Danforth's General Store, where she could puff to her heart's content. Danforth's was a great place, very tiny with a pot belly stove in the middle where we could warm up on a cold day and a back room with three or four booths. We boarders played many games of Pinochle, Whist and Bridge there in a smoke-filled haze with a small Coke as a token purchase. Smoking was strictly forbidden in the Villa or college building. Once, when cigarettes were hard to come by during the War, Gennie went to the tobacco store and bought a corncob pipe, "for my grandmother," she explained. Then she emptied the tobacco from the butts of the cigarettes into the pipe and smoked them that way (generally filter tips were unknown.) I only smoked occasionally, mostly Kools that were easier to get and I "never inhaled." Naturally, I never smoked at home. That would have brought a severe scolding from Aunt Marie. Some of the girls would try going out one of the girls' windows that had access to a slanted roof where they could smoke. Those who didn't would be on guard so that the Sisters wouldn't catch them. Being on a scholarship I had to be a little more careful about the rules.

In our freshman year we had the usual Freshman Mixer Dance when boys from the nearby Catholic College, St. Michael's, in Winooski were invited. In an effort to look more attractive, I removed my glasses, but after intermission, it was difficult to find the boy I had just danced with. I had a few dates with Frank Smith, a Michaelman (student from St. Michael's) as an aftermath of this dance. Aside from my pseudo-dates with Sonny, this was my first real date. The next year we put on the Sophomore Hop with a musical theme all in silver and black that we thought was just the best. Junior Prom and Senior Dance followed.

A classmate, Lily Bajda who lived in South Orange, New Jersey, and I used to meet at Grand Central Station under the big clock to take the train from New York to Burlington. On one trip we met two very nice servicemen in the Field Artillery—Gene Ford for Lily and Gene Ferry for me, both from Brooklyn. We double-dated them a few times until they were transferred. Another serviceman I dated was from the Air Force Cadets at the University of Vermont. A few other Michaelmen were dates, but I don't remember their names. Vermont was a blue law state, so Sunday dates were really limited. If you had a date on Sunday, you had a choice of going to the University Museum or taking a walk to look at the Green Mountains in the distance. A special treat was to go to the Howard Johnson's out of town and have one of their wonderful ice cream cones.

When the gentlemen came to St. Joseph's Villa to call on a date, Sister Bernarda, the house mother, would ring a centralized buzzer for each floor (of course after she had duly checked on the young man to see if he qualified.) The system consisted of one or more long buzzes followed by a number of short ones. That is if your number was 21, we would all hear two long buzzes followed by one short one. Of course this way everyone knew who had a date, so no secrets there.

Occasionally some of us girls would get daring and go to a local cocktail lounge, the Sugar House, to have a drink. Those of us under 21 (which meant most of us) had to take on another student's identity to get served. Sometimes a classmate would buy a bottle of gin and then we would add Orange Green Spot to mix with it. Leaving a jug of the Halloween cider (unpasteurized) for a while in the closet gave us a nice treat of hard cider that we enjoyed later.

I used to hang out a lot with other students in Peggy Magner and Catherine Smith's room on the second floor as it was bigger and we could take advantage of both of their talents in Math to get our homework done. We all chipped in for nightly snacks of crackers with marshmallow fluff and peanut butter. We listened attentively there to the weekly Hit Parade. The Big Bands were popular and we had to know which song or which band was on top. We prided ourselves on being able to recognize each one after only a few bars of the music. I used to wear Lily's brother's jacket and a bow tie, hold on to a broom handle and imitate Frank Sinatra's singing, for example, "I Couldn't Sleep a Wink Last Night," or "I'll Never Smile Again." The others dutifully swooned as I did some of his little characteristic trills. I got to be known as "The Thriller of the Third Floor." I had his photo in my wallet, but had Joseph Cotton's picture on my wall.

One of my favorite pastimes was to take a walk in the woods behind the college. The white birch trees along with the dark green pine trees made for a very peaceful and inspiring refuge. I also used to go to the woods behind the University of Vermont, supposedly to study alone for an upcoming exam. However, I found myself leaving my notebook under a pine tree and then going off to pick the many violets growing there. *I have always been a fan of wildflowers everywhere I lived and I guess it all started here, or maybe in the meadows near the house in Madison.*

After my sophomore year when I was finally eighteen I didn't have the worrisome Catch-22 of trying to get a summer job without working papers, and trying to get working papers without a job. I did apply and interview at several places, e.g. pharmaceutical companies, other businesses and finally got hired for my first paying job at Kresge's Department Store in Newark, NJ. I was hired as a waitress from 7 a.m. to 4 p.m. as they served breakfast and lunch. I had to wear a brown waitress uniform with yellow collar and trim and a "snood" (net) for my hair. The U-shaped counter-type restaurant was located in the basement with sixteen customers per waitress. There were about 8 stations in all. I liked the work and loved the food, but when I got up in the morning I had to be careful about putting my feet on the floor as they were sore from walking on cement every day.

During wartime there were a lot of government employees in nearby buildings, so everyone was on a half-hour lunch period. Everyone wanted to be served very quickly. The ladies, especially wanted to eat, shop, primp up—all in a half-hour. This was when being a "Jumping Joan" really helped. The fussiest customers however, were the store buyers who worked upstairs and had gotten used to having things their way. Coffee was rationed to one cup apiece. One lady pushed the cup at me and said angrily "I asked for a cup of coffee." Mystified, I looked at the cup and it looked like coffee. The only other alternative was tea, which was served in a clear, hot water pot, so I didn't know what she meant. She demanded: "Fill it up!" So I let some of it overflow into the saucer. After drinking a little from the cup, she poured the contents of the saucer into the cup and this way she could get her second cup, or close to it.

I noticed that men especially, always ate the same breakfast, day after day, and year after year. I still remember one man's special order was always—prunes, whole-wheat toast and coffee. I learned a lot about human nature and how to cope with all kinds of people, including the kitchen help. It was important to be "nice" to them as if they didn't like you, your order could sit on the spindle for a long time. If a customer found a worm in his corn on the cob, I returned it to the kitchen where they quickly flipped off the worm, turned the corn over and returned it to me for the customer. Once another waitress, afraid of serving a group of deaf customers, sent them to my station, as she must have thought I could handle them. Some customers would ask: "what flavors of ice cream do you have?" "Vanilla, chocolate, strawberry…peach, black raspberry and banana." "Do you have butter pecan?" "No." "Well, what do you have?" and I repeated the list again. "Well, I guess I'll have vanilla." It was easy to spot an overeater, usually women who would insist on a lettuce and tomato sandwich with no butter or mayonnaise and then order a hot fudge sundae.

I had to walk about a mile to the train station and then take the Lackawanna commuter train to Newark, then walk about six blocks to Kresge's. On Wednesday nights the store was open, so I was asked to work late that night. *In later years young women wouldn't dream of walking at night in downtown Newark, but during the war it was safe.* These were the nights when my college friend from South Orange, Lily, was working at Westinghouse, and we would go out to Borden's and get a great big sundae. Sometimes we would go to a cocktail lounge and have a Tom Collins (a gin-based cocktail.) This was the highlight of the week and of course, Aunt Marie did not know about these infractions. I sometimes was asked to help out at the soda fountain making sundaes and sodas and on Fridays help peel shrimp for the shrimp chow mein, which was always on the Friday menu. Most of my salary was turned over to Grandma to help pay for my household expenses. I had this job again after my junior year.

I think it was in my junior year when several of us received our income tax refund and we decided to give ourselves a treat. We went by bus to Montreal, stayed at a local "tourist home" and received information from the manager about a nearby dance hall called the "Palais d'Or" and danced with some of the local boys. Some of them walked us back to our tourist home and said farewell on the steps. It was a great weekend and we were glad that we hadn't frittered away our hard-earned money.

In college I once borrowed someone's skis and went down the hill at the nearby Mary Fletcher Hospital. I was afraid of breaking the skis as they were wooden and I couldn't afford to replace them, so never tried them again. Occasionally I got some money baby sitting for the Danforth kids, but I usually received spending money from my aunts according to what they could afford.

One year at Thanksgiving vacation I went with some other girls to Stowe where we ended up going to a big square dance at a barn. I really enjoyed being taken off my feet as I didn't know the steps but just let my partner lead me. A blizzard came up and the buses weren't running. The only vehicle available was a small mini-bus where we all piled in. This required that some of the skinnier (like me) girls had to sit on some guy's lap. This was a great adventure and when we got back it was hard for me to tell the Sisters what had happened and where I had been, as I did not have written permission from Aunt Marie to go there. They thought I had gone to Madison, so I held my peace. The Trapp Family Singers (of *The Sound of Music* fame) had not yet opened their big ski resort in Stowe, although we did see the parents and girls at the bus station in Burlington on occasion. We thought their clothes and hairdos were hopelessly out of style.

Career Decisions

We had to attend Mass every morning in the College chapel, wearing our academic caps and gowns. Actually these came in very handy for late risers as you could get up five minutes before Mass time, pull a few bobby pins or curlers out of your hair, don the cap, and the long black gown covered the pajamas underneath. We had dialogue Mass (the congregation answering the priest's prayers) and we would go to the local St. Mark's church where the pastor had permission to say Mass facing the people once a month. It took another twenty-some years for that to become a reality. We were all in favor of it. The pastor had a brother who was a Maryknoll priest, Father Mark. It was a modern church building with all the latest in liturgical art with special motifs that honored St. Mark.

Some of the Sisters, especially Sister Cyril, a convert, were very careful to inculcate Catholic social teachings of the Papal Social Encyclicals (like position papers from the Pope.) I think this is when my religious focus changed from pious Irish Catholic practices to a broader liberal stance on issues of peace and justice which has endured to this day. This stance differed from most of the Jollett family including my two brothers. What I learned in college also helped me to choose the path of religious life as a missionary, especially one with a more recent history. We studied Church History and had to be able to name the ten persecutions of the early church, along with the prominent martyrs. In May we had our May crowning of the Blessed Virgin, complete with a Maypole dance and flowers. It was truly a Catholic College in every way, and I was pleased with the education I received.

My classmate, Lily, from South Orange, New Jersey had a sister who was a Protestant missionary doctor and she spoke about her often. I had long been drawn to the religious life especially as a missionary, so her sister's experience piqued my interest. I had heard of the Maryknoll sisters and their work especially in China. Then Lily found out that there was a Catholic missionary order, the Medical Mission Sisters, who were located in Philadelphia. We were both interested in learning more, so at Easter vacation in my Junior year we both visited

8400 Pine Road in the Fox Chase suburb of Philadelphia. The whole place appealed to me instantly—the big trees on the grounds, the farm, the simple houses, the little lake and the boathouse nearby and the naturalized daffodils that grew on the walk to the boathouse. It didn't look like a convent or an institution of any kind. I had already "been there and done that." The Sisters I saw wore simple gray habits and a royal blue veil and a silver cross. The novices whom I saw carrying baskets of laundry wore a white veil.

I was also impressed with the Novice Mistress, Sister Agnes Marie, who had been one of the four original members of the Society. (The official name of the Medical Mission Sisters was Society of Catholic Medical Missionaries, thus the short name "the Society.") She was a nurse and spoke so glowingly about working in India and all the many needs in the missions. She stressed the difficulties of the missionary life but also the Society's dedication to professional care of the sick without a proselytizing goal, but only to share in Christ's healing mission to all peoples. I was fortunate to have a short meeting with the foundress, Mother Anna Dengel, an Austrian doctor, trained at the University of Cork in Ireland and who came to the United States after having worked in India to found the order in Washington, D.C. in 1925, the year I was born.

I returned to College to finish my senior year with the growing realization that joining the Medical Mission Sisters would be my choice of career. It was so thoughtful of Sister Agnes Marie to write me with no identifying return address on the envelope so none of the other students knew who was writing from Philadelphia, so for some time it was my secret and Lily's. Our mail was always put out on a little table in the rec. room so everyone could see what everyone else got in the way of letters. I read all the mission literature with great eagerness and felt that this was where God wanted me to spend the rest of my life. Just seeing the 8400 Pine Road address gave me a thrill, somewhat like that of the girls who had boy friends in the service when they got a V-mail from overseas. Lily decided not to join. She never married, but later became the Chief Sanitarian for the State of New Jersey. *As I look back, perhaps some of my motivation to enter the convent was related to my idea that I wasn't attractive enough to ever find a mate. My desire to get out from under Aunt Marie's strict surveillance may also have influenced me, even if subconsciously.*

In my senior year we were sent off to do our Practice Teaching. I went for two weeks with Peggy Magner to Swanton High School, near Lake Champlain, north of Burlington. We stayed at a comfortable boarding house. Fortunately for us, the two teachers who were our mentors were graduates of Trinity whom we both knew and were also staying at the boarding house. I taught English, Civics and French. It was hard to look mature when some of the students were about my own age. I liked teaching well enough. At that time the main discipline problems were gum chewing and throwing spitballs. I asked one student: "Would that be chewing gum?" As he had stretched it out, he rolled the gum into a neat little ball and deposited it behind his ear for later use. What could I do but turn around and attend to something else, trying not to show my amusement?

When time came for graduation and the parting of the ways, many of us girls had to sort out our skirts, sweaters and jackets as we borrowed from each other so much, we often didn't remember what was whose. We almost got to the point where we would go to another girl and say, "can I please borrow my sweater?" A last minute exchange was done and then we proceeded to assist each other on sitting on the overstuffed suitcases. As so many of us were not from wealthy families, this exchange gave us a more varied wardrobe than just our own. During my four years I had two wool dresses, two plaid skirts, a couple of sweaters and a maroon velveteen top. For the warmer season I had three dresses. I also had a light blue evening gown that I wore for all the dances and May Day. My last year I had a long black skirt which I wore with the maroon velveteen top. A lined trench coat helped in rainy and cold weather. It was the style then to have friends autograph the trench coats. Saddle shoes were de rigueur and never to be cleaned. Super large sweaters were the fashion. Slacks were rare. Shorts unknown.

I graduated from College with a Bachelor of Science degree cum laude in 1945 and because I was planning to enter the convent, I never got the beautiful blue graduation ring. I found a short-term job in a defense plant in Madison making resistors—a very boring job. It consisted of taking a small spool of copper wire, measuring it on a blade with an electric reading dial. If it was too low for specs, it was discarded. If over, we had to cut the wire at that point and then glue it down and return it to the finished box. That was it! The ladies at the shop mostly gossiped about clothes, movies and people they knew, but I didn't find it stimulating.

The job gave me enough money for two months to buy the required items that I needed to take with me to the Medical Mission Sisters. My Aunt Marie thought I was making a decision without sufficient information and suggested I go visit the Maryknoll Sisters in Ossining, NY. To satisfy her I did and had an interview with Mother Mary Rogers who was very cordial but the whole place looked too much like an institution to me and I wanted the more homey looking 8400 Pine Road. She also had me talk to the local parish priest.

My Aunt Marie took me to a religious goods store in Newark where I went down the list that had been sent me and bought what I could. The hardest thing to look at in my black footlocker was the pair of black "old ladies" shoes along with the black stockings and a pair of gray woolly slippers. We bought the gunmetal gray wool sweater at an Army-Navy store. I decided to wait until I got to Philly for the underwear, as that was an option. A missal, a fountain pen, a nail clipper and small scissors were also on the list. *The Imitation of Christ* by Thomas A'Kempis was recommended so I bought that. No personal photos, books or other reminders of our past lives were allowed. Not that I had much. My prize possession was Richard Halliburton's *Book of Marvels* (Richard Halliburton was a very popular travel writer at the time) and it was hard to part with my high school yearbook *Sesame* and the college yearbook, *Tau Kappa*, and a few mementos from college dances and programs. At this time I did not even have photos of Mother and Dad or my brothers to allow me to renounce them.

I had one last date with Lily and her brother Jim and we went to Olympic Park and went on the roller coaster and other rides. Jim said: "You'll be back home in two weeks." It was Jim's jacket and bow tie that I wore as Frank Sinatra, so his friendship had some sentimental value, but he had never been a real "boy friend." I was determined to follow my aspiration of being a missionary Sister.

CHAPTER 7

MEDICAL MISSION SISTERS

Then on August 9, 1945, the date of the atomic bombing of Nagasaki, a center of Catholic culture in Japan, I went with my Aunt Marie to enter the Medical Mission Sisters, dressed in my best celery-green wool suit and spectator shoes. These were kept in a suitcase in the attic in case I left. I stayed, so they were finally given to the Thrift Shop. I then donned the simple navy blue dress, black stockings and shoes, and underneath a slip made partly of striped mattress cover material and the convent underwear with buttons in the crotch. These were often made out of cotton feedbag material (for the chicken feed.) Old flour bag material was used for kitchen towels, dress shields, kitchen aprons and other uses. I was now a postulant.

As postulants and novices we had to hang out the laundry in the yard and were convulsed with laughter as we noticed Sister Anthony's bloomers had two big roosters on the seat. We all had been given laundry identification numbers, so we didn't have to guess whose bloomers they were. My number was 99. I was pleased, as it had been the number for the young Swiss Sister Hildegarde buried in the cemetery, and made me feel like I was still a pioneer—one of the first 100. Her gravesite was the only one in the cemetery. These numbers had to be embroidered with a chain stitch on every piece of clothing. It helped to have only two digits instead of three, as I was not enamored of sewing. For chapel we had to wear a small black lace veil.

Later during winter we were told to go to the closet and pick out a coat. This was on a first come, first serve basis, so we didn't always get the coat we wanted. There were some nice long ones that had been some postulant's brothers' light blue military school coats which were much in demand because they had style and were ideal for the cold walks we had to take. There were a couple of Navy pea coats too. Others were those given by the postulants who entered in February (cold month.) I remember Sister Brigid always tried to get the nice Kelly green one. Often a very tall Sister got a short coat and a short Sister got a long coat; the stout Sister squeezed into a tight one while the skinny one floated in a very ample one. Never mind, we weren't supposed to be vain about our appearance and we couldn't say that any coat was "mine." These coats were needed when we took walks to the nearby Pennypack Park or Larimer Woods near the convent grounds. These were beautiful with wild flowers and berries in the spring.

When our first shoes wore out, we went to the attic to the large "shoe box" and told to pick out a pair that fit us. Some of the more comfortable ones were those that had been worn but looked like military issue, so were well made. Some were quite new, but others showed the bumps and creases of the previous owner, and often even the smell.

Our training to be a full-fledged Sister consisted of six months as a postulant (Postulancy) then two years as a novice followed by the making of First Vows. These two years are called the Novitiate. The word Novitiate may also refer to the place where the training is held. After three years these vows were renewed for another two years. The Sister could leave the Society during this time. It was necessary to get permission from Rome to leave the Society after final vows (final profession.)

After six months as postulants we were able to receive the habit and given a new name. Some postulants left at this time, either of their own free will or recommended to do so by the Novice Mistress. This was always a painful event for the rest of us. We were told we could have no correspondence with those who had left. Eight of us received the habit in a simple ceremony in February 1946 (no bridal dress or hair cutting for this occasion as in some religious communities.) At my request I was given the name of Sister Mary Gabriel. I had always had a devotion to Our Lady of Sorrows and St. Gabriel of Our Lady of Sorrows was an inspiration to me. He was a young Passionist Priest whose feast day was on February 27th. I was familiar with his story as a big statue of him stood in our mostly Italian church in Madison. Unfortunately the name Gabriel was occasionally morphed into "Gabe" as in "Gabby Gabe" which they used to identify my tendency for gabbing but said in an affectionate way. *My priest friend, Fr. Boor, who I met in Venezuela later still addresses me as "Gabe." To my disappointment later with the changes of Vatican II, St. Gabriel's feast day was no longer listed on the church calendar. Even my beloved St. Joan of Arc's name no longer appeared.* In those days we did celebrate each Sister's feast day with a cake, greetings and prayers.

The habit was a long gray dress with a white starched collar (sewed to the dress, not with buttons as I had at St. Mary's) and a scapular. The Sunday habits were made of wool but the daily ones were a kind of denim. The veil for novices was white. At first we tied the starched headpieces too tight and it hurt, but we soon got the hang of it. *Later I heard that when the Society first got permission to wear the habit and veil that Mother Dengel, who was not too enthusiastic about it, would appear in the morning without it as she conveniently forgot it. No doubt it was uncomfortable for her too at first.*

As postulants and novices we were each given "obediences" (chores) to do, either every day a different one or sometimes the same one for a month. Everyone had to help with the laundry. Although we had washing machines and mangles (large commercial type roller irons), we still had to do some hand scrubbing on washboards with homemade brown soap. Items such as the starched headpieces, altar linens and handkerchiefs had to be scrubbed. As I mentioned before, we would hang the clothes out in the laundry yard. We weren't supposed to talk during work unless it was related to the work, so this was a hardship. We somehow managed to communicate with signs, giggles and pointing. Mangling was hot but relatively easy. We had to iron the altar linens, our Chaplain's shirts, guest linens and the starched headpieces that held the veil. Everything else we neatly folded and put into baskets, and later distributed to the respective owner (or number). Some of us got cleaning obediences, which were probably the most boring of all. Other chores were helping in the kitchen, washing the dishes and setting the refectory tables. Soon we would be introduced to completely new and strange "obediences."

The Farm

The compound which had once been an estate consisted of a 70-acre farm, with milk cows, steers, pigs, chickens, a meadow for the grazing cows, a corn field, vegetable garden and an orchard with apples, peaches and pears and a wonderful strawberry patch. Sister Anthony, who was the Society Treasurer, also had a couple of pet goats, one named Shirley Rose who was liable to eat anything available. There was a Main House, a large old-fashioned stone barn, a greenhouse (later used as a printing office), the Chaplain's house, Mother Dengel's little cottage, and another small building, St. Benedict's, that had served at one time as a stable/garage and then as a meeting room. There was a small lake and a Boathouse where we stored and packed equipment and supplies for the missions. It later served as a chapel and even later as our volunteers' thrift store.

We had our own milk, butter, cream, buttermilk, cottage cheese, pork, beef, chicken, eggs, lard, fruits and vegetables. The community was pretty much self-sufficient for food except for potatoes, flour, sugar, tea, coffee and spices. Sugar was mostly used for making jellies and desserts but not left on the table for adding to tea, coffee or cereal, except on big feast days, so early on I became accustomed to drinking coffee without sugar. The Sisters did all the farm work except for the plowing and other jobs that required farm machinery, which was done by our farmer, Mr. Burkhart. Those Sisters that had been raised on a farm were assigned to milking cows, feeding the animals, (all vegetable scraps went to the pigs), killing the pigs and butchering the steers. I guess the Superiors didn't want us city greenhorns to damage the animals, so we weren't assigned to those tasks. However when it came time to "put up" chickens, we all pitched in. We would have a chicken party, where some were assigned to catching the chicken, laying it on a board and chopping off its head, (with some of them escaping and running around with their heads off!) others to dipping the chickens into hot water and pulling off the feathers, then singeing the pin feathers. Others were assigned to gutting the chickens and cutting them up into the appropriate pieces for freezing. We saved the chicken fat for cooking. For all these dirty outdoor jobs we usually wore a "garden habit" which was very old, full of paint spots, patches and stains. If we were going to climb a ladder to pick apples we pinned up our skirts with a large safety pin so we wouldn't trip over our skirts or scapulars.

Another seasonal obedience was weeding the vegetable garden and harvesting the beets, carrots, spinach, celery, lettuce, asparagus, cabbage, squash, onions and green beans. Picking the beans was the worst, requiring a lot of bending down. Father Mahoney, our Chaplain, would say in Spiritual Life class—"when you weed, pull out the beets." He didn't care much for beets. Much of the cabbage was eaten fresh but some was made into sauerkraut in large crocks. The corn was mostly feed corn and we would have days of picking corn, stacking it in sheaves and shucking it for feed for the animals. I got some pretty bad attacks of hay fever from the dust so I would be assigned back to indoor work that I hated. I'd rather just sniffle and work outside.

The strawberries were Sister Agnes Marie's favorites, so only the "farm girls" got to work on them. One evening I had the temerity to ask: "How do I get to know how to care for the strawberries if I'm never assigned?" (Another Catch-22.) Soon after that I was assigned. The strawberries had to be trimmed, covered with straw and the shoots replanted each season. We were not allowed to eat between meals, so this job had the added feature of being a penance as the strawberries were mighty tempting. However, every June we had a Strawberry Festival out on the lawn when we gathered together and had strawberries with corn flakes, whole strawberries, strawberries and cream, cake and strawberries etc. and ate to our hearts content. This took some of the sting out of the penance.

The time for butchering pigs was very early in the morning when we would be sitting quietly in chapel during Meditation and all of a sudden we'd hear the awful cries of the pigs being rounded up to be butchered. When the pigs were butchered their blood was made into blood pudding (the Irish call it "black pudding.") The Sisters who did the milking had to do this early in the morning and make up their Meditation some time later. With so much milk, we churned our own butter with an old-fashioned butter churn, hung the milk in muslin bags to make cottage cheese and buttermilk. We also candled the eggs and put them into large barrels. We made jelly from the apples and strawberries. The foam that came to the top was often left out for our morning or afternoon tea time when we put it on our homemade bread. Some of the beef fat was used to make laundry soap by adding lye. We also used this soap to wash our hair and take baths unless someone had donated us bath soap.

The "Vegetables" obedience consisted mostly of cleaning, trimming and cutting up vegetables for the cook to prepare. When the apple season arrived, we were overwhelmed with apples from our large orchard, so the task of sorting out apples was usually undertaken during Spiritual Reading or even Evening Recreation time as we sat around outside in a large circle. The Sister assigned to "Vegetables" was in charge of hauling out the baskets of apples, providing each Sister with a paring knife, an old large tin can where the cores and peelings were put, and a bowl for the sliced apples. There was a whole "apple culture" involved. We wrapped the perfect ones individually in tissue paper and kept them aside for freezing or immediate eating. The rest we cut up for apple pies, apple salads, apple fritters, fried apples, applesauce, apple jelly, apple butter, apple cake and finally apple cider. We even had applesauce on our Sunday breakfast Corn Flakes. We sorted out the apples according to a system—"edible, soon edible, very soon edible" and lastly those that went into making apple cider. We had honeybees (which Sister Henrietta cared for wearing a big bonneted mask) on the compound and they were instantly attracted to our apples. I used to be terrified of bees, but constant contact, even to the point of neatly slicing a bee in two, cured me of that fear.

To get perfect apples for freezing and storage we had to climb up on ladders and hand pick each apple, and hand it down to another Sister as throwing it into a basket would bruise it. As skinny as I was, I got to be quite adept at hauling a bushel basket of apples away from the orchard. I was assigned to "vegetables" so often that one night when Sister Agnes Marie, the Novice Mistress, was announcing the obediences for the next day, she listed each Sister and her individual task, e.g. "Sister Judith—paint" etc. When she got to me she was pretty tired and said "Sister Vegetables—Gabriel" We all had a good laugh at that.

Spiritual Formation and Classes

Our days were full. We began with the recitation of the Office based on the Psalms for different hours of the day. Prime was the morning prayer. After a half-hour meditation we attended Mass in our chapel. *The meditation that we did at that time was of the discursive type according to the model of St. Ignatius, the Jesuit, with the selection of a part of the New or Old Testament appropriate to the season, where we pictured the scene in our minds and then made application of the text to our own life. This was not the popular "transcendental meditation" of today.* After breakfast, which was in silence with readings from *The Liturgical Year* by Abbe Gueranger or the Bible, our daily work began. The chores were interspersed with classes and prayers.

Father Mahoney taught the class on Spiritual Life, which taught us how to live a holy life with emphasis on the virtues and the way of perfection in our service to God. Father Mahoney was a Holy Cross priest, so on occasion he would keep us up to date on the Notre Dame football games. This did not go over too well with the Novice Mistress when she heard the conversation in the next room. He was duly reprimanded and came to the next class, ostensibly opening the book close to his face and reading Tanqueray's *Spiritual Life* in a very serious voice. We then surmised that he had been told. Our punishment was to spend an hour of our recreation time reading the Spiritual Life book. The Novice Mistress taught the class on the Constitution, Spiritual Directives (Rules) and Customs of the Society. When I was a novice the Rules were typed up and covered with cardboard from a large sanitary napkin box. Later they were printed and bound. As can be gathered, the Society was quite poor, being a missionary congregation and no local income, so thrift and making do with what we had was paramount. If we broke something we had to fix it if at all possible.

Sister Lucia, a Dutch Sister who had done her Anthropology thesis on midwifery in the Taos Pueblo, New Mexico, taught Missiology which is cultural anthropology applied to the missions. The mission in the Gold Coast (now Ghana) was just being started, so she taught us the anthropology of the Gold Coast. She was a wonderful teacher.

We also had regular choir practice for the Sunday and holy day Masses with Sister Henrietta, another Dutch Sister. She insisted we had to be able to put three fingers sideways in our mouth to be able to sing out. Gregorian chant was the most commonly used, but we also practiced polyphonic hymns for special occasions. The most emphasis was on preparing for Christmas. We learned not only Latin and English hymns, but German and French ones as well. Mother Dengel was Austrian, so we always sang "Silent Night" in the German "Stille Nacht" version.

Our prayer life revolved around the liturgical year. We even used to follow in procession through the fields and orchards as the chaplain blessed the crops on Rogation Days (from the Latin rogare, to pray) which fell on the three days before the feast of the Ascension. *This custom seems to have gone out of style after Vatican II.* Advent season was always very special to me. I remember our little services each Saturday evening reading the Psalms for the following Sunday and readings from the prophet Isaiah. For the eight days before Christmas we sang the beautiful "O" antiphons that are sung before the Magnificat at Vespers. One special example is: "O Wisdom, that proceedest from the mouth of the Most High, reaching from end to end mightily, and disposing all things sweetly: come and teach us the way of prudence." A special treat was the reading of a section of a book of unrhymed verse by John Lynch, *A Woman Wrapped in Silence*, which tells the story of the Virgin Mary's life from her girlhood to her death. It follows the Gospel story and avoids any legends and sentimentality. *It is now still available in paperback so I have bought many copies of it to give to priests and friends and still use it especially in Advent, Christmas and Holy Week.*

When Christmas Eve arrived we novices and postulants were surprised as we slept and were awakened by the singing of carols by the professed Sisters. This custom was always a closely guarded secret so we never revealed it to the next group of postulants. Then we paid a visit outside to the large hand-carved Nativity scene from Mother Dengel's own country of Austria. We then attended Midnight Mass in our beautifully decorated chapel.

Before lunch we recited a special prayer for the Society and made our private examination of conscience. Later in the afternoon we said the Rosary in chapel, and a short visit for silent prayer, followed by more chores and/or classes. Spiritual Reading lasted about a half-hour and was scheduled to fit in with the rest of the day. One Sister read out loud while we prepared the vegetables or caught up on our darning. Living on a farm, our lives were pretty much focused around the different seasons, so no two days were alike.

At Spiritual Reading time the books were usually about the Saints. Sister Agnes Marie favored stories of strong holy women such as St. Teresa of Avila, St. Therese, (The Little Flower) and some of the Abbesses like St. Hildegarde of Bingen and mystics of the medieval times. Another book was *Wives and Mothers of the Olden Times* (or a similar title) that featured women of the early Christian era. I always admired these women Saints and I couldn't help but wonder why women were not more honored and involved in the management of the Church. Carryl Houselander's *Reed of God* was published in 1944 in war torn England. The Reed of God is Jesus' Mother Mary, and Houselander explains how Mary saw and loved Christ in each and every person, no matter how poor or flawed, and how we can imitate that love. The book is still a classic. Her book inspired me much more than the older ascetic books that emphasized the way of perfection which only resulted in me feeling I could never be "perfect." I knew it would help me in my future work among the sick and poor. It also reminded me that I still had Mary, a mother figure in heaven who would care for me like my own mother would have.

We were given the assignment to write a small paragraph on "My Ideal Medical Missionary." Following what I had learned from our noon prayer and readings, I wrote that the ideal would be a person who practiced the virtues of charity, generosity, cheerfulness and simplicity. *Although now no longer a Medical Missionary, these virtues are still my ideals, even though not always fully practiced.* Letters from the missions and the *Medical Missionary* magazine always gave me inspiration and encouragement and I still remember a certain thrill when it would arrive and I eagerly read every page. I so admired all of the Sisters in their work, but never felt when I was in the missions that I too belonged in that same category of heroic and dedicated women.

Once a month we had a Day of Recollection and a Meditation on Death. The purpose of this was to think of how we lived our present life and to realize that "as we lived, so would we die." Once a year we had a preached eight-day retreat. I made many resolutions to improve, but these often went by the wayside in time. On Sundays we said or sang Vespers. After evening Recreation we recited Compline (Psalms for the end of the day) in the chapel. There were a few Psalms that gave us all trouble. One was the Thursday night Psalm that said: "Let them be turned away blushing for shame that say unto me 'aha, aha'." If we were tired we couldn't help but burst into suppressed laughter. The other tough one was when Sister Boniface or Sister Camillus got up and intoned Psalm 21 "many calves have surrounded me, fat bulls have beset me around." These two Sisters did the milking and other work with the animals, so the appropriateness was not lost on us postulants. We sang Vespers on Sunday afternoons. On Sunday evenings Compline was sung in Latin.

After Compline we had some quiet time before going to bed. This was called Grand Silence, which is stricter than silence at other times. If we broke Grand Silence it was one of the items we were told to report to the Superior at our monthly interview, so we could be given an appropriate penance. These penances were usually practical things, such as scrubbing the kitchen floor, or if we had broken something, we had to repair it. There was always so much work, there was no need to invent strange penances. The Psalms became a real part of our everyday life. I still remember Sister Martha exclaiming after a difficult task, "My strength is dried up like a potsherd." Sister Anthony heard her and quickly added (from the same Psalm) "Yes, but your tongue hasn't cleaved to your jaws."

We went to Confession once a week. I still remember repeating the same infractions week after week: being impatient, judging and criticizing others, complaining about my work, making excuses for my faults and distractions at prayers. *Now I wonder why I never confessed to the fault of envy, something that has often occupied my thoughts. Could there have been a commandment that read: "Thou shalt not covet thy neighbor's parents"?*

Recreation

After supper we had an hour's Recreation when we played cards, talked, darned our stockings (we all learned to darn very neatly using a burned out light bulb if no darning egg available) or other sewing and on occasion listened to letters from Sisters in the foreign missions. I remember especially those from Sister Alma Julia from Rawalpindi, Pakistan. Those written at the time of the India/Pakistan Partition in 1947 were especially dramatic. It was a dangerous time when over half a million were slaughtered in both India and Pakistan, but the Sisters were never harmed and often had to escort their patients to their homes on bicycles for their own safety.

A favorite topic of conversation was to ask the Sister assigned to the kitchen what we were going to have for breakfast the next day. For some, the announcement that it would be our home-made Philadelphia scrapple would put a pall on the rest of the evening, for others it meant anticipating a treat. *For those not familiar with that regional delicacy, it is composed of meat from the head of the pig with ground corn meal and pepper, made into a loaf, sliced, floured and fried.* At the end of Recreation the next day's chores were announced if they were different from the ordinary.

Recreation time also gave us the opportunity to work on plays or programs for the big feast days. I remember one we did with a song "In a Missionary Convent" a parody of the song "In a Monastery Garden." This was a history of the Society with great humor thrown in to keep it lively. We also practiced and sang "The Waltz of the Flowers" and "The Blue Danube." We looked forward to Holy Innocent's Day (December 28th.) We could go to the Boathouse and rummage through donated clothes and accessories and dress up any way we wanted to for a big party. We played tricks on the Professed Sisters, as this was a day for the lowest to be first. The Epiphany cake had a bean in it and the Sister who got the piece with the bean was queen for the day.

We celebrated Thanksgiving with the usual American turkey dinner with all the trimmings. The fun part was the annual basketball game before dinner between the novices and postulants against the Professed Sisters. Each side also had to produce a team mascot complete with a song or two. One year we made a huge worm or caterpillar made of chicken wire and gunnysacks. We postulants/novices got under it winding our way to the tune of "I am Willy the Wersatile Worm, and Today is the Day I've Elected to Turn..." If I remember right, we won that game. I was usually in the second string of the basketball team but enjoyed it anyway. Sister Benedict, a student in Medical School, always made the wonderful doughnuts we enjoyed along with cider after the game.

We all made our own habits, so we had to learn how to use the sewing machine as well as hand-sew the very fine stitches needed for the wool habits. The Irish Sister, Sister Veronica, was our guide in this task.

The Big Move

The old novitiate building (which had been the previous estate owner's home) was being stretched by the onslaught of candidates immediately after World War II, so we began saying special prayers to St. Therese of Lisieux, the Patroness of missionaries, to solve our housing problem. We also said litanies that had the response, "please send us a house." Finally on October 3, 1945, the feast of St. Therese, the Society decided to purchase the Crawford estate directly across from 8400 Pine Road. The acreage at 8403 was about 70 acres. Like 8400 it had once been a farm estate. It had a large amount of property including a barn and a smaller house. The main house, called Ury House, dated back to pre-Revolutionary War times with additions added periodically after that time.

There was a large boxwood garden and a wooded area with trees and blackberry bushes in the back of the house, plus some open farmland. A nice driveway with a circular plot completed the picture of a wealthy old country estate. The Society must have been able to buy the property at a very low price or its poor condition may have made it cheaper. Funds for buildings in the missions and at home were mainly from donations of Catholics and others, by sales at the Thrift Store, by the Ladies and Men's Auxiliaries, by church collections in many places, direct mail requests and by the magazine the *Medical Missionary*. For us it was to include also a lot of "sweat equity," commonly referred to by us as "the odor of sanctity."

The two-story house had a large basement. For our group this was the adventure of a lifetime and we willingly set to work like old pioneers to rehabilitate the property and house. I can still feel the excitement when we all trooped through the house for the first time and were given historical information—George Washington visited here; in the 1600s Swedes had built the first block house which was a small room with a low ceiling with rough pine wood floors; the more recent parlors had beautiful parquet hardwood floors; the elegant windows upstairs had small diamond shaped panes; interesting little built-in cupboards were everywhere; we had a lovely old-fashioned verandah in the back; a brick oven was found in the basement and best of all, legends of a hidden underground tunnel in the basement. Unfortunately the two Crawford sisters had papered over most of the walls with very dark wallpaper or painted surfaces with dark colors, giving the whole house a gloomy appearance. It had been neglected for some time, but the ugliness was just skin deep until we uncovered its original beauty.

Reality soon set in when from October until May we novices and postulants spent our days in our oldest habits with a new set of "obediences" announced every evening for the next day's work. These might be: scrape off old wallpaper; sandpaper painted or varnished surfaces; paint just about everything; remove old putty from the windows and put in new putty; some other chores were outdoors— pull out weeds in the garden area; trim the boxwood hedges; chop down some trees in the woods; clean up the blackberry patches and make the farmland ready for planting more field corn. Some chores required a little more talent, such as re-upholstering old donated furniture; mending broken window panes; repairing hinges, doorknobs and furniture knobs; carrying numerous items up and down stairs. One hired worker who had observed what we were doing, was heard saying to his companion as he was about to carry a bathtub into the house, "let the novices do it—they're strong." We did practically everything except plow the field. In addition to "garden habits" we now had "paint habits" and "paint shoes." Besides these interesting and ever-changing chores we still had our old boring obediences such as preparing vegetables, cleaning and kitchen duties.

During this work period someone tapped on the low ceiling in the old Swedish room and discovered it to be hollow. After further investigation we found beautiful pine wood rafters under the plaster ceiling. We tried but never did find the hidden tunnel in the basement.

In some way our spiritual life took a minor role, but Sister Agnes Marie, a great admirer of St. Benedict, would remind us "laborare est orare" or to labor is to pray. Many times we just ate our lunch out on the circular plot near the house. The kitchen Sister would bring out a big pot of stew and we sat on the cement border around the plot and ate our lunch. Even spiritual reading was done there occasionally so we wouldn't have to waste time changing our habits. When we finally got to chapel to pray, many of us just fell asleep from sheer weariness. We were not a cloistered community so all this work helped prepare us for the hard work of the missions and realize its spiritual value.

In February our group received our habits and we were now novices. The habits were a little longer than our postulant dresses but we soon adjusted to them and proud to wear the white veil and didn't have to worry about our hair-do. By May the house and property were more or less ready, so on May 31st Cardinal Dougherty of Philadelphia came to dedicate the new St. Therese's Novitiate. A few days later the Professed Sisters had a real mission departure ceremony for the novices and postulants, complete with ringing of the mission bell and we proceeded to walk across the street to our new residence. We still went to some services at 8400 but this was now our new home. When other candidates entered we were very possessive of the property and would scold anyone who inadvertently treated the floors, windows, furniture etc. carelessly—"Watch that, if you knew how hard we worked..." *Sad to say, several years later the Ury House and its surrounding property were sold by the community for financial reasons and the building of small houses at 8400. It is now a large apartment complex.*

Soon we had our classes here as well as our own chapel, parlor, kitchen, recreation room and bedrooms. For the refectory, Sister Agnes Marie commissioned beautiful hardwood monastery type tables that had a good waterproof polish so we never used tablecloths. Sturdy benches complemented the beautiful tables.

Little by little we cleaned up the boxwood garden and planted flowers. The field was planted with corn and we did all the chores related to the harvest, e.g. picking and shucking the corn and then stacking the sheaves in upright bundles to dry.

Life soon returned to some normalcy. Now, however, as we had our very own kitchen, we also had more "managerial" positions. One Sister (a novice) was in charge, one prepared the main dishes, one made the desserts and one was in charge of bread making. As soon as the bread would come out of the oven, the aroma filled the basement and the bread was promptly consumed at tea time. We each rotated these services for one month so we learned all the different cooking duties. Once I was making pancakes on the large griddle when Sister Agnes Marie came out from the refectory and asked: "do you think you're cooking for lumberjacks?" To her the pancakes were too thick and big. I had all I could do to not answer her that most of the novices ate like lumberjacks because we all did a lot of physical work. The griddle held about 24 pancakes at a time, so if we made them too thin they would get burned before we could flip them. Like a good novice I added more buttermilk to the mix and just flipped a little faster.

Sister Agnes Marie loved good food and would say that it was a sin if we took God's beautiful fruits or vegetables and ruined them by overcooking or other abuse. Sister Anthony occasionally made "snow ice cream" as a special winter treat. So, we did eat quite well. Two and three helpings of everything were the order of the day during this time. We got weighed once a month at recreation time and those of us that were skinny were tempted to put a heavy rock into our pockets so we could meet the guidelines. I weighed 95 pounds at that time and was told I would have to get to 100 pounds to make my first vows. (Loss of weight or insomnia were possible indicators of not being fit for missionary life. I guess I made the grade.) *If I ate like I did during the novitiate, I would now be a blimp.*

Soon we had a new Novice Mistress, Sister Pauline, who had served many years in India with the Indian Medical Mission Sisters. Also the Postulate was moved to the 8400 house. It was a whole new regime. We novices were surprised when we got several candidates who had served in the military as WACS, WAVES, or nurses in WWII and were a lot more mature than us greenhorns. In 1947 the Society counted 179 professed Sisters worldwide so space was at a premium.

CHAPTER 8

NURSING SCHOOL

On February 11, 1948 I took the vows of poverty, chastity and obedience for a period of three years along with six other Sisters and received the blue veil, gray habit and silver crucifix. *This ceremony is usually called "profession."* My thoughts at this time were that I would "live in the house of the Lord forever" and I was determined to persevere to the end and die in the Society.

Mother Dengel had interviewed me earlier and asked what kind of work I wanted to do in the Society. My first response was that I would like to study and teach Missiology. She answered that we already had Sister Lucia getting her Ph.D. in anthropology at Catholic University, so we didn't need another one in that field. (A year or so later Sister Lucia had a nervous breakdown and was unable to teach any more.) She asked me if I was willing to study to be a dietitian or lab technician which I declined. I already had a bachelor's degree and could finish nursing at Providence Hospital in Washington in a couple of years. They now had a bachelor's program in nursing through the Catholic University and the Sisters of Charity there were offering scholarships to our Sisters. Not knowing much about what nurses did and not having any negative feelings about nursing, I consented to studying nursing. *I now realize that I also could have asked to help with the Society's monthly magazine, the "Medical Missionary" which was always well written and maybe that type of work would have suited me better.*

Right after Profession I went to the Washington House of Studies on 6th and Buchanan in the Northeast section of the city. I enrolled at the Catholic University program that had its clinical practice setting in the old Providence Hospital (built during the Civil War) in the Southwest area on 2nd and D St. close to the Capitol. Sister Jacob and I were both bachelor degree graduates so only had to take Anatomy and Physiology and the clinical studies. In two months we were on the floors doing our clinical practice. We stayed in the Nurses' Residence on the fourth floor with the Sisters of many other congregations, some of them former teachers or from other professions. These Sisters had some spending money and occasionally would come around to each of us student Sisters and ask for money to buy a nice gift for Sister X's 25th Jubilee or other occasion. Our spending money was very limited to carfare and basic essentials, so we always offered a Spiritual Bouquet that consisted of various promises of prayers for the jubilarian. On weekends we took the bus and trolley from Providence to the Washington House. Another Sister, Sister Juliana, was already there in the diploma program, the last one offered at Providence, so we were fortunate to have someone to orient us to the place.

The first six months were tough for me as I started having a strange kind of "morning sickness" and could hardly get my breakfast down. If it weren't for Sister Jacob's encouragement I would never have stuck it out. By noon I was fine. *Now I think that the stress of nursing, with its heavy responsibilities and being in a career that was not my first choice had something to do with this problem.* I grew out of it and was soon "talking shop" along with all the other students with the usual comments at mealtimes about the most bizarre and disgusting aspects of nursing, such as wound care for bedsores etc., much to the distress of other non-medical employees. Sister Jacob and I were asked to sew our own white habits. Sister Veronica had cut out the material for us. We were given a portable sewing machine that fit on top of the radiators in our rooms but was only capable of a chain stitch. Somehow we made our habits between our classes, clinical duties studies and prayers.

Our program was excellent and we had good clinical experience, although Mother Dengel was disconcerted that we had nurse's aides to help us (this was a very new concept that was promoted by Catholic University graduate school.) It did help us in our future work as much of our careers were in supervision, administration and teaching. I was kind of a klutsy nurse but with dint of practice became proficient, but never a "born nurse." One big mistake I remember was when I misread the doctor's order for one dram (teaspoon) of whiskey in eggnog for a patient with hyperthyroidism and I prepared it with one ounce of whiskey. The patient complained that it was pretty strong but I told her to drink it slowly. Later I discovered my mistake and went to the Head Nurse. She said to wait until the doctor made rounds and see how the patient was doing. When the doctor arrived he said to the patient, "My, you're looking chipper today, Mrs. X." Her pulse had increased quite a bit, but the Head Nurse and I both breathed a sigh of relief that she was all right and I learned to be VERY careful about reading orders. The symbols for dram and ounce were easily confused. That old system has now been changed to the metric system so less mistakes possible. I was eternally grateful to that Head Nurse. (Later I heard that one of the student nurses gave a patient two Aspirins on a home visit, ordered verbally to the family but without a written doctor's orders, and she was promptly expelled from the school.)

Washington, DC was still segregated so we had "colored wards" and wards for white patients. I always enjoyed the men's wards as most of the men had a great sense of humor and would tease each other to keep up their spirits. When I came on duty one morning to a five-bed ward, the patients told me "you should have seen old McNamara leading his band down the hall in his hospital gown" or "Captain Kidd was shouting out orders to his crew," etc. The diabetic men patients enjoyed noting the reaction of the nurses when their urine was tested and found it to be 4-plus for sugar. Later we found out that they had put apple juice in the urinal.

The Operating Room was a favorite as I learned so much practical anatomy. After a full morning scrubbing, I fell asleep in the Anatomy class that was held right after lunch. We had a full month in the Diet Kitchen, another month in Central Supply, three months each in Pediatrics, Obstetrics and Medical-Surgical. We daily took the bus to the old Gallenger Hospital *(now DC General)* for our Communicable Disease clinical practice where I saw my first case of typhoid fever and was impressed with the new drug Chloromycetin which radically changed the outcome for these patients. The food there was so skimpy that some of us would bring a lunch with us or get back to the Providence cafeteria for a square meal. The District of Columbia depended on the federal budget timetable, so it was often left short with budgets based on the last years' prices.

We had Community Health Nursing with the Instructive Visiting Nurse Service in the city where we visited some of the same patients we had seen in our Out Patient Clinic. This is where we got a little dose of reality. I remembered visiting an elderly black diabetic patient and how I told her in the Out Patient Clinic to boil her vegetables, etc. and not fry them. When I saw the tiny one-room she was living in with a small heating stove in the middle of the room which served as the cooking stove for her and her husband, I became aware of how unrealistic I had been. It happened to be one of those hot and muggy summers when no one wanted extra heat in the house. The area we were assigned to was a poor area, in spite of being close to the Capitol. One time a patient told me: "Visit me at the house on G Street as my place ain't fitten for you to visit." When I saw the house on G Street, which was pretty bad, I wondered what *her* home was like.

Another time when I went in a backyard I spotted a lot of empty expensive brand whiskey bottles which the residents were using to make their own home brew. (I found out about this illegal activity when I saw an item in the newspaper that reported there had been a raid at that address.) Some of the homes did not have running water, but relied on a pump in the backyard, so they had to pour water over a basin for me to wash my hands. Sometimes I had to use a Sterno can to boil up a syringe to inject a patient. *Years later the old Providence Hospital was torn down for public housing and moved to the more upscale area of Northeast Washington so I guess the area is still poor.*

We spent three months at Seton Institute in Baltimore for our Psychiatric Nursing training. This three month affiliation helped us learn how to care for mentally ill patients, both acute and chronic. Some were occasionally dangerous. Here I realized that this was not my cup of tea, but I did learn a lot that I could apply to other types of nursing. To keep my sanity I wisely had a couple of books to read, such as Thomas Merton's *Seven Story Mountain*. This was a best selling memoir of a young man who became a Trappist monk after a rather worldly life. I found it full of wisdom, humor and inspiration. *I've always been a fan of Merton.* Seton was a Catholic institution and there were several priests, nuns and Brothers that were patients, and doctors and nurses as well. Our teachers told us: "There's a very thin line between you and the patients." I asked one religious Brother about his community and he replied: "We have everything from soup to nuts." I quickly responded: "I'm glad you said that and not me," because if I had, it would have meant a dismissal.

Student nurses came from all over the eastern seaboard to affiliate here and it was very well managed. One very intelligent manic-depressive patient spotted the bulletin board at the nurses' station and read a clipping about the need to have congressional lawmakers pass a psychiatric examination before being elected to office. She somehow managed to hand write on the clipping "and who will examine the Psychiatrists?"

My brother Bob was ordained to the priesthood in June of 1949 during my vacation time. I was unable to go to Canada for his ordination but went to Madison to attend his First Mass. I was still in Nursing School then. I remember the months before how I made a Communion pall (the stiff square linen that was placed on top of the chalice at Mass) for him that was adorned with my own cut-work. I got to call it "the appalling pall" as it was difficult following the design that Sister Veronica had given me. *On my recent trip my brother Herb told me that Dad and Bella met the newly ordained Bob in Newburg, New York because Dad did not go to Madison for his first*

Mass. I had always wondered about that and was happy to know that Dad had a chance to receive his son's priestly blessing.

In October of that same year when I was doing my Psychiatric Nursing clinical practice, I received a phone call from Aunt Marie that my Dad was dying. He had had a sudden massive heart attack. I was unable to reach the hospital in Elizabeth or his funeral there on time, but Aunt Marie picked me up at the Washington house for his burial in the Mount Olivet Cemetery in Newark. *Bob told me later that the only way he was able to receive the Last Sacraments was to promise, that if he survived, he would live with his wife as brother and sister. To me this was really a cruel thing to ask of someone who really loved his wife. This was another difficulty that I had with the Catholic Church's rules and regulations. More on this later and my thoughts about Dad.*

Our teachers in Medical-Surgical were top physicians in their field and then these classes were followed up with the nursing aspects by qualified nurse teachers. I'll never forget one doctor's advice on answering test questions—"I don't want a diarrhea of words and a constipation of thought." We even helped our Nursing Arts instructor, Esther (Nellie) McClain write her then famous *Scientific Principles of Nursing* book. She assigned each of us a nursing procedure and we wrote one principle (physics, chemistry, psychology etc.) for that procedure on an index card. I'm sure that this helped a lot in her book.

Living on 2nd and D Street had some advantages. We were able to watch President Truman's inauguration on the Capitol steps, and listen to the Marine Corps band on some evenings, as well as watch the many squirrels cavorting on the lawn. We visited the Mellon Art Gallery, the Smithsonian Institute, the Library of Congress and the Shakespeare Library—all within walking distance. Then on weekends in Northeast Washington we often attended Mass at the Benedictine Priory where the monks excelled in Gregorian chant which was so familiar to me from my boarding school days and which was very inspiring.

The Washington house was quite strapped for funds. When we would get a large package of brick ice cream left on our fourth floor and the other Sisters had taken what they wanted, we would wrap the ice cream bricks in newspapers and carry it to the Washington house in our briefcases. They survived quite well using this method. Sister Monica, the Superior, was always happy to get anything to help balance the budget and stretch the menu. When we returned to the Motherhouse (headquarters) in Philadelphia by train for the summer, we were told: "Bring back a suitcase full of green beans from the farm."

One day Sister Jacob and I stopped at a local shoe repair shop and after we finished our business, I remarked how courteous and friendly the owner was. Sister Jacob responded with assurance that she expected that when she saw the sign in the window that said "POLISH." She was not surprised, being of Polish descent herself. Her pride took a fall when I pointed out to her that the sign was referring to "shoe polish."

By June 1950 we had completed all the requirements for graduation except for two classes. We had to attend classes on Head Nursing and Public Speaking at Catholic University in Northeast Washington during the summer months. This was an exciting time for me as I soon would be assigned to the foreign missions. As yet I had no idea where it would be, maybe Africa or India, or maybe a whole new area, but I was ready to go wherever sent. Catholic University only had one graduation a year in June, so I was already in the missions when I officially graduated the following June. *Another graduation missed.*

CHAPTER 9

INTERIM

When I finished at Catholic University I was assigned for a short while to our Atlanta house while another Sister-nurse was on vacation and retreat. The Society had been asked by the local bishop to run the Catholic Colored Clinic in Atlanta, Georgia that served "colored people." During World War II the Sisters were not always able to travel to foreign countries so the Society accepted a couple of "home missions." The services consisted of an out patient clinic, with minor surgical procedures, mostly tonsillectomies once a week, and some major surgery, usually hysterectomies on another day. The patients were poor and very simple people who greatly appreciated the services and care. I still remember the look of pleasure and relief on the face of a diabetic patient. I had been telling her about what she could eat and not eat. When I said she could have a "poached egg," she thought I said a "po'k steak" and her eyes lit up. It was sad to have to correct her.

Local white doctors provided the medical services. We did have some "colored" nurses who were very helpful in educating us on the local culture, such as their food choices and common expressions for their complaints, e.g. "I got a fireball" meaning "I have a fibroid tumor" or "I have high blood" meaning high blood pressure or "low blood" meaning anemia. Patients that had more serious conditions were referred to Grady Hospital, the city hospital. It was not uncommon to see a child named "Grady."

My next assignment was to help in the Boathouse in Philadelphia, sorting out medical supplies and clothing to be packed for the missions. People donated medicines, bandages, baby clothes, old dental and operating room equipment, instruments etc. so we had plenty to do.

During the fall of 1950, it was announced that the Society was going to take over a newly built hospital in Maracaibo, Venezuela. This was a new modern hospital owned by Creole Petroleum Corporation, the Venezuelan subsidiary of Standard Oil, (now Exxon) for their employees. It was not in the traditional setting of a local Medical Mission hospital, but a contract was made with Standard Oil for the Society to run the hospital and receive payment for the services to the oil workers. I found out that my first mission would be Maracaibo. The contract with Standard Oil would allow us to take private paying patients and those who could not afford to pay.

This project was a new concept to many of the sisters and for some time, Maracaibo was considered a "home mission" without the cachet and mystique of a "foreign" mission. Although we provided a greatly needed monetary service to the Society, some of us felt like stepchildren when compared to the other mission hospitals. Those of us assigned to Maracaibo resented the fact that we were considered a "home mission" so could only have a two weeks' vacation, not the usual four weeks for those in the foreign missions. Being pretty close to the equator, and in a tropical zone, we did need more of a break from the enervating heat and humidity.

During the next few months I (as the only Spanish speaking nurse assigned) sat down in Philadelphia with Sister Miriam, a nurse who was appointed to be the administrator of the new hospital, to go over the blueprints of the hospital. We pored over these plans and tried to figure out the layout. Little details such as the "Sala de Trabajo" needed to be translated as the Labor Room and not a Work Room etc. The "capilla" (chapel) in the basement had us a little stumped, but later we found out that the chapel was placed next to the morgue for the visiting relatives. We later ended up with our own chapel on the first floor in a room that had been planned for a conference room. Some of the other Sisters assigned to other duties were busy studying Spanish. The hospital had been named by the Society as Hospital Nuestra Señora de Coromoto as we learned that Our Lady of Coromoto was the patroness of Venezuela.

On January 6, 1951 (feast of the Epiphany) we had our Departure Ceremony in the Boathouse chapel. It was a joyful day with the ringing of the mission departure bell, and special prayers said for us. As we all had expected to be asked to leave the U.S., we accepted the challenge of leaving our loved ones behind, even though considered a "home mission." Most of the other Sisters in my group were assigned to schools in nursing, medicine, pharmacy, and journalism or to other duties and missions, but none were assigned to Maracaibo.

CHAPTER 10

MARACAIBO, VENEZUELA

Some Sisters assigned to Maracaibo had already left and others traveled by air. On February 9, 1951 Sister Victoria, a newly professed

Sister from an English family in Brazil, and I boarded the Grace Line Ship, Santa Sofía. This was a medium-sized freighter that regularly took a limit of 52 passengers to ports on the Caribbean coast. We ate in the dining room and were seated with the ship's doctor and another passenger. As we approached the area of Cape Hatteras in North Carolina, a big storm came up and when I was eating breakfast I felt a bit squeamish. I thought the easiest thing to do would be to drink the orange juice and then work my way through the rest of the food. What a big mistake, as what went down quickly also came up quickly and I had to leave the table. This was the only time I ever experienced seasickness. If I felt strange I found that getting out on the deck was the best, watching the waves so my eyes could send a message to my inner ear about what to expect. We had excellent food and my first encounter with delicacies such as frog legs. It was also my first trip on the sea.

The ship stopped at the Dutch Island of Aruba where we visited Orangestad for a short while. Here I saw a sign on a church door in the local patois language called Papiamento, a mixture of English, French, Dutch and Spanish that could easily be understood by different people. With a little guessing I figured it out. Another stop was in Puerto Cabello that serves as the port city of Caracas, the capital of Venezuela. I was so thrilled at my first sight of the sparkling aquamarine waters of the Caribbean, the white beaches, the swaying coconut palms, the mountains in the distance and my first sight of the country where I would be working in my first mission.

After ten days on board we sailed into Lake Maracaibo harbor. Lake Maracaibo is on the northwest coast of Venezuela near Colombia, connected with the ocean by a narrow strait to the Gulf of Venezuela. The city of Maracaibo is on the west side of the lake with a harbor adequate for medium sized vessels. We had been told to look to the west to see the Sisters waving sheets on the hospital verandah as a welcoming signal. We stood on the deck with binoculars loaned by our co-passengers and we all cheered when we did see the white sheets in the distance. The Sisters met us at the dock and we finally saw our beautiful Hospital Coromoto (as it was usually called) near the western edge of Lake Maracaibo.

The landscaping consisted of a few coconut palm trees recently planted that had four branches which over time we watched as they grew to tall full-bodied trees. A row of red-blossomed ixora bushes lined the driveway to the hospital. The building looked out on the south to the Creole headquarters next door, a few hundred feet away where the company had their offices, a clubhouse and residences for mostly American employees.

Although the second largest city in Venezuela, Maracaibo only had municipal water for the past four years. Donkeys were still in operation on the streets carrying brooms and mops and other articles for sale. The lack of concern by the oil rich country and its political leaders in Caracas was always a bone of contention for the Maracuchos, as the residents of Maracaibo were affectionately called. They made all the money the country was running on, but received few of the benefits, as most of it went to the capital, Caracas.

Hospital Coromoto had 60-beds with two stories and a basement. There were covered verandahs on both the east and west sides of the hospital. The east verandahs had a beautiful view of Lake Maracaibo and the distant mountains. In my mind I can still see the reflection of the rosy colors of the rising sun on the green rubber-tile halls when I worked the night shift. Some American patients asked to have their beds moved out to the verandah at night and we both enjoyed watching the lights of the oil tankers as they entered or left the Lake. We also watched the peculiarly Venezuelan heat lightning called the Relámpago de Catatumbo (the lightning of the Catatumbo River) that was almost constant because of the collision of hot tropical air and the cold mountain air. It was also possible to use the flat roof, which we often did in the evening watching the magnificent sunsets and clouds especially in the summer. We would go there for recreation and sing songs accompanied by Sister Madeleine's guitar. When we sang "Deep in the Heart of Texas" we got an enthusiastic applause from the American families not far way at the Creole camp.

Sister Victoria, already knowledgeable in Portuguese, picked up Spanish quite quickly and I had my two years of classroom Spanish, but very little chance to speak it, so I had to listen carefully to the conversations. One of the first things we were assigned to do was to check out all the supplies in the storeroom. Sister Miriam and I had some good laughs on what the Creole purchasing officer, an American named Mr. Bonfiglio, had ordered. He was not familiar with hospital supplies, so apparently just went to a hospital supply catalog and ordered, e.g. one dozen of every size catheter listed and every size of gloves etc. As a result Sister Miriam said it's too bad we weren't treating elephants as we had a couple of dozen size 40 enema tubes. We also had dozens of sizes up to #9 of surgical gloves, etc. We set up a perpetual inventory system so we would know when to re-order. We were amazed that no one had ordered baby diapers. When we did open the Obstetrics Department, we had to tell the mothers to bring their own baby diapers and undershirts until our Sewing Department could make them.

The hospital had been very well designed and we only encountered a few problems. The water pipes had been incorrectly hooked up and in the beginning we had hot water in the toilets, so we didn't sit too long. The other problem was the blistering of the metal-framed doorways and windows. Apparently the construction workers had used water from Lake Maracaibo to mix cement and in time the metal blistered from the excess salt. Lake Maracaibo, although mostly fresh water, has a limited connection to the saltier ocean. Both of these problems were fixed as promptly as possible.

Sister Victoria was busy supervising the cleaning crews who constantly requested "polvo" or cleanser that they used in great quantities. Sister Samuel set up the laboratory and Sister Constance the X-ray Department, working with an English speaking radiologist, Dr. Pavan. I focused pretty much on the Operating Room and the Surgical Floor with the help of Pat Patton, an American volunteer nurse, (now Sister Patricia in Kenya, Africa.) An English nurse, Bessie Coombs, who had known Mother Dengel personally, offered her services to the community, and set up the Central Supply Department. Of course she kept using English nursing terms and would ask: "where are the spirit swabs and the strapping?" (Alcohol and adhesive) and used the term "receiver" instead of our American term "emesis basin." So we had to learn not only Spanish but also a variant of English.

The hospital was officially opened on March 5, 1951 at a ceremony blessed by the Bishop. Our first patient was a Manuel Kelso who had suffered a fractured leg in an industrial accident. However, our first operation was an emergency D. and C. on a poor woman, Rosa Suarez, who had miscarried. Fortunately for me, we had Dr. Pérez, the obstetrician/gynecologist who had trained at Charity Hospital in New Orleans and was married to an American nurse. He helped translate for me whenever needed, often coming to the O.R. for other doctors' cases just to help out. Once when a patient's blood pressure was dropping, I asked if they wanted me to prepare an ampoule of Caffeine Sodium Benzoate (commonly used in the U.S. for mild drops in blood pressure.) Dr. Pérez pointed out that this would not be of much help in a country where everyone drank coffee at every turn. By little incidents of this kind, I learned the culture of the country and how I needed to adapt to its ways.

In the early days because of our minimal nursing staff, Pat Patton and I would take our siestas at different times so that there would always be a nurse on duty. I quickly learned to take a siesta of 20 minutes very quickly and then back to work. We used the wards on the First Floor as a Sisters' sleeping quarters until about a year later when the Society rented an apartment down the hill from the hospital. I remember one early morning hearing a kind of groaning, cranking noise and thought it was the sound of the oil wells operating. When I remarked about it to some of the men patients, they laughed. The oil wells were far away on the other side of Lake Maracaibo. The noises I heard were the local donkeys!

The Medical Floor was opened, set up and supervised by a lay nurse from Switzerland, Marie Bachman, an older nurse who spoke broken English and because she knew a little Italian, tried it out on the staff and patients. One day the aides were almost in convulsions when she said "llame la cochina," or "call the pig" (cochina.) What she actually wanted to say was to "call the kitchen" (cocina.) She reigned on the Medical Floor without much interference from us. She would come back on duty in the evening to just "check things out." She never looked tired although she was getting on in years, and faithfully dyed her hair with liquid black shoe polish.

We Sisters weren't much better at the language. Sister De Sales, the dietitian in charge of the kitchen, would check the patients' trays with the diet girls, and once demanded to know "dónde están las cucarachas?" or "where are the cockroaches?" when she really wanted to say "cucharas" or spoons. We did have enough cucarachas to contend with but they weren't expected on the trays. Another time Sister Madeleine as circulating nurse in the O.R. told the scrub nurse that a specific instrument would be "mujer para el doctor," or "a woman for the doctor" rather than "mejor" or "better for the doctor." This got a happy smile from the doctors. Another nurse read the doctor's orders for "sopa tibia" as "soak the tibia" whereas it was an order for "warm soup." She thought the order a bit strange as the patient did not have a leg problem.

The Brazilian Sister Praxedes was a medical doctor but foreigners were not allowed to practice medicine in Venezuela so she was the anesthetist for all the operations and on call for those deliveries that needed anesthesia. She had been one of the first to arrive with Sister Laetitia.

Sister Laetitia was one of the original founding four of the Medical Mission Sisters and had spent much time in the missions. For a while she was the Superior. I remember her thoughtfulness during Lent when candy was not to be consumed. Sweet desserts were few and far between. If an American patient gave us a box of chocolate candy she would pass the box around at recreation time and say pointedly, "Sister, have some Maracaibo bread." We all dutifully partook of the Maracaibo bread.

Our cooks were all Basque immigrants and one, Carlos, was being trained to make cakes, pies and puddings. So when a new dessert would appear, even if it were a flat cake, Sister Laetitia would ask Sister De Sales, "did Carlos make this?" Our desserts consisted mainly of bananas, pineapples, mangos and papayas so even a flat cake was welcome. We learned to eat goat cheese and arepas (heavy corn flour biscuits) and plantains and "caraotas" or black beans, along with some dishes that were similar to what we were accustomed to. As Lake Maracaibo was full of fish, we often had delicious red snapper and roughy. Once when I was substituting in the kitchen for the vacationing Sister De Sales, the fishermen called the hospital from the dock and asked, "The fish are still breathing, do you want me to kill them?" "Of course" I replied and took whatever they had to offer. When Sister De Sales returned she found the freezer full of fish.

When new Sisters were going to arrive, the Customs officers always found that along with their luggage, they carried applesauce, peanut butter, white shoe polish and crucifixes, so word got around that that was all the Customs officers would find. No doubt they were disappointed at our choice of imports. After our major "apple culture" in Philly, we longed for some good old applesauce. White shoe polish was hard to find in Maracaibo and we wanted to put a crucifix in every patient's room.

I helped a local Venezuelan nurse set up the Out Patient Department and the newly arrived Sister Jeanne, a French Canadian, worked as the receptionist and record keeper. We had many displaced persons who had immigrated to Venezuela from Europe during the war years. Barbara, a Romanian nurse's aide, showed an artistic ability that was often used for decorations for Christmas and other occasions. An Italian nurse, Señora Della Salda, was in charge of the Newborn Nursery and tried to use her Italian as a lingua franca and I was often called upon to translate her Italian into Spanish. Once we had Greek sailors as patients and the nurse asked me to translate for them. Unfortunately, my Greek was limited to Kyrie Eleison, so no luck there. A young German woman, Margie Hartwig, worked in Central Supply and eventually fell in love and married our Hungarian orderly, Jose Kubic. We also were fortunate to hire Hubert Hummel, a German who had known Mother Dengel and was put in charge of maintenance. Eventually he too found his life-mate and married one of the local clerical staff and raised his family happily in Venezuela.

Two nurses staffed the Surgical Floor. One was Isabel Zuniga, a Costa Rican, and the other was Carmen Atencio, a Colombian. Señorita Atencio was very competent and as I was but a recent graduate (in fact not even officially graduated until June!) I learned a lot from her. I would ask her to "show me how you do it in your country" and proceed to imitate what she did. Señora Zuniga taught me the use of the "tico" expressions such as a "permisito" which would easily be granted rather than just asking for a "permiso" (permission.) We had hired a Spanish nurse, Manolita Ricart from Barcelona, who had been working at the local Nursing School for some time and she became our instructor of the Nurses' Aides and often worked as night supervisor. She had served as a nurse in the Spanish Civil War and was from a very aristocratic Catalan family, which showed in her every accent and movement.

For a short time an American nurse who had worked with the Pan-American Health Organization helped with teaching the aides. Venezuelan graduate nurses were scarce, but we were able to train many young women as Nurses Aides. The maintenance, cleaning and dietary staff was Venezuelan (except for our fiery Basque cooks.) An American nurse, Lillian Engel, became supervisor of our Obstetric Department when it was set up. Later two American nurses volunteered, Laura Rendziniak and Mary X (I'll think of her name some day.) Later another American nurse, Katie Hinnegan, worked on the Medical-Surgical floor and being an attractive young lady, was very popular with the male patients. So, our staff was one big United Nations all working happily together. Over time the obreros (workers), mostly local Venezuelans who worked at the hospital in the more menial jobs, formed a union and they did give us some difficult times but we tried to be fair. Even school books for their children were on their bargaining agenda, to say nothing of "aguinaldos" or Christmas bonuses and extensive sick leave, etc.

We tried to incorporate the employees as part of the Coromoto family when we had pageants, parties for their children and other celebrations. The day of the Secretary, Nurses' Day, Physicians' Day and others were all honored with cards and flowers. All the nurses in the city celebrated Nurse's Day, Florence Nightingale's birthday, May 12th with a special Mass in the Cathedral and a parade downtown. The nurses were all in uniform with caps and capes. The usual flowery tributes and the laying of a wreath at the statue of Simon Bolívar (the national Liberator) completed the events.

Sister Stephen had a ministry that focused on helping those in a common law marriage to formalize their union by receiving the

Sacrament of Matrimony. It was not uncommon to have a couple in the chapel with their children and grandchildren present. When a fifty year old man was asked why he hadn't been married before, he responded that he didn't want to be tied down, although he had been living faithfully with his "compañera" for over 30 years. *Remnants of my old Irish Catholicism came to mind as I was shocked at first, but I slowly began to understand some of the cultural aspects of Latin American religion and learned to take such events in stride.*

The poor telephone operator who made announcements on the intercom had a hard time with some of the foreign names, so Laura Rendziniak would be paged as "Señorita Laura" etc. Many of the Sisters' names were Hispanicized such as Hermana (Sister) Gabriela, or Hermana Constancia, etc. The operators on the night shift were especially helpful as they would listen in on the calls coming from the oil fields across the lake that were letting us know about a patient being sent over the lake on the "lancha" (boat.) When I was Night Supervisor they would often interpret my poor Spanish to people on the other end, and interpret their Spanish to me in a simpler fashion. I learned to imitate what they would say, so eventually I became reasonably proficient in the language (so much so that when I was transferred later to eastern Venezuela, patients would ask me if I were a Maracucha.) When we got a call that they were sending over a woman in labor, I never got too excited. I figured she would have either delivered by the time she got to Maracaibo or have been in false labor. If they said it was a possible appendix case, we were given time to set up the O.R.

I served usually as Day Supervisor of all the units except the Medical Floor and the Out Patient Department. Later I had to take my turn as Night Supervisor. We didn't have an Evening Supervisor as we worked a split shift with starting work at 7 a.m., then a break at noon for lunch, siesta and prayers and then returning on duty about 2:30 p.m. until 6 p.m. I would also be on call for Emergency Room cases and usually was the scrub nurse for any operations in the evening or night shifts. It was hard to be awakened at about 2 a.m. but the doctors were always in a better mood at night and easy to deal with, which was not always the case in the daytime. During the day shift they might be paged for an emergency or be asked for information on a patient's record etc. At night it was nice and quiet and cooler too. We pretty well understood that many of the doctors and others resented the fact that Sisters and foreigners to boot were administering a hospital. If they had a complaint I referred them to Sister Miriam, the administrator, but they knew she would treat them with respect but with firmness and good sense, and they would lose the argument, so they refrained from further complaints. *I now realize that one cultural factor that I found difficult was the pervasive "machismo" of the Latin culture. Having a woman run a hospital was a new situation for the Venezuelans to accept. This machismo showed in several other ways.*

Eventually we opened the Pediatric Department and after about two years we were a fully operational general hospital and it was considered to be one of the best run in the country. The Venezuelan doctors in town were happy to be on the staff. Little by little the hospital settled into a comfortable routine. We had two Sisters who drove the station wagon for trips into the city. We were the first Sisters in Maracaibo to drive, so the Venezuelan Sisters took the cue and began doing the same.

As this was a completely new hospital, and for me a whole new situation, I enjoyed the challenge of setting up nursing units, writing down procedures and establishing policies for ordering supplies and medicines, making out work schedules and many other routine procedures. The X-ray Department helped by providing us with cleaned used X-ray films which served as protective covers for the many procedure lists, such as the O.R. setups for each type of surgery; the different doctors own special requests; the Central Supply tray contents for various procedures; standing orders of each doctor, etc. We set up an American style Kardex system for nursing care plans for each patient, a medicine card system and a way to check narcotics and other medications. This type of organization was not something that the Venezuelan nurses took to at first, but soon they realized how the systems saved time and helped make their work easier.

On the other hand they taught me some ways to make do with what was on hand, e.g. making sanitary napkins by wrapping cut cotton batting with pieces of gauze; cutting and folding large rolls of gauze. We also made our own 4" x 4" sponges which were then wrapped in the yellow paper that came with the X-rays. This ended up being a chore for the nurse or aide who was sitting with a patient in labor and there wasn't much else to do until she delivered. They also had the custom of having notebooks for the reports for the day, evening and night shifts that were read at each change of shift. They taught me that courtesy was important. I learned that I couldn't just come running to give an urgent message to the head nurse, but had to make the customary remarks, such as: "Buenas dias, Señorita Atencio, como amaneció?" or "Good morning Miss Atencio, how are you today?" and then give the message. This had to be done at the first encounter with that person. Later, conversation could be more informal and business-like.

As a nurse, one unforgettable experience—the night a patient was admitted to the Obstetrics Ward for high blood pressure. She came with her X-ray report (but not the film) taken at the Creole clinic across the Lake that read that the fetus was in the head down position. What was my surprise when I was called as Night Supervisor that she had delivered a baby in the ward bed. My surprise later was even greater when I discovered that there was another baby coming. I rushed to awaken the doctor on night-call to hurry and come to the Obstetrics Department. This second baby delivered normally and then much to the astonishment of all, a third, stillborn baby was delivered. The fetus <u>was</u> in the head down position but no one had told us that there were three heads! *Several years later I took a course in Midwifery and would have been chagrined if I hadn't listened to the fetal heart, palpated the patient's abdomen and determined that she might have triplets.*

The two surviving babies were the pride of our Newborn Nursery as they were our first premies, María Coromoto (named for the hospital) and María Magdalena. The doctor, who was quite young and inexperienced, would order, say, one ounce of formula, but these babies were hungry, so we cheated a little and doubled each order so they thrived quite nicely. The doctor was quite proud of their progress (and so were we.)

I got used to patients holding up their five fingers bragging about their stool test report that showed they had <u>five</u> kinds of parasites (not uncommon.) One illness I contracted in Venezuela was Ascariasis or roundworm, which was not serious and quickly cured with medicine. The Venezuelan patients seemed to have a high tolerance for pain and many of the male patients would ridicule other foreign patients that carried on about their pain. I presumed it was part of their Indian heritage as most Venezuelans were mestizos or "café con leche" that is brown in color—a mixture of Indian, Black, and European.

In the beginning we discovered there were many petty thefts, for example missing light bulbs in the halls and wash cloths and other small items missing. Apparently some figured they were taking them from an oil company that was so rich it wouldn't miss the items, so we had to establish a strict accounting system. To get a new razor blade, the nurse had to turn in the used one, and dirty linens were counted and exchanged for clean ones, etc. After the employees (some of them had been responsible for some of these petty thefts) became more accustomed to the fact that it was also <u>their</u> hospital and they started missing the supplies to do their work, this petty thievery stopped being a problem.

Time Off

Occasionally we were invited to the Creole clubhouse to see a movie. One I do remember seeing was Rudyard Kipling's "Kim." This movie gave me my first glimpse of India, later Pakistan. For our first Christmas Sister Miriam bought us several pairs of roller skates. On a Sunday afternoon when all the Lab and X-ray Departments were closed, one of the doctors received quite a shock when coming to see a patient in the Emergency Room he saw some of us Sisters skating down the tile floor of the basement with our long habits flying. Once on the feast of the Holy Innocents, we put petite Sister Praxedes, dressed like a baby, in a laundry cart fixed like a baby carriage and pushed by her "mother," Sister Samuel, who was very large. I don't think Sister Praxedes appreciated this but she went along with it and we all had a great day. At our own recreation time we sometimes put on "radio plays" with a script in hand. One was *Brother Orchid*, the story of a wanted criminal hiding in a monastery. We even made up some commercial jingles for the breaks like "C-R-E-O-L-E, that's the oil for me."

Feast days were kept as in the U.S. with appropriate table decorations. I still have one that was based on the *Prayers from the Ark* by Rumer Godden and they appropriately chose the "Prayer of the Butterfly" as my place card. *I still have the card and say the prayer on occasion: "Lord! Where was I? Oh yes! This flower, this sun, thank you! Your world is beautiful! This scent of roses... Where was I? A drop of dew rolls to sparkle in a lily's heart. I have to go... Where? I do not know! The wind has painted fancies on my wings. Fancies... Where was I? Oh yes! Lord, I had something to tell you. Amen."* This prayer appealed to me as it expressed my love of Nature and gratitude to God for all it beauties, but also of my distractibility in my prayers and my constant interest in something new that challenged me.

We sometimes attended Mass at the various local parishes when we could, but ordinarily services were in the hospital chapel. We had to get up at 5 a.m. in order to say Prime (morning psalms,) meditation, Mass, breakfast and then on duty at 7 a.m. If I had been up at night, it was even harder to stay awake during meditation, especially as we were still fasting.

Sometimes on weekends we would drive to the Shell Beach on Lake Maracaibo, or even further north to Sinamaica which was on the ocean, where we changed into bathing suits in the recesses of the sand canyons and went swimming. On other occasions we crossed the Lake on a "lancha" and visited the small town of Altagracia or the Isla de Toas in the Lake.

Sister Laetitia spent a lot of time looking for a place for the "tiempo caliente" (hot time.) Our vacations were for two weeks. The climate was very hot and humid most of the time except for trade winds breezes in the winter months. This season was known as "los hielitos" or the "little ices" by the locals. For us there were two seasons, one when the fans were on high and the other when they were on low.

The first year vacation we went to the Creole Camp in Puerto Cumarebo on the eastern Caribbean coast and stayed in one of their

Quonset huts and had a sandy beach to enjoy. Vacation gave us all time to relax listening to music, light reading and sharing our thoughts about our life and experiences. Oil wells were close to the camp and I remember the consternation when one of the wells was being drilled and the diamond bit broke at about 1800 feet. This meant the well site had to be capped and abandoned. Little by little we learned about the oil industry, often by talking to sleepless patients on the night shift when they would tell us how it all worked. We eventually got to see many of the oil installations, oil wells, drilling wells, gas-pumping establishments, refineries etc.

For the second year's vacation we went by a local bus to the little Andean town of Boconó where we rented a house for our two week vacation. I just loved the surroundings, the local Andeans and the delightfully cool climate. The third year we were invited by a hacienda owner, Señor Febres Cordero, to stay at his hacienda in Mérida, the capital of the State of Mérida in the Andes. We were fascinated by the "fountain" in the bathroom. Sister Victoria with her European sophistication clued us in to the mechanics and usage of bidets. The Irish Sister Anne exclaimed, "It's a poor house that can't afford one lady" as she coped with our ignorance about the spirit lamps that we used and resigned herself to being the official lamp lighter. Her great Irish wisdom gave us the comment "might as well get hung for a sheep as a lamb" when we were skirting rules and regulations.

The fourth year we had our own little vacation house in the Andean town of La Mesa. Getting to these Andean towns was always an adventure, as we had to travel on the local buses, which were often very crowded and with chickens and goats on the roof. In spite of the narrow, dangerous and winding mountain roads, we were amazed that the buses never got in an accident (at least not when we were on them!) The drivers were very adept at fixing everything with chewing gum, matchsticks and bits of wire. The bridge over Lake Maracaibo was not yet constructed so we had to take a southern route around the Lake if we wanted to get to the road to Caracas.

In these Andean towns we learned of the farming and ranching that was the livelihood of the area. We drove near the highest spot in

Venezuela, the Pico Bolívar at 16,427 feet where we actually saw snow on the mountain tops and I had my first taste of artichokes along with a welcome cup of hot chocolate. It was in Mérida that we learned how to climb up and descend the mountains by watching a child quickly scamper down the mountain to deliver his father's lunch to where he was working in the fields. We discovered that the bent-knees walk (à la Groucho Marx) worked very well and saved the knee joints. Here too we encountered Andean hospitality as we were invited in for a juicy treat of fresh pineapple. I learned not to sit on banana leaves as they made permanent purple stains on my white habit.

In the evenings I loved to hear the sounds of the Venezuelan four-stringed guitars, called "cuatros," being played in the distance. Once I was sitting on a bench in the plaza doing a pastel painting of the local church and a group of children surrounded me. I was quite flattered when one pointed to the window I had drawn and exclaimed "mira la ventana" or "look at the window." Not being artistic, any compliment was appreciated. It was also a great way to get outside and relate to the locals.

Christmas was always a special time in Maracaibo. About November 18th on the feast of Our Lady of Chiquinquirá (the patroness of Maracaibo) we began hearing the typical music called "gaitas" which lasted until well after Christmas. Gaitas are lively, often humorous songs with chorus and verses accompanied by typical Venezuelan instruments—the cuatro, the maracas, the charrasca (a brass pipe with horizontal slits and struck with a nail) and a "furro," (a cylindrical drum with a bamboo stick that punctured the skin of the drum and was moved up and down.) The furro made a lovely thumping sound a little like the Irish bodhran (drum.) "Aguinaldos" or "villancicos" were Advent carols that were sung in preparation for the season. Some of the most beautiful were composed by famous Venezuelan musicians and were often sung in church, whereas the gaitas might be composed on the spot with verses made up for the particular occasion, often political in nature, and sung mostly on the plazas and streets of the city. Often these gaitas were written to complain in a very subtle or humorous way about the government or some bureaucratic problem. Occasionally the authorities banned a particular gaita, but that only made it even more popular. *Many years later one of my students at the University of Zulia, Margarita Jimeno, gave me a record of a very popular gaita group, Los Cardinales del Éxito, (The Successful Cardinal Birds) which I still enjoy every Christmas season. The songs instantly bring back nostalgic memories of the people of Maracaibo and their special homespun humor and infectious rhythms.*

We always put on a Christmas play or pageant for the hospital employees and shared songs with the patients. At Christmas every Venezuelan family made "hallacas" which were like tamales only wrapped in banana leaves and the "masa" made with corn meal, pork, potatoes, onions, ripe olives and spices. They were not made at other times of the year. Many workers got time off for the whole season so official business was difficult to conduct at this time. Most workers were used to their annual Christmas bonus, so it helped them celebrate in style. Once a Czechoslovakian patient didn't have enough money to pay his bill so we negotiated with him to teach us how to make puppets. He was very talented and as a result we put on a Christmas puppet show called *The Littlest Angel* that was well received by our patients and employees.

Politics, Geography And Culture

When we first arrived in Maracaibo, the government consisted of a "Junta" of three military officers, called the triumvirate. They had obtained those positions in 1948 by a coup against the elected President Romulo Gallegos, a famous novelist. By 1952 General Marcos Pérez Jimenez (one member of the triumvirate) took over as dictator until 1958, when he was overthrown by another coup. This was a "law and order" regime with some of the previous party politicians languishing in prison. Much emphasis was placed on the military as evidenced by their very posh clubs and their visible presence. Honking horns was forbidden, so the locals learned to slap the doors of their vehicles when they would have previously honked. Many loved the "law and order" but others were happy when democratic elections came about as they enjoyed what they called doing what they liked or "lo que me da las ganas." We used to read *Time* magazine's Latin America edition and when we knew there was something critical of Venezuela it would be censored. We easily found out the true report from the American oil workers who often went to Miami and brought back the original uncensored version. In spite of the strict regime, bribes were still the order of the day. Even <u>we</u> had to resort to paying one to facilitate getting our identity cards. Otherwise we would go to the government office day after day and find out that we would have to come back the next day.

The regime also strongly pursued the exploitation of the country's oil resources. It was finally in 1960 that the Oil Minister, Juan Pérez Alfonso, along with four other oil-producing countries, Iran, Iraq, Kuwait and Saudi Arabia, founded OPEC. The foreign companies, Standard Oil, Shell, Gulf, Texaco, etc, were required to pay big royalties to the government and to provide many amenities to the areas where they worked, such as roads, schools, churches, hospitals and clinics. In spite of these big royalties they complied and still made money. Pérez Alfonso often advised that the country should "sembrar el petróleo" or "sow the petroleum," that is to take the income from the oil and put it into development of agriculture and manufacturing as he saw that a one-product economy was too risky. This advice was rarely followed. The fact that the oil industry was not very labor-intensive limited the number of jobs in the country.

Some German immigrants started vegetable and fruit farms in the Andes and elsewhere and many Italians and other Europeans were the principal craft workers, e.g. plumbers, carpenters, electricians, mechanics, etc. Maracaibo was a very cosmopolitan city with many nationalities including Chinese who set up restaurants. Middle-Easterners (they called anyone from the Middle East a "Turco") were the ones with the clothing and textile shops. Actually most of them were from Lebanon or Syria.

We would often see the Goajiro Indians who lived on the Goajira Peninsula north of Maracaibo. The Peninsula included part of Colombia so they traveled back and forth especially with their flocks of sheep. The women wore colorful long flowing caftan-type robes with sandals with huge wool pompoms. Some did not even speak Spanish. More primitive Indians such as the Motilones and the Perijá Indians lived in the forests and were seen occasionally. There was a certain amount of discrimination against the Indian population as I found out later when a Goajira patient in the University Hospital was very upset when her roommate was discharged. She was very concerned about who her next roommate would be. When asked about her concern she answered: "por la raza" or because of her race she feared rejection.

Over time we began to learn the history, geography and culture of the country. Maracaibo had been founded in 1571 (the dates vary by different authors), so had a long and colorful history. In fact, Américo Vespucci noticing the Indian dwellings on stilts on Lake Maracaibo named the country Venezuela, or little Venice. As I was really a frustrated anthropologist, I collected as much information as I could from books, magazines, (some excellent ones put out by Creole and Shell) and by asking people about events and customs. Unfortunately in the Novitiate our Missiology classes were all about the Gold Coast (now Ghana) and news from the missions was usually about India, and next to nothing about Latin America. I did struggle in the beginning with culture shock, but I put so much effort into getting to know the country, that later I found it very hard to leave a country that I had begun to love.

As this was my first mission it also became my favorite. I loved the Lake, the city, the mountains, the people, the fiestas, the history and everything about the country. Some aspects of the culture were difficult to understand, but little by little I began to respect the Venezuelans for their good characteristics. The Maracuchos were noted for their optimistic spirit and good humor, always ready for a joke and always willing to help. I had gotten to know many doctors, nurses, workers and even patients who had become a part of my life. Most of all, I knew when I came to leave I would miss the Sisters that had pioneered with me and whom I had come to love with all their wonderful characteristics and even idiosyncrasies. *Sister Miriam, the administrator and superior was such a talented woman that I really loved working with her and was not surprised that later she became the Mother Provincial for the North American group.*

It came as a great shock when the Society superiors decided that they needed a nurse with a degree who could teach in the Nursing School in Rawalpindi, West Pakistan. Sister Kathleen who was teaching there was needed in Philadelphia as Postulant Mistress, so I was selected to replace her. Rawalpindi was the original mission when Pakistan was still India and where Mother Dengel had first worked before founding the Society. In some ways it was a great honor, but it still was hard to say farewell to my first mission. This time it was another Grace Line ship, the Santa Clara, which was to take me away. The Sisters came to see my cabin and wave me off (teary-eyed) to another mission. So after four years I left Maracaibo on October 9, 1954. Seeing the Statue of Liberty from the New York harbor was an emotional moment, especially when I realized I had been living under a dictatorship (Pérez Jimenez) and was now coming back to the land of the free.

CHAPTER 11

RAWALPINDI

I spent a short time in Philadelphia and a one-day visit to my aunts in Madison. Herb had joined the Navy so was not there at the time of my visit. Bob was in Canada. I was sent out "on the road" with one of the more experienced Sisters to help with the mission collections that we often had in parishes in several states. We received hospitality at the local convents where the Sisters were always generous. Sometimes the Sister assigned was asked to go to the pulpit and give a short talk on the mission experience and why we needed the funds. It was during this interim period that I came down with mumps, probably contracted on one of the trips, so again I was isolated for a couple of weeks. I wasn't very sick, but did find it hard to swallow foods such as apple sauce which the kindly infirmarian gave me, thinking it did not require any chewing. Of course, the acid in it just caused my salivary glands to ache. No one else had the disease.

I was one of those that were asked to go to the missions by ship so that I could help with the "unaccompanied luggage," mostly donated medical supplies and baby clothes. It was very costly to pay for transportation by ship of these supply crates to Pakistan, so the "unaccompanied luggage" saved a lot of money. I embarked alone on December 3, 1954 on the President Line ship, the S.S. Andrew Jackson. This was a U.S. Steel Company freighter with a maximum of 13 passengers. My aunts Marie, Anna and Sister Raphael joined my brother Herb to see me at the dock. I didn't know it at the time, but the trip was to last over five weeks. I had a lovely large cabin by myself and sat at the dining table with the First Mate and the Radio Operator ("Sparks") *I learned many years later that all radio operators were called "Sparks."*

On the same ship were several veteran Protestant missionaries, who were on their way back to India. One was a middle-aged woman whom the crew called "The Bible Thumper" when she wasn't within earshot. The other was an elderly man, also a missionary, who was an expert in Hindi/Urdu. (Hindi is written in one script and Urdu in another, but both have pretty much the same vocabularies.) He kindly offered to help me with my little Urdu grammar book and I did learn some useful phrases from him. As I had plenty of time, I did my best to become somewhat familiar with the language, including the Arabic script.

I had also brought with me the Liber Usualis or the Latin Hymnal for all the Divine Hours and the sung Masses in Gregorian chant. As it was the Advent season, I was happy to have a chance to meditate on the beautiful "O" Antiphons that are so often read during Advent. They helped me really prepare spiritually as I had in the Novitiate for the coming days of the Christmas season.

Our first stop was in Beirut, Lebanon. This was a beautiful cosmopolitan city that had not yet been touched much by the Israeli-Arab problem. We were allowed to debark and I took a taxi to the Catholic hospital there. The Sisters were very gracious and offered to have one of the clerical persons conduct me on a short tour of the city. Here's where my French came in handy, although I found myself making up French words out of words that were actually Spanish, e.g. saying "teche" borrowed from the Spanish "techo" whereas the correct word was "toit" meaning "roof." The Sisters also offered me a very nice light lunch. Unfortunately, I ate the nice fresh lettuce salad and a short time afterward back on the ship I came down with a bout of diarrhea. The First Mate who acted as the medical officer gave me something for my diarrhea and I stuck to a diet of apples and soda crackers for a few days until I recovered. *After I had been in Rawalpindi a few months I began to show signs of anemia (8 gms. of Hemoglobin) and the Sister-doctor discovered I had amoebic dysentery that I must have contracted in Beirut as we never ate unpeeled fruit or raw vegetables.* A course of medicine quickly cured the problem.

The next stop was Port Said where we watched from the deck as the local workers unloaded the crates onto the dock. This was where a perennial entertainer, Spud Murphy, operated a shell game for the tourists and ship passengers. We also stopped in Alexandria to unload freight. We discovered when we got to the Suez Canal that there was a ship embargo due to the Israeli-Arab conflict at the time. Each ship was given a priority number and the captain said ours was 52nd in line. So we spent quite a few days in line to go through the Canal. This had some advantages as it was during the Christmas holidays and the ship staff didn't have much to do, so we all enjoyed the time off. The Captain asked me to lead a small prayer service for Christmas. I read the Christmas gospel of St. Luke, said a few prayers and we sang "O Come All Ye Faithful" and "Silent Night." The crew seemed to appreciate the service. The "Bible Thumper" also had a service, but most preferred mine, whether they were Catholic or Protestant as she came on a little too strong for some of the crew. The Church Seamen's Service gave us all, passengers and crew, little Christmas presents and of course we had a special Christmas dinner. When I was alone in my cabin I sang the Christmas Mass and hymns and read the mail I had kept for this occasion. I had been given the packet before I left and it was good to have Christmas greetings from my family and news from some of the Sisters in Maracaibo. I was reminded by the Gospel readings that Egypt was where Mary and Joseph had to take the Child Jesus to avoid the threats of Herod. I loved standing on deck and watching the waves break against the ship and thinking often of what my new assignment would hold for me.

After we sailed into the Red Sea, we had a freight stop in Jedda but were not allowed to get off, so we spent our time watching the workers unload the crates. This was before containers were used. I watched while one coolie spilt a barrel of some kind of oil onto the deck and with his bare hands proceeded to scoop it back up into the barrel. Another interesting scene was watching a dock worker wearing only a loincloth, and seated on a cart, carefully plucking his beard as he looked into a small broken mirror. This was my first contact with the Arab world and for the first time I saw women wearing mostly white burkas. We finally sailed into the Arabian Sea and landed in Karachi, the port city, and at that time, the capital of West Pakistan. I was told that the Sisters from our Holy Family Hospital in Karachi would meet me at the dock. It was difficult to make out the Sisters, as they looked similar to the burka-clad Muslim women, both all in white. However the Sisters did not have their faces covered, so I could pick them out.

Sister Ursula met me at the dock and then helped with the customs and my 26 crates of "unaccompanied luggage." Karachi was a bustling commercial city with every possible means of conveyance— camel carts with their clinking bells on their ankles, donkey carts, ox carts, cycle rickshaws, motor rickshaws, bicycles, tongas (two-wheeled one-horse carriages) and victorias (four wheeled carriages with horses) as well as buses, cars and taxis. I stayed five days in the Karachi Holy Family Hospital and then Sister Ursula got me a ticket for the 24-hour long train-ride to Rawalpindi (commonly called "Pindi"). As a possible holdover from colonial days, all clergy, Protestant, Catholic and Muslim, were given free tickets for the trains, a considerable saving for our Society as we often had to travel by train. Of course we had to go through a few hoops to get these clergy tickets but they were worth the trouble.

This was another exciting and challenging experience. The intermediate class compartment was just for women and children and I had an upper berth. I proceeded to try out my little Urdu to make small comments to the ladies, some of whom just smiled, probably speaking only Punjabi, or my Urdu wasn't the greatest.

The trip was freezing cold as we went through the Sind Desert and on north up to Pindi which is located on the high desert plateau in the foothills of the Himalayas, so warm in the day and cold at night. As I settled down to sleep for the night I wrapped my legs in my wool shawl to stay warm. Later I was told I had gotten my first touch of frostbite in my feet. The dust seeped through the closed windows, so the one bright spot was the hot tea at stops at the different stations. The waiter would come to the window and take orders at one station and then another waiter would show up at the next with a full tray with a teapot, tea cozy, cups, sugar and milk and some bread. This was very welcome as we were told not to drink the water, but tea was safe. The Sisters had packed me a box lunch but I was more thirsty than hungry. . *When traveling we never drank the water or had drinks with ice in them for fear of getting any number of gastro-intestinal diseases.* After going to what appeared to be "the ends of the earth" the train finally arrived in Pindi in the dark.

Sister Dolores, the hospital administrator and Superior, and the driver of the hospital tonga, Nur Din, met me. It was very cold and when the student night nurse opened the door of the hospital to meet us, she was dressed in the usual Punjabi dress of shalwar (trousers) with a white uniform over it, instead of a kamiz, and covered by a navy sweater and a white nurse's cap, covered with a wool scarf. It was definitely cold inside and outside!

The hospital was named Holy Family Hospital but was not the one (Old Holy Family) where Mother Dengel had worked. (Although this had been converted to a Catholic boy's school, the locals still would call it Old Holy Family, much to the chagrin of the Reverend Fathers, as they didn't want to be identified as a hospital but as a boys' school.) The newly built 200-bed hospital, was made mostly of local brick, with a large tower which served as a water tower, bell tower and one small room for the Night Supervisor to sleep in. A beautiful stone statue of Mary graced the front of the Out Patient Department. This symbol was not considered disrespectful of the Islamic culture, (although their religion forbade the use of images) as I found out later. The Muslims revered Miriam (their name for Mary in Urdu) and women in labor often invoked her for a safe delivery. Very tall poinsettia plants adorned the sides of the building. This hospital was a little outside the main part of the city and close to the Jhelum River, a branch of the Indus. Rawalpindi had been the

British military headquarters before Indian independence in 1947, so became the Pakistani military headquarters after Partition.

After a short orientation by Sister Kathleen, the Sister in charge of the Nursing School, I was put in charge and was the only teacher for the entire program, with the exception of some medical lectures by Sister Elise Wynen, our Dutch Sister-Doctor. The curriculum was based on the English nursing system, so again I had to use the words learned from Bessie Coombs, e.g. spirits, (alcohol) receiver (emesis basin) etc. Fortunately, the classes were in English as Urdu had very little technical language at the time. English was the business and second language of the country and the tests by the Pakistan Board of Nursing would be in English. To deal with patients however, I had to learn Urdu. Every day at siesta time I would sit at the bedside of Sister Elise who was a real linguist, for my Urdu class for a half-hour (I took my siesta for the next half-hour.) Later a local Urdu teacher taught me the language. The New Testament in Urdu helped me learn the script and I could guess the meaning of a lot of the words.

One word I learned was "Abba" meaning "father." It also had the meaning of "Daddy" as I discovered from a toddler who stood up in his crib holding on to the rails and crying: "Abba, Abba!" In our New Testament we find the words, "Abba, Father." Now I had a real live example of the sentiment behind the word.

Some patients spoke only Punjabi, a language related to Urdu, some patients spoke Kashmiri and others from the Northern Frontier spoke Pushtu. A few of our nurses spoke some of these languages, e.g. Mr. Khan, Head Nurse on the Men's Ward, who spoke Pushtu, and some of the nurses from the villages who spoke Punjabi. We also had a few Anglo-Indians, a heritage of the British colonial days, as well as a sprinkling of other foreigners from the embassies, the U.S. Military Aid Group and the local business community who knew English as a second language. Often English and Urdu were mixed together in common speech. I still remember Mr. Khan telling a relative of a patient "apna mind make up karo" or "make up your mind." "Apna" means "your" and "karo" means "make." They got the message!

Aside from the Head Nurses who were graduate nurses, (mostly graduates of the Protestant mission hospitals,) the student nurses provided most of the care. The Pakistani curriculum called for teaching the application of leeches, cupping and mustard plasters, all new to me. For the leeches I just read the procedure but never actually demonstrated it. The class on Health and Hygiene called for a section on the requirements for building a safe latrine, and the characteristics of a safe well, all topics that I hadn't studied in Nursing School.

The features of our practice doll, Mrs. Chase, had faded and contact by many students had long worn off her skin. For anatomy classes we had some bones whose protuberances were quite worn out. One poor student taking the practical exam (one from another hospital) did a great job describing the hipbone but it was actually the scapula. Unfortunately the scapula was so worn that the blade part had a hole in it which confused the student.

Sometimes in winter it was so cold inside as we had no central heating that we would have classes out on the flat roof of the hospital. As Pindi had a semi-desert climate, the sun made the roof much warmer. As our beds were the local string beds or "charpais" (four-footed) it was easy to move them to the roof. Inside I had the habit in winter of wearing wool gloves with the fingertips cut off so I could write on the blackboard.

I was one of the examiners for the Anatomy and the Medical-Surgical tests for the Punjab Board of Nursing. These tests were both written and practical. One student wrote that you feed the tetanus patient through the tracheotomy tube! I corrected the paper but had to inform the student that her patient would be dead. Bandaging was something I had to learn myself as they used bandages a lot more in Pakistan than we had in the U.S. The bandages were made of torn up old white sheets, so the students had to learn circular, spiral and figure-of-eight bandages. Bandaging was always included in the practicals. Frankly, most were more adept at bandaging than I was.

After about two years, another Sister who "needed a change" was assigned to the School of Nursing—a disappointment to me as I loved teaching and the close contact with the students. *Years later I consoled myself by finding out that one of my Anglo-Indian students,*

Margaret Strudwick, had been appointed Sister-tutor (Director of the Nursing School) and did a remarkable job of teaching.

New Duties and New Ways

I was assigned to the various services—men's floor, women's floor, the Obstetric Department, Pediatrics, the Operating Room and the Out Patient Department. I also rotated as Night Supervisor. I remember complaining once to Sister George, the administrator, that I hardly got used to one department when I was changed to another. She wisely replied, (probably aware of my "Jumping Joan" makeup) and suggested that if I were in a position more than a year at a time, I would probably be bored to death. She had a point, so I got used to being called "Sister Substitute."

Sadly, I soon found out that it was not "cool" to talk to the other Sisters about how we operated in Venezuela even if I mentioned a point that might be useful to operating in Pakistan. They thought that the management of an oil company hospital couldn't be compared to a foreign mission hospital. This made me feel like an outsider for some time, so I tried to limit my comments and ideas.

One of the duties of the Night Supervisor was to observe the midwifery students in their practice, so Sister George asked me if I would consent to studying midwifery. I was a little puzzled as usually Superiors just told us what we would be doing without asking. I found out that the 1936 Canon Law decree from Rome allowing religious to practice Obstetrics read as follows:

No Sister may be obliged by her Superiors to undertake obstetrical work; only those are to engage in this particular form of work who are willing to accept this special charge of mission charity from their Superiors. ...but above all, they must be protected by special spiritual safeguards to be determined by their Superiors.

What these special spiritual safeguards were none of us could ever figure out. It seemed to me more reasonable to be "safeguarded" when working with male patients, but this was never mentioned.

The Church's patriarchal and all-male hierarchy found it hard to understand the role of women and issues of sexuality, and of the professional practice of medicine and nursing.

From March 1957 to March 1958 I too became a student of Midwifery along with some of my former nursing students. I also had duty on the men's floor and/or the Out Patient Department, so had to squeeze in my cases between my regular duties. The students were quite competitive especially if it was a case they wanted to observe or actually do the delivery, so I had to be sure that I kept in touch with the Labor Room. However, we were very fortunate that in August of that year there were five sets of twins to be delivered within a couple of days, so we all checked off our twin deliveries on our list. The local paper was intrigued and had a photograph published of the five proud fathers and the sets of twins "nursed by their fathers" in the local paper. It would not have been modest to have photos of the proud mothers. As midwifery students we were allowed to deliver twins, breech births and even do episiotomies when necessary. We would call for assistance from the doctor for difficult labors, Caesareans and for repairs of the episiotomies or tears.

I remember supervising one of the students deliver the Princess of Swat who had married the son of the Pakistan Prime Minister, Ayub Khan. *When Swat recently had a serious earthquake, the Princess came to mind... was she still alive and involved with her stricken country?* There were a few patients who wanted a doctor for their delivery but most preferred a midwife. Occasionally the companion who comforted the patient in labor was the patient's husband's other wife. Plural wives in the Muslim religion were permitted if the husband could financially care for them, which was not too common. I probably delivered over fifty babies so I felt well prepared. I supervised many other deliveries. Our text was the large English midwifery book by Miles that was very complete. We went to the city of Lahore for our Midwifery written exams.

Sometimes during the practical exams we were helped by the practice patients themselves (patients from our own Pre-Natal clinic who consented to help with the exams, where we had to palpate the patient's abdomen.) The pregnant ladies would kindly point to where we might hear the fetal heart, what position the head was in, or hold up two fingers to tell us they were going to have twins. Was this cheating? We didn't ask them to do this but I guess they felt sorry for us. The tests were not that easy so I did have to study.

Many patients who could not afford hospital food would have their relatives bring their meals in a tiffin carrier. A tiffin carrier is a series of tin containers, usually three, one atop the other and held together with a metal handle. This also kept the cooked food hot. Otherwise the diet was quite adequate with chapattis (a tortilla kind of wheat bread) and curry and fruit in season. We had excellent fruits such as plums, oranges, and loquats. We received American food from CARE such as powdered milk that we gave out every week but in liquid form so that it would be drunk and not sold. We also had American cheese and clarified butter (ghee). We made a point to see that our tuberculosis patients received the cheese as they were so undernourished and needed the protein. We noticed when we went to the bazaars that all the containers for these products were recycled into cups, plates, spoons and even medicine dishes which we used in the hospital.

We could learn so much from the thrifty Pakistanis. I remember we used to get one ½ inch roll of adhesive to use on the wards for a whole month. We used to split even this small piece in half to fix the I.V. tubing to the patients' arms. The dressings in the O.R. were sewn together with a large tension suture through the tissue and holding the dressing in place, so it stayed on until the stitches had to be removed. This worked very well at saving gauze and adhesive and also helped prevent wound infections, as they never got exposed. For small clean wounds we used collodion without any covering dressing. *I got so indoctrinated into this kind of recycling that when I visited my aunts years later, I had to ask them what they did with their paper bags, a question they found strange (this was before the age of recycling.) When I returned to the U.S. I was amazed when I saw 3-inch adhesive being used to stick a notice on the refrigerator door at the Nurse's Station. Health Care Reform bureaucrats, please take note!*

Sister Elise, with the help of the U.S. Agency for International Development, constructed a sewage system behind the hospital that used the purified effluent as an irrigation system that watered the peanuts and citrus trees that had been planted in a plot behind the hospital. For the babies in Pediatrics we used the very rich water buffalo milk. It was not uncommon to see a one-year old baby who weighed only 8 or 10 pounds. Those babies that could not breast feed were often susceptible to diarrhea, dehydration and malnutrition. Often they had been drinking watered down milk or contaminated milk that caused diarrhea. Breast feeding mothers always stayed in the hospital with their babies so they would still be able to breast-feed. They usually slept on a mat on the floor next to the baby's crib.

Anemia in women was very common, mostly due to constant bouts of malaria. Among the poor, men ate the small amount of meat first and the women ate the little that was left. Some women were walking around with a very low count of two grams of Hemoglobin (a normal level is about 10–12 grams.) Just looking at their completely white eyelids, we could easily make the diagnosis of anemia. These women needed blood transfusions not easily obtainable. It took a lot of persuasion to convince family members to donate blood. Some would ask if we could use goat's blood. Those with less severe anemia received intravenous iron injections in the clinic. I was very edified by the story from our Lab technician that one woman who had been told that "blood is life" offered to give her blood for a relative. After the procedure she asked: "when will I die?"

Tuberculosis was very common, not only of the lungs, but lymphatic, abdominal (of the mesentery and peritoneum), bone, meninges and reproductive organs. Body casts for spinal tuberculosis were common. For abdominal tuberculosis just opening up the abdomen would have a curative effect in conjunction with Streptomycin injections. Streptomycin was just beginning to be used but sometimes caused serious side effects, such as deafness. The students had their own way of diagnosing a baby with tuberculosis. They would say "look at his long straight eyelashes." They were often correct—the child had tuberculosis, probably abdominal. *It's possible this may be related to an effect of the disease on the hormonal system. I never heard the cause explained scientifically.*

Occasionally we encountered a case of tetanus. As it is usually fatal, immediate treatment with Tetanus Antitoxin was instituted and we saved a few cases. Some of the tetanus cases were due to poor hygiene during delivery and the custom of putting cow dung on the baby's umbilical cord and other unhygienic practices.

We saw many pregnant women with osteomalacia (softening of the bones) due to lack of Vitamin D in the diet and the fact that wearing a burka prevented them from getting Vitamin D from the sun. The Christian women and the Gypsies were spared this, as they did not cover their faces. This condition caused bone deformities and made for difficult deliveries and often Caesareans were necessary. We administered Calcium intravenously in the prenatal clinic as a preventive measure.

Gypsies sometimes came to our clinics. They often camped out on the banks of the Jhelum River. The local people were afraid of them as they were very adept at sitting next to a woman whose coins were tied up in her dopatta (scarf) and making off with the coins. In general, however, because of their outdoor lifestyle, they were a healthy group.

Speaking of the river reminds me of some days when we were allowed to shorten our siesta time and take a walk down along the river. I still remember fondly one beautiful spring day when we were looking across the river at the blossoming fields of mustard and grain, we were enchanted with the almost biblical scene—a man guiding a donkey with a woman holding a baby. It looked so much like the Holy Family on their road to Egypt. As Pindi is in a high desert, in the month of February for example, we could be nice and warm on the walk, but very cold inside the hospital. We used to say: "It's the only place you can get sunburn and frostbite on the same day." In the summer we would close the windows with "chiks" (dark blue curtains) to keep the heat out and then open them at night to let the cool air in. A Kenmore stove in the middle of the wards made the patients more comfortable in the winter.

The Sister who worked as Night Supervisor slept during the day in the hospital tower room that had an air-conditioner in the summer.

What a blessing! Otherwise, we would take a shower in our night-gowns and lay down on our charpais (string beds) to cool off—sort of an evaporative cooler system. Our nightgowns dried out very quickly. Sometimes we slept out on the hospital roof but used mosquito nets, making it even hotter. We took precautions to avoid malaria, common among our student nurses. They were so accustomed to it that they would come shivering to the Head Nurse, and say, "I have malaria, can I please go and lay down for an hour or two?" They would take some aspirin and have a break in their fever and soon return to duty. Every morning at roll call we administered Chloroquin to the nurses as a preventive measure, but still some came down with malaria. *Malaria is still a very widespread disease in the developing world and causes not only many deaths, but loss of productive work. Our hygiene practices prevented us from contracting the disease, even though mosquito nets and malaria pills were an irritating part of life in the missions.*

During my time in Pakistan I had the opportunity of visiting some of the sights in Lahore, such as the Shalimar Gardens, and also Taxila, north of Rawalpindi. Taxila is the site of ruins of several ancient civilizations from the seventh century B.C. to the seventh Century A.D. Alexander the Great had been here and later it became a Buddhist center. A few years later I visited Mohenjodaro near Karachi—the even more ancient Indus Valley civilization dating back to 3000 B.C. I have always been interested in archaeology and was impressed by the Pakistanis pride in their ancient culture.

During the summer we were allowed four weeks at our vacation house in the hill station of Murree north of Pindi (where the British colonials used to go). We took the local bus up the road past what is now Islamabad, the capital. In the 50s we drove past water buffalo grazing in the pastureland. Now it is a bustling capitol city. Our vacation house, Oxford Villa, was a cozy, rustic house in the foothills of the Himalayas. The high altitude and pine trees made our house delightfully cool and breezy. We had our own little chapel and a priest from a missionary order came to say Mass for us. One day, a priest spotted a flying squirrel (they were often seen on our rafters) on top of the tabernacle. "Oh, that's an interesting tabernacle," he exclaimed until he saw the frightened squirrel finally jump off to its own place. He mistook the squirrel for a small carved ornament on top of the tabernacle. We would take hikes in places like Natiagali that was even higher where we could see the "real" Himalayas. Sisters from Karachi joined us at this vacation house.

We had some very good times here. We had an old wind-up Victrola with some equally old records, such as John Philip Sousa's marches that we played when we were doing cleaning chores and a real popular song entitled "My Adobe Hacienda." If we picnicked out on the rocks behind the house we had to watch out for the crows and jays that would steal our sandwiches if we left them for a moment. I can still remember the initial feeling of bliss as I lay down on my cool charpai and relaxed. No more worries about very sick patients or complaints about the student nurses or any other responsibilities and not being so tired after a very hot day. Our Pakistani cook who had his big iron wood stove in a little shed outside the house fixed excellent meals. We had our own chaukidar who served as a general caretaker, guard and assistant to our cook, as well as a mehtrani (sweeper) who emptied our outhouse potties down the gully. It seems strange that a poor mission community had servants, but that was the culture of the country, and it gave some needed employment to the people. Besides none of us knew how to tend and cook on a wood stove.

We had other employees at the hospital, besides the nursing staff and allied health professionals, such as durzis (tailors) who made all our sheets, towels, O.R. linens, and even our habits; dhobis (washermen) who beat the clothes on rocks and then hung them out on twisted clotheslines to dry or on rocks. This method did not require clothespins. We also had our own tonga-walla, or the man who drove the one-horse carriage. The cleaners did their jobs by hand mostly as we did not have any mechanical floor scrubbers or other modern devices. When we needed new chapplis (sandals) we would go into the parlor while the shoemaker from town would put down a newspaper and trace each foot. Thus we got a perfect fit on our sandals. This was the usual procedure in Pakistan as commercially made shoes were even more expensive than handmade ones.

We never had white shoe polish but used ground-up chalk as polish. For sanitary napkins we used folded-up diapers, also made on the premises. For toilet paper we used torn up squares of newspapers. One happy Christmas one of the Sister's parents sent her a large box of toilet paper. We often saved this for our vacation house. Toothpaste was rare so we used the tooth powder made up by our pharmacist, Sister Renee. A tube of toothpaste from the U.S. was a much-appreciated gift found on our Christmas tree. I also remember some chocolate bars sent by ship that arrived a few months later. These usually had a little mold on them, but we were happy to scrape off the mold and enjoy our "Mounds" (not "molds.") At Christmas we received all of our Christmas cards and letters from home and from our Sister friends. Of course, our beautiful poinsettias made us feel more at home.

We found living in a Muslim country not as difficult as we would have imagined. We learned about the Muslim religion and its customs and discovered that they had great respect for "people of the Book," meaning those who read the Bible or other holy book. As I mentioned earlier, Mary, under the Arabic/Hebrew name of Miriam was venerated during childbirth and Jesus was considered a prophet along with Mohammed, but not revered as the Son of God. We only had a few Muslim nurses, as their religion did not approve of them caring for male patients. When the Pakistani Army was left with few nurses after Partition, they were happy to send us Muslim students who would later join as nurses in the Pakistani Army. Most of our nurses were Christian converts from the lower classes, and a few Catholics of Anglo-Indian or Goan extraction. We also had an occasional Parsee (Zoroastrian) nurse. The Society had the policy of avoiding proselytizing. Our religion was to be expressed in our healing and educational mission. This mixture of religions sometimes had its advantages, as the Muslim nurses were willing to work on the Christian holidays, and the Christian nurses worked on the Muslim holidays or on the night shifts during Ramadan.

We sometimes had a few problems, such as when a Christian nurse mistakenly put her sandals on a shelf in the cupboards above a shelf that held the Koran, respectfully covered with a beautiful cloth. Muslims so respected their Koran that nothing unclean, such as shoes, should be placed above it. Muslims do not eat pork so we never ate it either. Some Muslim women, especially widows, expressed a desire that their religion would also have some kind of dedicated women to serve the sick and poor as we did. *Now that we are at war in Iraq and becoming familiar with the two branches of Islam, Sunni and Shiites, I remember we had three Muslim students in one class—Tyaba Hyder, Zohra Khan and Mubarika Malik. The first mentioned was a Shiite and the latter two were Sunni, but they were great friends and got along with each other in contrast with the present hostilities between the two groups. At that time Pakistan was mainly Sunni.*

I have a theory about "culture shock" and decided that once you had adapted to your first foreign culture, the next ones would be easier. I had adapted with some effort to the Latin culture so found it not too difficult to adapt to the Eastern and Muslim culture. However, it would have been easier for all of us to serve in the same culture for longer periods of time, but the needs of our missions did not always allow that. For some of us "reverse culture shock" proved to be more difficult when we returned to the U.S. after years in the missions.

Some of our Pakistani nurses excelled at eastern dances that they performed with recorded music and camel bells on their ankles. These dances were part of celebrations for the Superior's feast day or other occasions when the guest of honor was garlanded with marigolds. Again my anthropological interest was piqued and occasionally a private patient (one with more money than most of our ward patients) would leave a local pictorial magazine with interesting articles about the country and its customs. I cut out many of these articles, for example, colorful pictures of Pakistani weddings, and saved them in a scrapbook along with other items. *When I returned to the Motherhouse I gave them to the Sister who was teaching Missiology, but unfortunately the scrapbook was never seen again and probably never used—another frustration for me.* I also learned to sing the Pakistani national anthem and to say the Our Father and Hail Mary in Urdu.

We sometimes took the nurses on picnics on the riverbank. Unlike us with a basket of sandwiches and chips or cookies, they insisted on spending the early hours of the morning cooking chapattis, samosas, rice and curry and putting them in tiffin carriers so they would have a regular hot meal. They even ground the curry spices that morning so they would be fresh—not exactly fast food but very tasty. *They would be horrified by our tin cans of "curry powder" that had been sitting on the shelf for months.* They donned their best clothes for the picnics. There may not have been a person in sight when we went to the river, but like spontaneous generation, the local children would come out of nowhere and watch us, no doubt wanting to share some of the picnic spoils.

I remember two very sad events. The first was the news that one of our Anglo-Indian student nurses, Marlene, was killed in a train wreck on her way back from her vacation in Karachi. It was a very difficult time for us and mostly for her fellow students. The other sad event was when our own Sister Regina suffered from ovarian cancer. She inspired us all as she tried to continue her work as nurse in the Newborn Nursery. The students really loved her and even felt free to tease her about her big "tummy." She knew her days were numbered and she would casually tell the nurses: "Don't forget to hand-wash the baby clothes when I won't be here." Finally when she was bedridden, we Sisters took turns sitting at her bedside. She would remark how it would be a relief not to have to read *Time* magazine any more to find out what was going on in the world. I remember sitting at her bedside as I went through her "things" and she would decide what should be done with certain holy cards and other little treasures. She died very peacefully with many of the Sisters praying around her bedside. The funeral was one of mourning for all, the Sisters, nurses and even patients who knew her. She was buried on the hospital grounds. *This was the kind of "happy death" I always envisioned for myself especially on our monthly Meditations on Death... with the Sisters around me with prayers and support and being buried in the missions or in Philadelphia. The purpose of The Meditation on Death was to think periodically about our death and how we should live to be ready for that important day. In other words, "as you live, so shall you die."*

Our chapel was finally finished and furnished with a beautiful green marble altar that came from a quarry in nearby Afghanistan. Our pews were designed so we would stay cool. They were like caned chairs attached to each other to make a pew. This made them a lot more comfortable than if the seats were solid wood.

After the 1957 General Chapter (a special meeting held every five or six years to discuss needed changes and make decisions for the future of the Society.) It was decided to divide the Society into Pro-Provinces. The Society had grown much bigger than when I had entered. We had Sisters in India, Pakistan, Africa, Indonesia, South America, the Philippines and also in Europe and it was decided that governance needed to be more decentralized. One of the Sister-doctors, Sister Benedict, (she of the Thanksgiving doughnuts when we had our basketball game) was appointed the first Pro-Provincial for the American Province which included the missions sponsored by that Province. The other two Pro-Provinces were the one for the Netherlands and later one for South India. New decisions and changes were made when Mother Benedict took over. Most of the larger hospitals soon had a separate Sister in charge of hospital administration and another Sister as local Superior. Although this system helped in sharing the heavy burden, it sometimes made for confusion for the Sisters who were not always sure of the demarcation lines. The Motherhouse was moved from Philadelphia to Rome and most decisions were made at the Pro-Provincial level. Many changes in assignment were made about this time.

In October 1959 I was overwhelmed when I received a new "obedience" as "Acting Superior of Holy Family Hospital, Karachi." That evening was the first time that I ever lost my appetite and could hardly eat my supper. It seemed like an honor but I also felt (and later Mother Benedict herself reminded me that "the willing jackass gets the load") that it was a burden I was not ready for nor qualified to carry. Also the word "Acting" seemed like a vote of no confidence, or a responsibility without full authority. As with every other assignment I acquiesced and this time "Holy O" (as we called holy obedience) entailed a real challenge. It was not to be easy as Sister Dolores was the administrator in Karachi and I had worked under her some time in Pindi, so knew she had a very strong personality and one that sometimes clashed with mine. Also I felt very intimidated by Mother Benedict who could come down pretty heavy on Sisters, especially Superiors, who did not conform to her way of thinking. Again I had to say goodbye to the Sisters I had worked with, the student nurses and others to move to the more metropolitan city of Karachi and a whole new role.

CHAPTER 12

KARACHI

The Karachi Holy Family Hospital was founded in 1948 (a year after Partition) and was in the process of adding a new wing to the 60-bed hospital. It did not have a Nursing School, but did have a simple training course for nurses' aides. I was given assignments as Nursing Supervisor, rotating Night Supervisor, and duties in the Delivery Room. My role as Local Superior was to look after the Sisters' spiritual welfare and lead the community in prayer; to supervise the Sisters' care when they became sick; counsel them when they had complaints or problems that were not directly related to their duties (these were the domain of the Administrator). Sometimes the lines of authority here would overlap, but I was expected to support the Sister and if necessary request a change of assignment. I had to schedule community retreats and conferences, and interact with the local Bishop and other Catholic communities in Karachi. I was charged with keeping the Chronicle that recorded the events of the day, and meeting Sisters who were traveling through Karachi to other destinations. I was expected to have a monthly one-on-one meeting with each Sister to inquire into her concerns and problems. Sometimes decisions I had to make were painful for the Sister involved and caused me to worry about the wisdom of what I had recommended.

As Nursing Supervisor I attended regional nurses meetings and one sponsored by the World Health Organization Middle East Region which had nurses from countries such as Egypt, Iran, Iraq, Jordan, Syria and Lebanon. At one convention I demonstrated the Kinney method of hot packs for polio patients (polio was still endemic in Pakistan and many other countries.) These meetings broadened my horizon to other Middle East and mostly Muslim cultures. They also made me aware of the close bond that nurses all over the world have with each other, that they face similar concerns and experiences and are willing to help each other. I learned to respect the role of the World Health Organization and its efforts to eradicate disease and improve the health of its members. *At later meetings some very*

ambitious goals were made in regard to health, such as "by the year 2000
X disease would be eradicated" or "X number of nurses would be trained
by the year 2000 or" or "80% of the world's population will have potable
drinking water." Unfortunately the year 2000 has come and gone and the
only disease that has been eradicated is smallpox and we still need more
nurses even here in the U.S.

The hospital had occasional fund-raisers for the completion of the
new hospital wing and I was asked to preside at the tea table on the
front lawn where dignitaries were served. I do remember one occasion when both the wife of the Prime Minister (Ayub Khan) and the
wife of the President (Mohammed Khan) were served—two very
gracious ladies. Many women from the various foreign embassies
also attended and were very generous in their support of our work.

The Society had a policy that each Sister should have at least one
day off a week so the Sister-nurses often got a day off during the
week and sometimes a Sunday off. Usually two Sister-nurses took a
motor rickshaw and went to the fishermen's beach on the Arabian
Sea. I remember especially taking a camel ride on the beach, (a
unique experience) enjoying our picnic lunches in the sand and reading a favorite mystery story. As a group the Sisters sometimes took a
ride on a bunder boat in the Karachi harbor. Karachi, being on the
seacoast, was much more humid than Pindi and therefore a bit more
enervating, (no taking of showers with our nightgowns on here, as
we would stay drenched) so we were very happy to take the train to
Pindi, then the bus to our vacation house in Murree and join our
Pindi Sisters there.

We attended classes given by the Oriental Institute (sponsored by
the local Catholic diocese) that informed us of the history of Islam
and its beliefs and customs. These classes helped a lot in understanding our patients and employees as most of them were Muslim. I was
surprised to find that like Catholics, they too had their folk religion
and little shrines to their "saints" whom they prayed to for certain
favors. These shrines were visited mostly by women of the poorer
classes, often to pray for a safe delivery, for a sick child and more
often to plead to be able to bear a child, especially a son. Being
childless was almost a sure excuse for a divorce or for the husband

to find another wife. At the hospital we often tried to help these women to determine the cause of sterility and perform needed surgery when indicated. The men were reluctant to find out if perhaps they had some condition that might cause sterility.

In January 1961 Mother Benedict made a visitation of the Karachi hospital and made many recommendations. I found this a very trying time as apparently I was not coming up to her expectations. Some of the Sisters probably reported to her that I had been impatient with them or did not understand their needs. She told me in an angry and curt voice that I was the worst superior in the region. Then in July of the same year there was a meeting in Poona, India of all the Superiors from Pakistan and India. It was here during coffee breaks that I mentioned to some of the Sisters that I had been told I was the worst Superior in the area. One after the other exclaimed: "She told me that I was the worst!" so there was some comfort in being part of a group of Sisters whom I admired but who had also suffered similar experiences. *In time I realized the pressures that Mother Benedict was under as everything was so new to her.*

In March of 1962, (I was not told why) I was relieved of my duties as local Superior and told to return to the U.S. I had no idea as to what my future assignment might be. I was relieved that I would no longer have such burdensome responsibilities, but also dejected at what I perceived as rejection of my best efforts.

CHAPTER 13

ST. VINCENT'S HOSPITAL

The Society had a custom of giving each Sister a kind of sabbatical renewal about every seven years so I had hoped to have a restful break. I had been in the missions for eleven years but discovered when I arrived in Philadelphia that one of the Sisters told me they had seen my name on the assignment sheet at St. Vincent's Hospital for Women and Children. This came as a big shock, but in April I moved to our residence at St. Vincent's in Southwest Philadelphia.

St. Vincent's was a home and hospital for unwed mothers and their babies, previously run by the Daughters of Charity. The Cardinal of Philadelphia had requested the Society to take over this hospital which was not exactly a "mission" hospital. Because of my midwifery training, the work was not difficult but we were very understaffed. I remember one time when I was called on night duty for a post-partum patient who was having convulsions. As I was administering oxygen to her and checking her blood pressure etc., I could not leave her to call for help so had to rely on one of the patients to go to the next floor (no phones in the patients' rooms) and get help from the nurse on duty there. Most of the mothers intended to put their babies up for adoption so the great joy of a delivery of a healthy baby was not always celebrated. We did not allow the mothers to see their babies so they wouldn't have such a hard time deciding if they really wanted to give them up.

This was the era of Dick Clark's "American Bandstand" on TV, a favorite program for the patients (and why not, the show originated in Philadelphia) and my first real experience of TV (except for the World Series I had seen in Baltimore when I was having my Psychiatric Nursing experience) and my first acquaintance with the new musical culture of Rock and Roll. Welcome to "reverse culture shock!"

I was only at St. Vincent's for about six months when I was given another new assignment. I was to return to Venezuela, but not to my beloved Maracaibo but to eastern Venezuela to another small Creole hospital, Sagrada Familia, in Caripito. Generally, in the Society, Caripito was considered a kind of "Siberia of the missions" because it was a difficult place to work having been managed for several years by the oil company, unlike the new hospital in Maracaibo, and the employees were pretty set in their ways. This only reinforced my idea that my new assignment was somehow a punishment or a lesson I needed to learn. I had become almost used to these abrupt changes, but just as I was getting familiar with Pakistan and its Muslim culture, I was going back to Venezuela. I know most of these changes were usually based on a need for a Sister being replaced because of some other need, but it didn't make it any easier. After all, my vow of obedience did invite me to accept whatever came along, so I tried my best to comply without complaint. *Now I can sympathize with our military when ordered to transfer abruptly to a new and unfamiliar location.* I was relieved that I would not have the position of local superior.

CHAPTER 14

CARIPITO

I arrived in Caripito on October 7, 1962 and found it to be a smaller and much less elegant hospital than Coromoto in Maracaibo. It was named "Hospital Sagrada Familia" (Holy Family Hospital) a translation of the name given to most of the Medical Mission Sisters' hospitals in India, Pakistan and Africa. It was in a rural area close to the San Juan River, which is a branch of the great Orinoco River. The patients were mostly oil workers and the local population, mostly with much less education than those in Maracaibo. This hospital was not new and had been functioning under the Medical Mission Sisters only since 1956, so it was sometimes difficult for employees to understand that we did not operate under the same policies as Creole Petroleum Corporation. I did the usual rotations of Day Supervisor, Night Supervisor, Central Supply, on call for the O.R. and even substituted for the Pharmacist (a Venezuelan) if he was on vacation or absent.

I also accompanied Sister Anita, the Administrator, to the nearby State capital of Maturín for the discussions on the annual labor contract renewal with the hospital union leaders. This was a real education for me on how political discussions were conducted. You give a little on your issue, and they'll give a little on their issue. All issues were finally worked out to the relative satisfaction of both parties, but the process could get painful at times. (This was a process that our mission training had not covered.) On a few occasions I substituted for the administrator.

Mother Benedict made a visitation in April 1963. One question she asked me was "what do you do all day?" referring to my duties as Day Supervisor. I found the question to be quite threatening, so after she left I wrote a letter which I never actually mailed, describing a typical day in the life of the Day Supervisor. I had worked the 7 a.m. to 3 p.m. shift so typed it up in my free time in the afternoon. Here it is, if you want to be bored by reading the "exciting" and glamorous life of a missionary. If you choose not to read it, skip ahead. My comments or translations of some Spanish terms made now are put in brackets [ ].

A Day in the Life…

Dated approximately 1963 reproduced as written without edits:

"What do you do all day?" It seems to be a question that I have never been able to answer so I thought just once in a while I would try and write down just what I did in a day as Day Nursing Supervisor. I can't put the things in chronological order exactly but it all happened sometime between 7 a.m. and 3 p.m. on a rather ordinary day. There have been worse days, and busier ones but the following is just more or less typical…no two are alike. After report I went upstairs to Mujeres [Women's Dept.] to discover that Señora Azocar, the aide assigned to Pediatrics did not show up…was she sick as she was the day before or would she come in later??? The assignment list then had to be changed and a nurse taken from O.B. [Obstetrics] to do Pediatrics. The mensajera [messenger or ward clerk] having to help out on Mujeres and Isolation. As there were eleven patients on O.B. they were left quite short handed with only one aide…when a patient was scheduled for induction it was obvious that they would need another one…what to do?…just wait and see. As it turned out, after all these changes were made Señora. Azócar turned up about 7:40 a.m. and then further changes had to be made. Later when the patient on O.B. started induction the O.B. aide was sent over to O.B. again…leaving Mujeres pretty short handed with all the old ladies, etc.

The mensajera had to take 228 Isolation and Doctor was doing a spinal tap on a child there she had to help with that…this necessitated also calling the enfermero (orderly) from Hombres [Men's Dept] to help out as he was quite a big boy and wouldn't stay still. I saw that he came and helped out. Then I explained to the aide that she had to be careful about sending the spinal set back to Central in a bag for sterilizing as it was contaminated. I took the specimen personally to the lab as the aide was in Isolation still fixing up the child and the graduate was continuing rounds with the doctor. When I got to the Lab the door to the Lab was locked... what was going on... what holiday was it..?? so I had the telefonista (switchboard operator) call the Lab and ask them if they were there and would they please open the door... apparently there were some Hermanas de los Ángeles [Sisters of the Angels] getting blood work done and they had closed the door... gave in the specimen.

Meanwhile, checking the pharmacy slips of "Dados" [stock medicines that had been 'given'] on the different services... as it was Monday they hadn't been changed since Saturday... the graduate from Pediatrics told me that they had two extra Largactil I.M. ampoules which had been sent up by mistake and 2 Fenergans... these were kept in the narcotic drawer to be checked. Apparently what had happened was that Largactil I.V. was used from Emergency (?) and the pharmacy helper sent up I.M. as that is all that is in stock on Mujeres... also as Fenergan is not stock on Mujeres it must have come from Emergency but the pedido [request] was left on Mujeres... this took some investigating and explaining in the Pharmacy. The counts on O.B., Hombres and Pediatrics checked out all right.

On Mujeres there was a new graduate who had only worked two days with another grad. so there were many new things to check with her. I helped her check the pharmacy basket when the boy brought it up... discovered that the bottle of Serpasol of 0.25 was still in a patient's box with some pills in it although the dose had been changed to 0.10 the day before... which was in an envelope as it had been given out on Sunday from Emergency... pointed out that this had to be checked.

I explained the discharge routine on patients. One was only in for Metabolismo [Basal metabolism test]... she said she would wait for the Creole car, but as it happened she went out on her own and when they called up from the office I looked all over the floor for her and couldn't find her so presumed she had gone. The other patient was discharged only by about 11 a.m. and by that time the car had gone off to Q.Q. [Quiriquire, another town] and she was hanging around until 2 p.m. getting nervous. I checked on this to make sure that the office knew about it and the car was coming. I told the staff nurse the routine for surgical admissions and discovered that a patient from Q.Q. had been admitted with her lab work done for a hysterectomy to be scheduled for the next day but that she had just about everything done except the HGB and Htco., [Hemoglobin and Hematocrit] which were very important as she was also bleeding at the time. By 2 p.m. I personally took the slip for it to the Lab so they could do it then as if she needed blood we could ask for donors at visiting hours. As it turned out the Lab was too busy and said they would do it in the morning.

Meanwhile…in Pediatrics one of the little girls was discovered to have full blown mumps so arrangements had to be made to put her in Isolation also…thus giving even more work to the mensajera…one basin was missing for the room so had to look around for this…found one in the utility room which apparently belonged to no one. The nurse from the O.R. came to inquire what she should do about doing an EKG ordered on the boy in Isolation, so I went to the doctor and asked him about it…he said it could wait until later after the results of the spinal tap came back. Discovered in Central [Central Supply] that the aide had taken the whole spinal tray into Isolation complete with the plastic tray card which of course was completely ruined in the autoclave so another one had to be taken from the card which belongs in Central. I went back to tell the aide about this and also explained to the graduate in Pediatrics not to take the tags inside but to leave them out on the table in the anteroom. Also a syringe had been broken on the spinal tray so had to make out a slip for this and exchange it.

Meanwhile…Father Gualberto [hospital chaplain] was looking for Sister Timothy to take his B.P. (a daily occurrence) and as she was busy on O.B. I took it…as Father was complaining of a headache he asked me to find out from Sister Timothy what injection was he supposed to take for his brain. Sister Timothy said she didn't know and so Father had to go down to his house to get his prescription…when he came back I went to give him the injection…what was in the icebox in Emergency was not enough so went up to borrow some from Mujeres. Father told me at this time that he wished we had informed him of moving Señora Gomez' room as he went to her old room and asked the patient there if she wanted to go to communion and discovered it was somebody else.

Meanwhile…Señorita Rodriguez from O.R. reported to me that some joker had written on the O.R. blackboard for an "extracción de muelas" [tooth extraction] and discussed this with her and tried to investigate from the enfermeros [male nurses]…who of course knew nothing of it. This was someone's idea of a joke as there were no operations scheduled. Señorita Rodriguez was rather upset about it. Made note of it to investigate further and report to Sister Jeanne.

Meanwhile...was told by the Linen Room that the laundry had not all come back and so there was a shortage of draw sheets...so had to go around especially on Mujeres and tell the aides to only change those that were absolutely necessary. Sister Jeanne asked me about where I thought the new wheelchairs should go...we figured about a list which she would present to Sister Samuel [the administrator]. She also asked me if I knew anything about the glass marking gun which was on Sister Benedicta's desk and which Sister Benedicta did not know anything about...I vaguely recalled that months ago I heard Sister Patrice mention that Sister Joseph said it wasn't working so I thought it had been turned into be fixed...how it ended up on Sister B.'s desk, I don't know. So I took it to Señor Bellabarba (maintenance head) who tested it and said it seemed o.k. Took it up to O.R. and asked Señorita Rodriguez to try it out...as it seemed o.k. I gave it to the O.R. as I think that is where it belonged. I reminded Señorita Rodriguez that I would like the sample gauze drains that they use in the O.R., so the aides could make them from roller bandage.

Also discussed with Sister Jeanne the shortage of aides on second floor and made some suggestions. Apparently Señora Manriquez had been missing from night duty due to illness so I had to find out if she were planning on coming that night or not, otherwise other arrangements would have to be made by having someone on 3–11 work an extra shift. I sent the driver to her house to get the answer...he returned saying she wasn't at home but they said she had gone out. So I asked her husband who works in the pharmacy what he thought...he said he would let me know after dinner. As it turned out later the message was that she could come, so no changes were necessary.

Sister Timothy was on O.B. and didn't know all the routines...explained what papers the discharged patients were to get etc. I discovered that in spite of having been reminded since Saturday the birth certificates were not signed by the two doctors. As Sister was busy and only one aide, I called the Doctora who came up to sign hers...Dr. Rojas was in Consulta [clinic] with a patient so I went down with the papers for him to sign as the discharged patients couldn't go without them. Sister Timothy asked me to check with Sister Carmelita about changing burned out light bulbs in the Delivery Room as it might be needed soon. I was surprised at this as I thought we always went to Señor Rivas and discovered that Sister Carmelita was now in charge of the cleaners and orders had to go through her...got upset about not knowing about this. I reminded Sister Carmelita about the order...no written pedido [requistion slip.] She thought Sister Timothy had said O.R. so this was taken care of.

Discovered the Communion box was still up on Mujeres in the duty room left there by the Night Supervisor so took it back to the sacristy. The telefonista said there was a special call for an O.B. patient and as I thought she said, from her husband, so I gave permission for her to take the phone, but discovered when I walked over to O.B. that that was the patient getting induction so she couldn't get out of bed...I understood the message to be that he was going to Caracas...as the lady seemed rather surprised at this news and also that if she was a problem patient it wouldn't be a good idea to have her husband away. I had to call back to the telefonista. Found out that it was a Señor Lares who was only a nephew of the lady so no cause for worry there.

Sister Jeanne had the duty list papers and asked me to bring them up to Sister Timothy on O.B. as she was working on it in her spare time. Sister Timothy asked me to make some changes on this week's schedule due to the fact that one of the aides had to work on her day off last week...had to ask another one if she would mind working evenings instead of days on one day. Sister Samuel phoned and wanted the English translation of some Spanish medical terms. Met Mister Burke [the Creole engineer) in Central and he said the autoclave was working very slowly and would I put in a pedido to the maintenance department to have the filter changed...did this. When I was in Central gave out the daily supplies and checked the returned pedidos.

I was called to the Caja [bookkeeping office] about a discharged baby whose father was not willing or able to pay the bill even though they had promised to do so. Discussed this with the father and the cashier...it was referred to Sister Samuel and the baby was allowed to go. When down there some lady wanted to visit the t.b. patient in Isolation but had to refuse her as it was still early in the morning and the patient was not serious. Sister Mercedes had left a note in the Nursing Office with the chart of the same baby that had been sent to Archivos [Record Office] without being signed off by the nurses. I discovered that this was the same baby who had been discharged on Saturday but had not yet gone. I investigated and found out that the Caja had called the Pediatrics nurse and told her the chart was ready after the bill had been made out...the supervisor had also been informed. Nobody ever came to pick it up. I went up to Peds. to investigate and found that the baby had a chart back with his name on it and inside was one sheet of nurse's notes which had been kept up since Saturday afternoon. No one informed the supervisor that it was still in the office...so took this up and told the nurse to finish it off only when the baby went home.

Sister Jeanne left an ophthalmoscope in the Caja by mistake which was supposed to have been fixed by the taller [repair shop]. The cashier brought it to me and I found that Senor Bellabarba had the pedido so I explained that I wanted the corroded batteries removed without ruining the case. He brought it back later but forgot to return the ruined batteries which I needed for replacement. Took two new batteries out of the closet and tried out the ophthalmoscope...it apparently worked but had to investigate why the doctors would never use it. Asked Dr. Garrasini who explained that the other type was far superior so they all preferred that one. Checked on the ones in Peds. and Mujeres...he made the suggestion that I leave the inferior ophthalmoscope in Peds. as they hardly used it there and send the otoscope and separate ophthalmoscope to Peds. Discovered that the otoscope on Mujeres was not as good as the one in Peds, so had to wait to discuss the problem later with Sister Jeanne. Also checked spare parts kept in Supervisor's closet on Hombres.

Sister Carmelita called and wanted to know if the cleaners could de-bug the duty room on Hombres which would mean emptying out all the medicine cupboards etc. I said yes and informed the nurse on Hombres. Also room 205 was to be cleaned out. When Señor Rivas was finished I had to check it was O.K. Some confusion in Room 205 as the aides were working in there at the time and had to be rushed along. Was also asked to find out what places needed to be done next...was told by Sister Timothy that Peds. was very bad especially around the bedside stands...checked this and made a note of it to be done the next day.

At various times took out of the supervisor's closet...talc powder for Newborn Nursery, TIG soap for cleaning baby bottles, urine specimen bags for Peds, and Central pedidos for the Emergency Room. O.B. aide sitting with patient getting induction so got gauze to fold from Central for her. Was called to receive a package from Avensa [local airline] but when I got downstairs the man had gone leaving the package in the Pharmacy. Went down there to check and discovered it was a big empty milk can which they thought belonged to Sister Benedicta...waited til she came up at 2:30 and informed her of it...it really belonged to Creole but the Lab had used it to send blood to Cumaná in it.

I noticed that the drum lining on the formula drum was very dirty so reminded the aide to ask in O.R. for a clean one. Also aide making formulas said some child's formula in Peds hadn't been given the day before...told her to throw it out. There was an urgent blood transfusion ordered on Mujeres and as the nurse was new I checked in the Lab for this for her. Was called by the telefonista about three times for patients to receive phone calls or visitors. Also one aide was called by the Inspector de Trabajo [Labor Inspector]...referred the problem to Sister Samuel as it wasn't exactly personal and could be a touchy situation if refused...o.k.'d.

As the mensajera was quite busy with 228 and Mujeres I did most of the messages...took slips to Pharmacy etc. Other aide was also tied up so checked the dressing cart for her. Made out the patient assignments for the 3–11 aides. Went around again to each service to get complete report for supervisor's report...three new admissions on Hombres and one on Mujeres. Checked little notice about making out Central pedidos with Sister Jeanne.

Took a quick look at all the patients and talked for a little while to Candelaria [an agitated elderly woman] to calm her down. Three o'clock and gave report to the evening supervisor.

Reading this report now, it sounds like a real life "Comedy of Errors" but it was just a day in the life of a missionary.

The Times They Are A-Changing

The sixties were a time of student and worker political protests against the government and the oil companies. Many of the local young men joined the guerrillas in the mountains and jungles and sometimes would blow up an oil pipeline in protest. The National Guard had a station nearby and would come to our hospital to pick up their first aid packs and gloves that we had sterilized for them. They would land by helicopter near the hospital and once offered a trip for us to view the local area. Sister Thomasina and I volunteered for this interesting tour where we saw parts of the jungle inaccessible by road and followed the snaky San Juan River as it meandered to its connection to its delta and the ocean. Ocean ships could come up the San Juan River and dock, but had to wait for high tide to turn around and go back.

We also had contact with the guerrillas when they would come in periodically from the mountains to replenish their food supplies and visit their families and girl friends. If they were injured they were hospitalized with a National Guard officer watching them. I remember one young man who reportedly had shot himself in the foot as a means to avoid the perilous duties of a guerrilla. We never took sides and did not discuss the political situations with either the National Guard or the guerrillas. To us they were just each doing what they thought was right, and our purpose was to care for the sick and injured. Besides, we were foreigners and we knew that any political involvement would mean expulsion from the country.

We took an occasional day trip to the beach at Carupano on the Caribbean and once to the Island of Margarita. We even visited the Cueva de Guácharo, or the cave of the oilbird, where we pinned up our habits and went barefoot as the floor of the cave was quite muddy. We walked through the cave that was a home for the oilbirds, blind mice and insects. On another outing we explored the Canaima Falls area and Cerro Bolívar, near the Orinoco. This was a mountain of nearly pure iron ore that was currently being mined and shipped on rail cars to the ships for export.

Eastern Venezuela and the jungle to the south were rich in gold, diamonds, iron, aluminum and other minerals. Unfortunately we never got to see Angel Falls, at 3,212 feet, the highest falls in the world. It would have taken an expensive airplane trip or a two-week trip with Indian guides to find and it could only be seen if there were no rain, a rare occurrence. Strangely enough, Angel Falls was named for an American adventure flyer, Jimmy Angel, who crash-landed on the top of the mesa and was the first foreigner to report the falls to the rest of the world. His plane is still there and a replica made of it for a Caracas museum. *Recently there was a popular animated movie called "UP" which featured a waterfall in South America that was called Paradise Falls. That name was definitely inspired by Angel Falls but no credit was given for the original story—"political correctness?"*

For our summer vacations we still had our two weeks vacation at La Mesa in the Andes along with the Sisters from Maracaibo and from another small hospital in Judibana. Once we took the local airline to La Mesa. It was an especially turbulent flight. A passenger across the aisle leaned over to ask if we had an extra sickness bag. I quickly pulled out the one from the back of the seat in front of me and was surprised that it was already filled. The contents spilled all over my white habit. The stewardess came immediately to my aid, thinking I had vomited so she was trying to get me to inhale an Amyl Nitrite crushable capsule. I protested that I had not vomited but she insisted. We had many a laugh at this event as the story was told and retold.

The Sisters organized a small clinic in San Pablo, one of the rural areas where local volunteer doctors and nurses could see patients once a month. Venezuela did not allow foreign doctors to practice so we never had Sister-doctors there and nurses were not allowed to study or practice midwifery. We collected free medicines to be distributed to the poorer patients.

One day I will never forget was November 23, 1963. I was working in the Pharmacy as the pharmacist was on leave. Suddenly our O.R. nurse anesthetist, Violeta, came rushing into the room exclaiming: "Se mató á Kennedy!" (They killed Kennedy.) The Venezuelans, as many other Latin Americans, loved Kennedy and I was amazed at the respectful condolences we all received. Many of the doctors, nurses and employees attended the special memorial Mass, all dressed in their black suits or mourning clothes. It was as if we had lost a member of our own family (and indeed some of us felt that way). The government declared three days of official mourning. This meant among other things, that only classical music could be played on the radio. This truly was a sacrifice for the Venezuelans who loved their loud local popular music. It was indeed a sad day for all of us. We all watched the funeral ceremonies on TV and mourned the death of the President who offered so much promise to the world.

The North American Provincial, Mother Benedict, made a visitation in April 1963. Fortunately I had no position of authority so was not the object of her advice and corrections. However, a year later I wrote her a letter, partly inspired by the new openness in our Society and my concern for our role in the missions. The letter focused on my interest in missiology and the messages of Vatican Council II on the Church's role in adapting to the needs and realities of the modern world. I reviewed what was being done during our formation time, but also the need to extend this education once in the missions. I pointed out examples of the lack of familiarity of the culture, for example in Venezuela. I quoted the Society's Directives that stated: "The Sisters should study the customs, beliefs, the language and character of the people among whom they work." I made suggestions on how a comprehensive program could be planned and adapted to each mission. This program could include formal classes, availability of reading material and even field trips. I offered suggestions for an initial survey of the Sisters on their present needs, attitudes and what opportunities they were using to increase their knowledge and what topics they thought might be most useful. I offered to assist in establishing such a program if approved by the superiors and experts in the field. (*If the reader would like to see the entire text, I can give them a copy.*)

Mother Benedict never answered or acknowledged my letter. Later when I did have a chance to speak to her, I eagerly awaited her interest and enthusiasm for my suggestions. I expected her to pick it apart or point out some unrealistic goals, but was unprepared for her short and dismissive comment: "Sister, we're already doing that." I had been hoping that even if she was too busy to read it, she might have delegated the task to another Sister. I would have appreciated her acknowledging my efforts even if she thought that my concerns were not valid. I felt discouraged by her lack of confidence in my sincere efforts to serve the community.

Vatican II Council was in session and news trickled in of the position papers and decisions that were the result of the Bishops' deliberations. I still remember how happy our people were when they actually could understand the words of the Mass, when they heard the prayers said in Spanish and the priest said Mass facing the people. Some could not even use the translations in the Mass prayer books, as they were illiterate. In the U.S. there was some resistance to the loss of the Latin Mass, but we never heard those complaints in Venezuela. *I must admit that I truly did miss the Latin Gregorian chant that I had sung so many times.* These changes and others were just the beginning of a new revival in the Catholic Church and everyone was full of hope for its future. *Now forty years later, I believe some of these external changes have survived, but unfortunately some key theological concepts,— such as collegiality (more input from different Bishops than just those in Rome and less top down government) and the option for the poor—(it was often perceived by many of the lower classes that Bishops and priests spent too much time and energy on the rich and influential than on their needs) have taken a back seat or have been actually opposed by conservative Bishops and even Popes. These are still issues for many Catholics and have divided the Church. It is hard to find a parish that has a priest and congregation that is truly committed to peace and social justice. Now problems of priestly sexual abuse and the controversy over priestly celibacy and women's ordination have caused much discussion and divisions within the church. I am still hopeful that slowly things will change for the better.*

The writings that came out of Vatican II and the years after helped to advance my spirituality from one of submission to rules and regulations to one of a mature and responsible adult and a reminder that we, the people of God, are the Church.

CHAPTER 15

THE UNIVERSITY OF ZULIA

In September 1965 I was transferred from Caripito back to Maracaibo. It was a happy day for me to return to my first mission, Maracaibo. Sister Juanita had started a Nursing School at the Coromoto Hospital and she needed another instructor. There were only four students and they were very intelligent and a real challenge. In the meantime, the University of Zulia (Zulia is the state where Maracaibo is located) began discussions on beginning a Bachelor's program in Nursing under the auspices of the School of Medicine. Up to this time, Venezuela did not have any Bachelor level of nursing schools, not even in the capital city of Caracas. All the national schools, as they were called, accepted students from the ninth grade, whereas the University would require a complete high school (eleven grades) education as an entrance requirement.

Sister Juanita worked with the Dean of the Medical School, Dr. Molina, for some time and then in February 1966 classes started at LUZ (La Universidad del Zulia) with the same students we had been teaching at the Coromoto plus some newer qualified students. I helped teach some of the introductory courses, such as History of Nursing and Nursing Arts and by February of 1967 I had a contract with the University as a Professor of the School of Nursing teaching the Medical-Surgical Nursing course. I received a Professor's salary that was considerably higher than the usual salary of hospital nurses. This salary went directly to the Medical Mission Sisters.

In the beginning the University asked us to get a revalidation of our nursing diplomas. This required writing to my schools, Trinity College and Catholic University for my records and having them officially legalized by the U.S. State Department, (signed by Dean Rusk), with a red seal of the Venezuelan government and a gold seal of the U.S. government. These were translated into Spanish and then notarized. As some were in Latin, I had to request the Bishop's office to help with the translation. Then I had to take the exams (equivalencia) in seven of the high school subjects that I had not had, such as Spanish, History of Venezuela, Geography of Venezuela, Venezuelan Civics, Professional Ethics and Art Education. I took four of these exams and then was studying Art Education (all of these in Spanish, of course.) Soon I would not need to take all these exams as with a Master's degree they would not be required by the University. Soon we had a new Mother Provincial, namely my former Superior in Maracaibo, Sister Miriam.

I wrote her and asked if I could return to the U.S. to get my Master's degree in Medical-Surgical Nursing. Although I was 42 at the time, I was eager to go back to school. I had kept up pretty well by reading the nursing journals and occasionally attending local medical conferences and lectures. Preparing for my classes with clinical practice also helped. The Nurses Training Act during the Johnson administration provided for stipends for living expenses in addition to tuition scholarships for qualified nurses who wanted to do graduate studies. So I went to the American consulate and took the Graduate Record Exam and was accepted by the University of Pennsylvania.

CHAPTER 16

UNIVERSITY OF PENNSYLVANIA

I returned to Philadelphia in July 1967 and began the two-year Master's Program in Medical-Surgical Nursing at Penn. Four of us Sisters lived in an apartment in an older house specifically for students in Philadelphia on 43rd and Walnut Street, close to the School. Sister Lois and Sister Patrice were studying nursing at Penn in the Bachelor's program and Sister Luke Marie was studying at the Wharton School of Business in Penn's undergraduate program. On weekends and when we could, we would go back to Fox Chase, the Philadelphia Medical Mission Sisters headquarters. Classes and preparing for exams and term papers kept us all busy. We somehow managed to have a good time when we weren't studying. We attended daily Mass at a local church where we got acquainted with some of the women who also attended Mass there. In addition I had some planned practical experience at the different Philadelphia hospitals.

The summer of 1967 was a year of the Medical Mission Sisters General Chapter (meeting) which was deciding on major changes due to the new Vatican II thinking and the recommendations of Rome. The document "Perfectae Caritatis" especially encouraged Sisters to adapt to the "modern world." One of these changes was that the Sisters could wear lay clothes if they wished. Some Sisters opted to stay in the traditional habit or a "modified habit" but many others chose to wear lay dress. I decided it was more practical to go straight into lay clothes rather than graduate slowly into different versions of modified habits and then lay clothes. Some of us went to our Thrift Store and tried on dresses and suits. During Christmas vacation I picked out a blue wool dress and then later went to a Goodwill Store for additional outfits, wearing my "new" blue wool dress. I almost got hysterical when a lady asked me: "How do I look in this outfit?" I was so tempted to say "lady, I haven't worn a dress in over twenty years, so don't ask me." However, I held my tongue and was flattered that I didn't appear to be a recent escapee from a convent. My classmates at Penn were pleasantly surprised when I returned to classes in lay dress.

Later we were also allowed to use our given names instead of our religious names. In Venezuela I decided to remain Sister Gabriel as it was easily used as Hermana Gabriela, rather than my more Anglo name of Joan Jollett. My classmates at Penn took it all in stride, so I had no problem there. Occasionally, I would almost panic when I felt that I had forgotten to put on my veil...but not to worry, veils were no longer worn. It was gratifying to be accepted like other women for my character and personality, rather than by my uniform.

The classes were quite challenging especially Physiology. I protested when I had to take all the Education classes as I told my adviser I had had the same ones in my college years at Trinity. I was told that things had changed since then, so I had to take them. My teacher for the Philosophy of Education was an older gentleman who mostly read out of his own book (as I found out when a classmate was reading his book in a whisper, before he even had a chance to say the words.) He was very kind, however, when I asked for special permission to write my term paper on someone who was not part of the curriculum. I chose to write on Marshall McLuhan and his influence on education. Marshall McLuhan was the author of *Understanding Media* and *The Medium is the Massage.* I got an A on the paper with his comment "very interesting." *Even McLuhan couldn't predict the major revolution that the new computer "medium" would have on all aspects of our society.*

Another class, one of my two electives, was one in Community Culture in the department of Anthropology. My term paper was based on Oscar Lewis' books on the culture of poverty. The title was

"A Maracaibo Barrio—A 'Community' in Transition: Implications for Planning a Health Program." *Several years later I used some of the concepts when I compiled "profiles" for the ten rural counties I supervised in Colorado.*

My Master's thesis to fulfill the requirements of the Research class was entitled" The Nurse's Perception of her Role in Rendering Spiritual Care to Patients." I did surveys in five different hospitals and interviewed thirty nurses who were asked to respond to several open-ended questions and then to a questionnaire that asked them to indicate which activities were to be: a) functions primarily of the clergyman; b) which functions primarily of the nurse; c) which were to be shared equally by both nurse and clergyman. *Reading it now I realize how far we have come in topics such as death and dying, the more spiritual aspects of religion and the role that religion and spirituality play in the healing of patients.* The biggest difficulty in this study was typing up the 43 pages plus the questionnaires using the old style typewriters that did not have a correction tape and needed to depend on "Whiteout" to make the corrections. We were graded not only on content but also on correct presentation.

There were no summer classes at Penn, so I asked to go a Catholic hospital in Youngstown, Ohio to observe and learn more about intensive care nursing. I was there about a month. One sad event of this time was the murder of Robert Kennedy. We now had lost "Martin, Bobby and John" and many of us were disheartened.

The next month I was asked to go to Dayton University in Ohio where they were sponsoring a program for returned missionaries. I gave a class on "Health for Missionaries." It was a great group and I made several friends among the Sisters, priests, seminarians and a young couple from a Protestant Bible Society, some of whom I still correspond with at Christmas time. I kept writing to some of the priests, Father Simon, and Father Alan, who had been in the Philippines and one young seminarian, (now Father Jim Weyker) who later was ordained and used to send me a report in his letters on how he was trying to inculcate healthy habits among his parishioners in Tanzania. He even was glad that I had included what to do for an emergency delivery as he was able to help a sow in distress on their farm when she was delivering her piglets! I also was enchanted with Dr. Colby Hatfield's Anthropology classes. *Later he was to help me find a place to stay when I moved to Boulder and is still one of my good friends.* The priests were somewhat envious of us Sisters whose communities seemed to have grasped the teachings of Vatican II faster than their Superiors had. It was a heady time for all when we questioned everything, both political and religious in the Catholic Church and we had high hopes of new days ahead.

About 1965 one of the Medical Mission Sisters, Sister Miriam Therese, was composing and singing scripture songs and hymns which later were recorded and publicized. Her first album, *Joy is like the Rain,* was popular even among the non-Catholic audiences, (actually sometimes more popular than among some of the more conservative Catholic churches.) These songs became an integral part of the Medical Mission Sisters liturgy and other prayer services. *I still have some of these many recordings and they still inspire me. Many songs have a strong social message and focus on peace and justice issues related to Christ's teachings and actions as portrayed in the Gospels. They are like prayers in song.*

My two years at Penn (1967–1969) were at the height of the famous "Sixties." The student body, although at an Ivy League school, was often involved in protests and actions. I attended one full day event sponsored by MIT and locally chaired by the Dean of the Medical School and faculty called "The Misuse of Knowledge." The protests were directed especially against the Antiballistic Missile System (The ABM.) Incidentally later these nationwide protests led to the ABM Treaty in 1972. *Unfortunately, the Bush administration revoked the Treaty in 2001.* As part of this "Day of Conscience" (as it was called), the item that the Medical School Faculty focused on was the outreach of the School and the University to the local low-income community of West Philadelphia, heretofore mostly neglected. Eventually that discussion resulted in some changes in all the programs at Penn including Nursing. *The Philadelphia Inquirer* published a scathing editorial on the event calling it the "Misuse of Education" and berating the "disgruntled student minority and their faculty advisers" for their "birdbrain tactics." I got permission to write a letter to the editor describing the details of the events and suggesting that the media needed a "Day of Conscience" as well. The Inquirer published my letter and I still have a copy of it. A Community Health Nursing student and I were the only ones in our class that attended this event. The irony was that we had to cut our class of "Nursing Issues" that day. Our role in the community could have been a topic of conversation for the class, but the instructor didn't get the point.

I was fortunate to have the opportunity to attend lectures by prominent authors, such as Elizabeth Kubler-Ross on "Death and Dying," Barry Commoner, a leader in the new ecological movement, and Margaret Mead the famous anthropologist who gave a challenging talk on "Parenting." She was in favor of having parents-to-be obtain a license before becoming a parent. Another speaker was Robert Kennedy at a rally for the Democratic presidential candidacy. Some of the students were for Eugene McCarthy but many also for Kennedy, so when he came to the podium he said, "I know you were waiting for McCarthy, but you're stuck with me!" That comment endeared him to the assembly. *I still have my Robert Kennedy bumper sticker.* I felt privileged to hear a presentation by the anti-war activist and poet, Father Daniel Berrigan. It was at a student play protesting the racism and prejudice prevalent against the Negroes (soon to be called "blacks") that I heard some new four-letter words I had never heard before. I was really getting an education to help me relate better to the "modern world."

A couple of books that I read during this time were Teilhard de Chardin's *Phenomenon of Man, The Divine Milieu* and *The Hymn to the Universe*, bringing the role of science, especially of evolution, into a broader spirituality. I still love one of his quotes: "Someday, after we have mastered the winds and the waves, the tides and gravity, we will harness the energies of love, and, for the second time in the history of the world, man will have discovered fire." Another encouraging event of the sixties was the publication of a new weekly Catholic newspaper, the *National Catholic Reporter*, managed by lay people. It has been a wonderful source of information of national and world happenings from a truly Catholic point of view. Its views on most issues are liberal in contrast to most of the diocesan newspapers that often try to return to pre-Vatican II thinking.

Among secular literature many books focused on interpersonal issues. Among these early ones were Erich Fromm's books on freedom and Martin Buber's writings on the "I-Thou" relationship in our dealings with all people. Catholic writers such as Louis Evely and Henri Nouwen adapted interpersonal philosophies to our Catholic spirituality. These writings helped me share a little bit more of my inner thoughts but always with a certain lack of transparency and trust. I am still working on this defect and this autobiography is a step towards sharing my story if and when it might be helpful to others.

Towards the end of the program I was honored, among other nurses, with membership in the nurses' honor society, Sigma Theta Tau. In June of 1969 I graduated with a degree of Master of Science in Nursing.

CHAPTER 17

LUZ AGAIN

Shortly after graduation, I returned to Maracaibo and renewed my contract with the University and was teaching Medical-Surgical Nursing and the Advanced Medical-Surgical Nursing for the seniors. The students had had a very comprehensive basic science background, taking Anatomy and Physiology, (working on cadavers) Biochemistry, Biophysics and Pharmacology from the same professors who taught the medical school students. In many ways I think our program prepared nurses on a par or above those in the U.S. with their solid scientific background. We also had a doctor who specialized in Physical Medicine (Rehabilitation) who taught one class on each topic of our medical-surgical curriculum. We had supervised the students' clinical experiences in all the local hospitals, so we found it easy to relate the classroom material to their actual contacts with patients. If I taught about hepatitis, for example, the students' eyes would light up as they said "Oh yes, Señora Lozada in bed 16."

By this time our first students had graduated and gone on to get their own Masters degrees, either in Puerto Rico or in Colombia since there were no graduate programs as yet in Venezuela. Two of my former students, Vickie and Pilar, were assigned to assist me in both the theoretical classes and the clinical practice. We operated on a team teaching concept, and we all sat in on each other's classes, made up the exams together and corrected them together. We introduced the students to Nursing Care Plans and the problem solving methodology. *In 1976 when I made a return visit to Venezuela, some of my former students, now teachers, told me they were still using the concepts and the Nursing Care Plans in their teaching, although at the time they had rebelled at the extra work involved.* We also enjoyed each other's company and shared a lot of stories and jokes. I learned as much from them as they did from me.

In Venezuela, as in many other Latin American countries, education is free except for a small registration fee. There were no student dorms so our students lived at home or with relatives or friends. This arrangement made them much more responsible and mature and less of a burden for us teachers (and less expense for the government.) The students in the National Schools had to live in a student Nurses' Residence. We taught our students to try to elevate the profession of nursing, which generally was not held in high esteem. I still remember one student who reported to me that one of the doctors told her to bring him his "cafecito." She replied "I didn't study for four years at the University to get you your coffee, and furthermore I have my charting to do." It was a bit daring on her part but I couldn't scold her for her words, but rather was quite pleased that she seemed to have understood the importance of her profession. After graduation our nurses were in great demand by the local doctors who respected their expertise.

The Big Decision

From 1969 to 1971 our community of Sisters had moved out of the Sisters' quarters at the Coromoto Hospital and broke up into several different small communities. So when I arrived from the States to return to teaching I was temporarily assigned to one group. We were trying to follow the Vatican II instructions to insert ourselves more into our local community and become more acculturated. One group opted to live in a somewhat upscale apartment complex where I was first assigned; another group lived in a small house in La Limpia, a poor local barrio, while another lived in a house in a working class neighborhood. I chose to live in the last named. In a little aside I'd like to share with my readers an article I wrote when living in that neighborhood. It evokes the sounds of a typical day in Maracaibo:

How to describe our neighborhood? Perhaps it might be easier to describe the various sounds we hear through the course of the day. Before we even get up we hear the various cocks crowing at different distances—one that seems right next door. Their schedule is often erratic as they have been heard at eleven p.m. as well as at five o'clock. Perhaps a cock has awakened from a romantic dream and is in the mood for courting. Nearly everyone has chickens here, although it is an urban area.

On a few days of the week we are rudely startled by the heavy motor of the Aseo Urbano (garbage collectors) chugging along and then the clanking of garbage cans. We then have to remember if we have put out the garbage or not—hoping that of course someone else has done it, or our next door neighbor, Señor Medina, will take care of it for us, as we turn over for another forty winks.

Once we are up we can hear the morning squawks of the many parrots that belong to the neighbors two doors away. They are very clever too, as they can say 'momentico' (just a minute) as well as any of us (and for the newcomers, probably better.) These squawks are well-mixed with the more soothing voices of the pigeons that nearly everyone keeps in their backyard.

Our neighbor Señora Medina is scolding her children or declaiming her rights in a voice 'that shatters glass' and using language which we are told would be better for us not to use in polite company. Soon the school bus is outside to pick up the boy next door and usually has to honk a few times to get him moving. As the neighborhood begins its daily work, I hear the sound of cars screeching around the corner. They have to honk to warn others as the visibility is poor and the street is narrow. As we are sitting down to breakfast we hear the clank of the front gate—that's our little newsboy, Victor, with Panorama, the daily Maracaibo newspaper which we can't be without.

The day wears on and the noises vary—perhaps it is the little motorized cart of 'Tio Rico' (rich uncle) who sells ice cream and plays his lively tune. Later the man who sells lottery tickets cries out 'Yaracuy, hoy para hoy' (today's special.) Various peddlers come by with rickety carts, selling perhaps carpeta (fish of the day,) plátanos (plantains are one of the Maracucho's daily staples,) Ariel, the current laundry soap powder, Coca-Cola, or the popular chicha (a drink made of corn.) Each shouts out his own product or slogan accompanied sometimes by his own special bell. These shouts and bells easily attract the many dogs and cats of the neighborhood that add to the cacophony. As the afternoon progresses the kerosene man will present his wares to the waiting housewives who run out with their own metal containers, or the knife sharpener man comes by with his grinding stone and revs up his wheel to a high pitch for the next customer.

As the windows are usually open we can have our choice of music from the various radios going full blast with lively music or the housewives' favorite telenovelas (TV soap operas.) As evening falls and the children are home from school, we might hear the crack of a baseball bat out in the street, until the mothers yell to bring them in to wash up for dinner.

Some days we might hear the sounds of Señor Medina who has had a little too many 'palitos' (drinks) and is expounding loudly to everyone on his views of the local politicians and his many grievances. Soon we can hear the clack of the dominos on the card tables under the trees as the day's work is done and the men relax. If someone has a birthday, the sounds of a backyard fiesta begin with the ladies preparing the treats and the musicians tuning up. Most families have someone who can play the four-string 'cuatro' (four-stringed guitar) and its sound, a little tinnier than a regular guitar, begins to be heard in the night air. As the cool breezes blow in from Lake Maracaibo and the Frangipani (Plumeria) blossoms seem to be even more fragrant, the romantic strains of the Venezuelan folk songs fill the air. All's well in our neighborhood.

I soon found out that a lot of concepts that had been dear to me in the Society were changing to practices that made me feel uncomfortable and threatened. The fact that we had to evaluate the new Sister coming to Maracaibo, or a Sister in need of changing her location, and then make a decision if we wanted to accept that Sister in our particular small community or not, was confusing at best. I had always believed that we were all Sisters and in it together. The fact that some Sisters were difficult to live with was not an issue previously. We all accepted each other without distinction and grew strong in the effort to get along with everyone. Now we were faced with focusing in on another Sister's suitability and compatibility, a concept which could be very threatening and for me a departure from our traditional community and family spirit. I remembered one Sister in Pindi that I didn't like, but decided to make every effort to get over my dislike. After trying hard to be more kind to her, eventually I found her to be easier to get along with and we became friends. *I think the fact that I spent most of my formative years in group situations made this change difficult for me. I also remember how the lure of group camaraderie and loyalty to a common goal appealed to me, for example in my love of stories such as those about the French Foreign Legion. Later the many trials and hardships the Medical Mission Sisters had endured together to establish hospitals and schools in the missions resonated with me as well. I didn't feel that I would fit in with this new life style.*

The other difficult situation was the decentralization of authority with no fixed Superior in each house. The effect of this was that, even though there was a "coordinator," the end result was that the "informal leader" took over. This meant that a Sister, who was the strongest in her opinions and most able to convince or even manipulate others, was the one whose opinions and actions prevailed. This did not suit me, as I had been willing, having made a vow of obedience, to obey my "superiors." However, I was not happy with obeying the "informal leader" and did not take well to being manipulated. Possibly, my own background of boarding school and college living also influenced my reactions. Perhaps I lacked the necessary social skills that come from living in a family environment. *In later years many Sisters chose to live in an apartment alone, or with only one or two other Sisters. This lifestyle I found even more difficult to understand and accept.*

We had also been encouraged to have frequent formal discussions on many items of religious life, that is, prayer life, our liturgies, practice of poverty, choosing a particular type of work or to work with a particular class of people, or in a particular place. Sometimes these discussions became endless and were very frustrating. I missed saying our prayers in common and common Spiritual Reading and saying of the Rosary. Often during these discussions I felt that my ideas and opinions were not given much worth.

This was a time when many religious priests and Sisters were leaving their communities for various reasons. Priests and some Sisters often left to get married and many religious left to be more autonomous or because they found the changes too radical. Perhaps, those with a stronger character could ride the tidal wave of change, but for me it became very uncomfortable. After much thought and anguish and some feeling of guilt to go back on my "permanent" vows, I finally asked permission to be dispensed from my vows and return to civilian life. *I still find it hard to explain all my motives but one analogy comes to mind: A young couple, Mary and Jim meet, fall in love, date for a while and share their plans for the children they hope to have once they marry with name choices, activities and plans. They marry and after a couple of years, Jim decides he does not want to have any children. Mary still longs to be a mother and the two are unable to reconcile their differences. Mary divorces Jim, although she still loves him. This may not be the same, but for me it is the best type of explanation I can give.*

This was a very painful decision because I had always dreamed of living and dying a Medical Missionary, and the Society was really my true family. I had been a Medical Missionary for 25 years, so it was like a death for me to leave. Already a couple of Sisters in Maracaibo, among them Marcy Bachler and Carol Bilsborough, had left so I was not the only one. My letter to Rome and the Church authorities for this dispensation or Indult of Secularization (necessary as I was under perpetual vows) was as follows: "...humbly asks dispensation from her perpetual vows, because she does not feel any longer able to observe the obligations of the religious life. The Superior General recommends this request." My request was accepted and I decided to leave on January 6, 1971, sadly exactly twenty years since my departure ceremony for the missions in 1951.

Later I wrote a letter to the Medical Mission Sisters newsletter that now had articles by the Sisters but also by those who had left the Society. An excerpt from my letter which was published gives a picture of how I felt at that time:

It is really difficult for me to explain why I have chosen to leave the Society of which I have been a member for over 25 years. In summary, it was a decision made after much thought and based mainly on considerations of my own personality, temperament and a realization that at this time NOW for me, I no longer find that the religious life is where I should be. This does not mean a lack of confidence in the value and important role of religious life. On the contrary, I think it has an ever more important role but only certain individuals fit in this new role. I am very grateful to the Society for all I have learned over the years and to the Sisters here in Maracaibo for their understanding and acceptance of my decision and wish to make it known publicly that I still value all the friendships I have made in the SCMM and wish to continue any contacts I have had in the past.

I wrote a letter to Fr. Lyons, an American priest who had a parish in Caracas and who had visited the Medical Mission Sisters several times. I asked his advice on leaving the Society and later wrote him about my thoughts on the difficulties of life. It was entitled "Conflicting Thoughts." What follows gives an insight into how I was thinking at the time. *Reading this now I notice that everything is in the third person, whereas it would have been more honest and helpful if I had written it in the first person. However, the following is what I actually wrote and without changes:*

To love it is necessary to have been loved by someone first. To love God it is necessary to have loved man. To know God's love it is necessary to know man's love. When one searches for love one does not find it. It is not enough for love to be shared, it must be shared freely (Merton.) How can this vicious circle be broken—to feel unloved (or be unloved in reality)—to be unable to love—therefore unable to be loved—therefore unable to love man—therefore unable to love God. Yet in looking for love one pushes it further away—yet the need is there—how can it be met without destroying the person and the love that is trying to grow? How can the person feel God's love and help in this struggle if he is unable to believe in it from experience.

One must accept one's past as part of oneself and the material with which one forges one's own life and character and destiny. Yet even this past is denied one if one has been trained to ignore certain facts, forget certain events, not react to others, to keep much secret. In trying to reveal these things to another, one is caught in a trap—of acting as if looking for sympathy (which may partly be true,) of making a mountain out of a molehill, when the past should be forgotten and one should live in the present with an eye to the future, of becoming morbidly introspective and touchy, of not realizing that many others have had similar backgrounds and have learned to survive them without trauma. Once the front has been put on, the mask adjusted, it is extremely difficult to take it off and to appear unmasked, showing a completely different picture than the previous one. With the change of mask or rather the removal of it, would entail a whole change in a way of life, of the way one is perceived by others, and although this is what one truly wants, the old habits have become engrained and comfortable to a certain extent and one feels suddenly naked and defenseless with the mask off.

Yet if the mask is never removed, one is never really quite at home in the role one has adopted but doesn't quite fit...sooner or later the mask must come off, it becomes more and more uncomfortable, and somehow one feels dishonest in continually wearing it. Yet to take it off one must have the assurance that on doing so one will not be despised, laughed at, pitied, analyzed or rejected. Where will one find this assurance if there is no one whom one can really trust, who can be with one long enough to bear out the long and tedious process of removing the mask which has now become so stuck to one's face that it must be removed slowly and carefully, and with someone nearby to soothe the painful spots where the skin has come off with the mask.

Yes, the mask must come off—no one can love a person who is continually hiding behind a mask, never revealing his true self to anyone. But who will give one the courage to do it once and for all? How can one find this help without turning that person against one? How can one be reassured that one will not be rejected? This is the crucial question which if answered would break the vicious circle and enable one to start on a new path—a straight one which would lead to true love of self, love of others and love of God.

I realize that writing my story, regardless of reactions of others, is one way of removing the mask. It is not easy.

CHAPTER 18

OUT IN THE WORLD

The Sisters were kind to me, but now I was on my own. I was given the usual $500 to get settled. I used this for a down payment on a used Ford Cortina that I bought about a month later. (I had taken driving lessons from Mr. Simone, a travel agent, in a Ford LTD so already had my license.) Besides the down payment I had to pay for insurance and an anti-robo (alarm system.) I then was receiving my own paycheck of about $800 a month as a Professor at LUZ so I was not without resources and kept making my monthly car payments. However, at the end of the pay period I often had to count my pennies (or centavos). At first I had to get to the University by "carrito" (taxis that had specified routes and more than one customer.) The car had many breakdowns and repairs and kindly passersby often helped me when I got stopped in traffic. These repairs were an added expense. Often I was asked to give a "colita" (ride) to one of the Sisters, teachers or students, so I was grateful to be able to return some favors to others.

I decided one major change was enough, so I stayed on in my job as Professor and did not return to the U.S. Unlike most Sisters leaving I really did not have a home to go to. My decision was accepted easily by the University staff and students. I was now called "Profesora" instead of "Hermana" (Sister). Even the Director of the Nursing School, Dr. Romero Paez, just said "felicitaciones" (congratulations) and went on with the business of the day. I sent letters explaining my change to my aunts and two brothers who accepted my decision. My Aunt Marie had died in the early sixties and her opinion would have been the only one that I dreaded.

I looked around for an affordable one-bedroom apartment that I found on Cinco de Julio, one of the main streets of Maracaibo, in a building that had a few small stores on the ground floor, next to the large Citibank building and on the convenient "carrito" line. As a woman, I had to get a letter from the Director of the School before I was accepted as a renter—an example of the prevalent machismo of the Latin American culture. Over time I bought the minimal amount of furniture and household items. The Sisters very kindly gave me a set of plastic dishes, a teakettle and a set of towels, so I was not left without some essentials as I began my new life. The apartment was on the second floor with windows on opposite sides with great breezes cooling it off. However, summers could get quite hot so I bought a window air-conditioner for the bedroom.

I shopped at Todos (the local Supermarket,) did my laundry at a nearby Laundromat, and found kitchen items at the newly opened Sears store and other local shops. *I still have those stainless steel pots and pans.* I bought a royal blue file cabinet and a yellow fiberglass telephone stand. *I still have both—the stand still has marks of a cigarette burn on the top, where one of my smoking colleagues left it.* It wasn't until October that I did manage to get my own phone. Living alone was very different from community living and sometimes I was lonely, and I especially missed the camaraderie, but most of the time I found it a challenging and adventurous experience. Fortunately, I had already changed into lay clothes, so externally I appeared pretty much the same to others, and kept the same job.

I signed up for an evening Yoga class taught by a local young man. I started going to the movies, local plays, concerts, ballets and other events at the Teatro de Bellas Artes and the Venezuelan Folklorico dancers at the sports arena and went to the beach with the Sisters or some of the students. I attended Mass at the nearby church of San Jose or sometimes at Coromoto Hospital, and occasionally at an English Mass at Los Olivos with Ann Skelton who was a Peace Corps volunteer and teaching English at the University. I often invited the Sisters, visiting Medical Mission Sisters, other visiting persons, my colleagues and occasionally a student for supper and lively conversation.

One of my visiting friends was the same Sister Cuthbert who had taught Missiology in Philadelphia and had left the Society and later as Doctor Monika Hellwig, studied Theology at Catholic University and wrote several books on the Church. She never married, but adopted a mixed-race girl who accompanied her on her trip to Maracaibo. We had a great evening discussing the post-Vatican church and the Society. *(I recently read in the* National Catholic Reporter *that she had died in 2005.)*

All of us who had left the Society were welcomed by those who had stayed, for which I was grateful. For many of us who left, it was like coming to a bittersweet family reunion when we met. We also shared many stories of the "old days" and had some good laughs. Across the street from my apartment was a small ice cream shop where I used to watch enviously as families with their children enjoyed an ice cream cone. Here I was with no family and few real friends, although I did get an occasional invitation to a colleagues' home, but I still felt left out. Unfortunately in Venezuela, even a person who obtained Venezuelan citizenship was called an "extranjero nacionalizado" or a nationalized foreigner that had the tone of not being fully accepted. This fact kept me from ever considering getting naturalized. Also as a foreigner, I was on a yearly renewable contract so was faced with the fact that my contract was renewed each year but with no raise in pay. Some of my students, now instructors, were making more money than I was as they received their yearly raise.

I helped with several projects at the School including the publication of the first Nursing Procedure Manual in the country that became widely used. The artwork on the cover was done by one of the nurses who had graduated from the Coromoto Hospital program. I attended curriculum meetings to determine what we needed to teach. Fortunately we had no predecessors so we could invent the programs and change them when they didn't work or add to them when we saw a need.

Two American Sister-nurses, Sister X and Sister Y from another order of Sisters in San Antonio, Texas came to determine if the Project Hope could stop in the port of Maracaibo with a teaching program for the nurses. Project Hope was a hospital ship and we were all excited about the possibility of having them help our students with some new concepts, such as an Intensive Care Unit. Plans were being made to have the ship come in 1973. It was not to be, however, as the frequent student unrest scared them at the time and the possible disturbances they expected at the upcoming elections. I doubt if this would have hampered their efforts, but they apparently had to get an O.K from the State Department and it was not given. The State Department never approved the program for 1974 either.

Sister X also helped us with our curriculum planning and some new concepts in nursing education. The two Sisters were in Maracaibo for about three months and usually I was the chauffeur and gofer for them. Sister Y did not seem to connect very well with the Venezuelan culture and sometimes I was embarrassed by comments she made, such as an exasperated "these Venezuelans." Sister X mentioned casually that she also had an assignment from the State Department, as this was a time of great concern about the infiltration of communism in Latin America and elsewhere. I stopped confiding in her as I thought she might be working with the CIA or other U.S. agencies.

In most Latin American countries universities are autonomous and student representatives are always included in major faculty decisions at every level. There was some communist influence especially among university students, with occasional protests with burning tires and cars in the streets and "Yankee Go Home" signs. Once some high school students stopped me in my car at the entrance to the University medical school complex near some burning tires. I sat there quietly and finally I called one of the students, pointed to my watch and said "I have to give a class at 2 p.m., can I please go?" They told me to go ahead and that was that. In the long run, it often was just adolescent rebellion acting out and often in imitation of student protests in the U.S. They went to see the movie *The Strawberry Statement* (about the sit-in at Columbia University) and learned to sing "Give Peace a Chance" in English. I remember one student group who said they were protesting the bombing of Cambodia and when asked where Cambodia was they said "maybe in Africa?!" If an American agency were giving out scholarships to an American university most would immediately drop their signs and accept the offer. We noticed that soon after graduation they became part of the "bourgeois establishment." When the Caldera government legalized the Communist Party and they had a few representatives in the National Assembly, many students were no longer interested in being communists.

Like most teenagers they enjoyed being against the government in power, whether left, right or center.

The labor unions at the University often staged strikes and we were asked to support them. We did suspend classes but not the clinical practice as we already had a commitment to the nursing care at the local hospitals. I remember when my Medical-Surgical Nursing teaching team was planning the schedule for the next year, we had to allow maybe a couple of weeks for strikes. I guessed they might occur in the month of May since December was the Christmas holiday, February and March had Carnival and Holy Week holidays and school exams were in July, so somewhere in between the students needed a time to blow off steam. My prediction proved true.

Being Americans we might have been afraid at all these protests, but we were never really threatened personally. We didn't take sides in any of the political discussions which were evident at Faculty meetings when the professors decided to dole out key positions on the faculty according to deals between the various parties, for example, "you vote for our candidate for the director of the School of Nutrition and then we'll vote for your candidate for the director of the School of Bioanalysis (Lab. Technician.)" Class presidents were not based on popularity or good grades but on which party needed to be on top after the deals were made. Even the student council was elected on political party lines. We Americans would call these appointments political "plums." In Venezuela they are called "cambures" (bananas.)

Vacation in the U.S.

The University had a month's vacation in August of 1971 so I took the opportunity to make a visit to the U.S. I first stopped in Barquisimento to visit the Medical Mission Sisters who had a small clinic there and also Fr. Colin Boor. Then on to Caracas where I stayed with Carol Bilsborough, a former Medical Mission Sister who had left the Society before I did. She was a very talented person and was now working as a consultant for doctors and health institutions in Caracas. *Later she adopted two Venezuelan Indian children and moved back to Maracaibo where she recently died.* She and I had spent one vacation in La Mesa and became good friends, reading the story of Maria Montessori's life and work with young children and sharing much.

Then I took the plane that stopped in Kingston, Jamaica. Here I was lucky enough to get permission to board the Project Hope ship. (See the notes on the previous pages. The decision not to come to Maracaibo had not yet been made.) It was a wonderful experience and I was really looking forward to our chance to have the program too. When I got to the Miami airport I wanted a book to read on the plane or bus, but was overwhelmed by the huge choices of books so ended up with none—welcome to reverse culture shock.

I made my way up the coast by first stopping to see my brother Herb who was married to an Italian-American lady he had met while in the Navy in Brooklyn. He was living in Maryland and working for the Naval Intelligence at the time. They seemed to be a very happy couple. They had been married since the late 50s. I had met his wife Anna once in 1962. She was 20 years older than he and they had no children. *Thinking about this fact now, I realize that the Jollett family name will soon be extinct, in spite of the fact that my Jollett grandparents had eight children.*

When I got to Philadelphia I went to Fox Chase to visit some of the Medical Mission Sisters I knew and the place I had loved so much. I can still remember sitting in the back of the chapel and crying about all I had lost in leaving the Society. Everyone was kind to me, but it still was very painful. I had a great talk with Sister Pierre who at one time had been my Superior in Pindi and we shared so many stories together. *Shortly after this she left the Society as Jane Blewett when she began working with the Jesuit Center of Concern and eventually married an ex-Jesuit priest she had met there. Both she and her husband Lou have been active in social justice issues and mostly with the link between the environment and spirituality. Both are also active Associate members of the Medical Mission Sisters. We still keep in contact by letters and phone calls and a recent visit.*

I finally got to Madison, New Jersey by bus where my two surviving aunts Loretta and Anna were living. It was a tiny upstairs rented apartment in town, much different from the house I knew. My grandmother and my Aunt Marie had died previously while I was in the missions so I never attended their funerals. Anna sold the house. My Aunt Loretta had married Bill Milligan and had lived in upstate New York and then Florida where Bill died of emphysema. She moved back to Madison after his death and lived with my Aunt Anna who had retired. The visit was friendly and I was pleased to see that they lived happily together. They never gave me a hard time for having left the convent, for which I was grateful. I also visited my old college friend, Lily Bajda, in South Orange, NJ, but have since lost contact with her. My Aunt Mildred was now living in West Orange, NJ and retired from being a secretary of the principal at an elementary school. She had a tiny apartment and had never married. She was my one connection to my mother so she was very special to me.

I then went west by bus to Alvernia College in Milwaukee for a workshop there on the Catholic Church in Latin America and visited Father Alan Rieger who had been one of my students at Dayton. *Father Alan once visited David and me when we lived in Desert Hot Springs. He was still working in the Philippines.* I stopped overnight in St. Louis to visit some Sisters I knew at the Medical Mission House of Studies there. Sister Sheila Parker, an occupational therapist, was one that I had become very close to during my time in Philadelphia when I was at the University of Pennsylvania. It was good to see her again. She was a kind, motherly type of person and made a dress for me that I took back to Venezuela. She died several years ago after working many years in Indonesia.

I returned to New Jersey and my Aunt Mildred drove us to see my priest brother Bob who was stationed as librarian at the seminary in Watertown, NY. We then drove on to Burlington, Vermont to visit my old college roommate, Gennie McKnight Pike, who was now the mother of four girls and one boy, who were all out of the home. She and her husband Ernest (Buster) lived in a lovely typical New England home in Craftsbury, Vermont where he was the local postmaster and she was teaching at the high school. This was our first get together since 1945!

We drove back to New Jersey and then I visited Marilyn DeCoster (another former Medical Mission Sister) who was now living in the Chelsea district of New York City. She offered to be the go-between for me to have an account in the local Seaman's Bank. I began sending checks to her from Venezuela so I could have an American account when I needed it. I returned by plane to Caracas and stayed with Carol Bilsborough a few days and by the first week in September I was back teaching at LUZ.

Local Involvements

I belonged to the Venezuelan National Nurses Association, but as yet there was no professional magazine or journal for nursing and very few nurses were proficient enough in English to read the American journals. This concern led me to start planning the possibility of publishing a small magazine under the auspices of the University with articles by local nurses. When I went to the Director, Dr Romero Páez, he seemed very skeptical and negative, but after many talks with him, he finally gave in and said to go ahead but I would have to find funding for the printing costs. I proceeded to contact local businesses and others who might pay for an ad in the magazine. I was allowed to approach the printing department at the University and The Department of Culture and request their help. They replied they were pretty busy but could get around to it sometime. I also talked to the graphic artist about cover art for the magazine that I had decided would be called *Perspectivas*. I gave him some ideas and he came up with a modern style cover in two shades of blue.

I then had to proceed to ask nurses I knew to write articles on a topic that they were familiar with, for example, on the new procedure for central venous pressure used in the new Intensive Care Unit at the University Hospital. I soon learned that I had to give each writer a specific deadline or I would never get the article. Selling the ads was a time consuming project as often the manager was out and I had to return many times to the same business before getting a promise for an ad. I wrote an article myself in Spanish but had to make a deal with the professor of Pharmacology—I would correct his abstract in a medical journal in English if he would correct my article in Spanish. It worked out quite well for both of us. Eventually the magazine *Perspectivas* was printed in 1972 and we had a champagne "baptism" ceremony of the magazine with the Director of the School of Nursing officiating. Finally, Dr. Romero Páez was proud to be part of the first Venezuelan nursing journal. The magazine came out quarterly after that and I contributed some articles to it as well.

After I left Venezuela the nurses at LUZ published a few more sporadic issues and they sent copies to me in the U.S. For the fifth anniversary of the magazine I was asked to review the story of the beginnings of "Perspectivas" which I did for the 1977 issue. I was pleased to see that the magazine included articles written by the students themselves. The cover date of the last issue is 1981 but I noted on the last page that it was printed only in November 1983. I noted with pleasure that by 1981 there were now two other University programs in Nursing in Venezuela. One was in the University of the Andes in Mérida and one in the University of Carabobo in Valencia, closer to the capital, Caracas, which still did not have a bachelor's program in nursing. I was also gratified to see on the editorial page my name listed as "Director Técnica Fundador" (founding technical director) although Dr. Romero Páez was listed as Director Fundador (founding Director). It reminded me of the days of "acting local Superior" only here the reason for the titles was probably political rather than any doubt of my competency.

I also submitted some articles for *El Graduado*, the magazine for the medical school graduates, which I wrote in Spanish and had corrected by Dr. Olivares, the Pharmacology professor. I wrote one, "El Hombre Olvidado" (The Forgotten Man: the Patient) and another "Deprivación Sensorial" (Sensory Deprivation). I translated an article from English into Spanish from the American Journal of Nursing on the care of patients with kidney transplants. This activity had kept me pretty busy but life in Maracaibo was not all work as we did have our Holy Week vacation.

During the Holy Week vacation of 1972 Otilia Mariña, a Cuban and a former Medical Mission Sister studying Medicine at the University of Zulia, joined me in my car for a trip to the Andes which turned out to be quite an adventure. When we got near to the ranching town of Santa Barbara at the lower end of Lake Maracaibo, my car stalled. A kindly rancher, Señor Méndez, came by with his pickup truck and attached a rope to our car and hauled us to town. As it was Holy Week everyone was on holiday including mechanics so he invited us to stay the weekend with his family who offered meals and their daughter's room since she was away at college. Finally on Monday morning we found a mechanic and our car was ready to go again. *When we arrived back in Maracaibo, Señor and Señora Méndez came by to visit and I drove them the next day to Otilia's house.*

On the way between two towns we were asked to give a "colita" (ride) to a National Guard soldier. After going through several Andean towns, we crossed over to the "llano" (plains) states and then on to the city of Barquisimeto where the Medical Mission Sisters had a small community clinic. We stayed overnight with the Sisters and then went to visit an American priest, Fr. Colin Boor, who had been a patient at Hospital Coromoto and was now assigned to a parish church in Barquisimeto. On our return we saw people on the road stuffing the Judas figure to be used during the Holy Week processions. We also saw many car accidents on the way.

A real treat was to see the many kinds of flowering tropical trees such as the Araguaney or Yellow Poui (a cloud of yellow blossoms.) In the State of Barinas we passed many truckloads of huge logs and we crossed many rivers. We went through some heavy rainstorms and discovered that the windshield wiper was out of order. Our entire trip was about 1,000 miles and about 20 hours of driving. My only souvenir purchase was a small square Andean stool with a goatskin cover that I still have. It has served occasionally as a stool, a drum, as a side table and as a place to park my current reading material. What a way to see the country! Venezuela is a country of great contrasts—from deserts to high mountains, from beaches to jungles, from cities to flooded plains. Otilia was welcome company and we both planned to visit Grand Canyon some day.

Shortly after this trip the School of Nursing began a "Complementario" program for those nurses who had graduated from a National School who wanted to get a bachelor's degree. This had been planned for some time and many were outraged that they had to spend about 2 1/2 years to get their degree. They didn't realize they had to take all the basic science classes that entailed a longer time in the classroom. We found that their attitudes to nursing needed some changes as well. This whole process had been quite difficult but we were getting used to problems by now. The nurses bit their tongues and complied with the requirements and we put up with their displeasure and complaints.

I was very fortunate that Maracaibo was becoming a very good place to further my own and our students' education. During the four hundredth anniversary of the founding of the City of Maracaibo several medical conferences were held where we took our students to be exposed to new ideas and research topics. Sometimes the organizers had invited American specialists to give lectures, which, although in English, were translated directly by very competent translators. The students acted as ushers but could hear all the lectures and the time was counted as classroom hours.

The Latin American Bishops had just met in Medellín, Colombia and Catholics in Latin America were reading the Medellín documents stressing collegiality, the preferential option for the poor and other concepts stemming from the Vatican II council documents. I joined a group of Venezuelans (mostly young people from the University and others) with Father Belandria, a Jesuit, for frequent meetings to discuss an upcoming meeting called "Desarollo Integral Del Hombre" (The Development of the Whole Man"). The first regional meeting was held in 1971 in Maracaibo and then later a national meeting in Barquisimeto. The Bishops had called the meetings but were somewhat unprepared for the criticism they received for being too allied with the rich and not enough concerned about the poor. They were also not accustomed to getting so much input from lay people.

Our little group from the School of Medicine that included the School of Nursing had focused on the topic of "dependencia" (dependence). We asked serious questions about whether the medical and health providers were remembering the patient as the center for their concerns. Some doctors found these comments about the "forgotten" man, the patient, as threatening, but had to admit that the medical community in general did not treat most patients as persons, but as a disease. I learned so much about grassroots politics at these meetings and realized that I too had a role in helping our nurses to understand the dignity of the patients they were caring for. It wasn't just a case of cirrhosis in bed 8, but a living human being with family and needs of his own.

Other topics addressed in these conferences were the role of politics, theology of mission, socio-economic issues, means of communication, and religion and the family. Stress was placed on the role of dependence in many areas. The cultural dependence of Latin Americans on the United States was pointed out and solutions suggested. Many position papers were written up and voted on. I was impressed by the variety of people at these meetings—bishops, priests, professionals, young people and persons from all walks of life with viewpoints ranging from the far left to the far right. The conferences were interspersed with Mass and other lively prayer services with songs and hymns accompanied by guitars and other local instruments and heartfelt spontaneous prayers, sharing of personal thoughts and even hugs. It all amounted to a truly spiritual experience. It was a three-day marathon of discussions and meetings. One message I did receive was that as much as possible we Americans should let the Venezuelans take over in positions where they could. This thought stayed with me for the next two years when I began to see that my services would soon not be needed as our students obtained their graduate degrees. Later some of the Bishops became more open to the laity and to the cause of the poor, but the recommendations were not universally accepted. Later, however Liberation Theology became more popular and small basic church communities were founded that still exist in much of Latin America.

Making Plans for the Future

The Nursing class of 1972 consisted of 25 students and they very kindly chose me to be the "Madrina" (godmother) for their graduating class. They gave me a beautiful plaque to remember the occasion. I was very moved by this gesture as sometimes the complaints I heard were that I was too demanding, others that I was too lenient, so it came as a surprise. The class of '72 had been my favorite—a lively group of smart and fun-loving students. Later Marialcira Quintero taught Medical Surgical Nursing, as did Emma Villalobos and others taught Obstetric, Pediatrics or Psychiatric Nursing. I felt the time and efforts I spent with them really paid off for nursing in Venezuela.

During 1972 I began thinking about my future. The Venezuelan nurses were beginning to become qualified to teach at the university level, and I realized that the nationalistic spirit included a certain amount of anti-American sentiment. Perhaps it was time to return to the U.S. I had inquired about possible jobs with the World Health Organization or Project Hope and other agencies that worked in foreign countries. Then I heard about the Nurse Scientist grants that were being offered during the Johnson administration for nurses with Master's degrees. These grants would allow a nurse to study certain disciplines and eventually obtain a Doctorate in Nursing Science. One of these disciplines was Cultural Anthropology adapted to Nursing, so I decided that would be the one I would choose.

There was a twelve-page application form to fill out for the National Institutes of Health. It included what the focus would be for my doctoral thesis. I wrote: "To study and identify cultural attitudes toward health, sickness and acceptance of health services among the Spanish speaking in the U.S . . . to explore ways of incorporating this knowledge into practical courses of study and guidelines for health professionals with emphasis on adapting knowledge and skills learned in formal programs to the expectations, fears, beliefs and customs characteristic of the Spanish speaking." I had to send for transcripts of my grades and courses from the three colleges I had attended as well as references from my various instructors. I took the Graduate Nurse Exam at the American Consulate in Maracaibo.

I was thinking of applying to two University programs, one at the University of Arizona in Tucson and one at the University of

Colorado in Boulder as both of these would provide access to the Spanish speaking culture. So I planned to visit these two universities on my August 1972 vacation. At that time Greyhound bus was offering a $99 trip anywhere in the U.S. as long as the ticket was purchased outside the U.S. I took advantage of this opportunity and flew to New Orleans and for the rest of the trip I was a guest of Greyhound. As I only carried a small suitcase I was able to get on the bus with my luggage and usually picked the seat behind the driver—for safety reasons and also to make it easier to ask questions—sort of a cheap tourist guide. No reservations had to be made and if the bus was too full they always added a second bus so it was very convenient. This was my first acquaintance with the U.S. west of the Mississippi and it appealed to me immensely. In all I spent over 130 hours on the bus. I also took a Grey Line tour bus in New Orleans with a quick overview of the important places. My first stop on my trip was San Antonio, where the Project Hope Sister X lived and she kindly gave me a nice baby pillow that I could use if I needed a snooze on the bus. *I still have that pillow and it has been a great companion on many trips since.* Of course I took a wonderful side trip to see San Antonio and the River.

My next stop was Tucson where I spoke to the Director of the Nurse Scientist program, Dr. Beverly McCord, and talked to Dr. Margarita Kay, noted anthropologist. They were very helpful and the city seemed like a good place to live. I visited one of my former students, Diana Peñuela, who was studying graduate psychiatric nursing at the University Hospital in Los Angeles.

At Flagstaff I took a quick look at the Grand Canyon. On the bus I sat next to a beautiful elderly lady, Betty Achuff, who shared with me the story of the great love of her life, a young sailor she met during World War II, but then lost track of him and later married another man. She was obviously still in love with the young sailor. She later sent me a card to thank me for being so kind as to listen to her story and sharing our first view of the Canyon. As we were driving north of Flagstaff, the bus driver stopped at a little wooded area and told us to walk a few steps. I couldn't believe it when right there in front of us appeared this huge canyon. Again I made the resolution then and there that one day I would hike down the Canyon.

From Arizona I traveled into Colorado. My first impression was that Colorado was just one big State Park with so many beautiful places. I visited Denver and had an interview with Dr. Janelle Krueger, the Director of the Nurse Scientist program at the University of Colorado. Their program in anthropology seemed more to my liking as it had a more Hispanic orientation. Another incentive was that my friend, Dr. Colby Hatfield, from the Dayton, Ohio days lived there. He assured me that I could probably live with the Lang family in Boulder. He had boarded with that family until he married another boarder, Cathy. The Langs were a wonderful family. Friedl, a native of Bavaria, was a professor of anthropology at the University. He and his wife, Martha, had seven children, five of whom were still at home—a truly generous and hospitable family and lots of fun. After these professional meetings, I took the bus back east to visit other friends and family again.

When I arrived back in Maracaibo I planned on resigning my position at the University of Zulia in July. Unfortunately, I received a letter in March 1973 from the University of Arizona informing me of President Nixon's decision to cancel any new grants for the Nurse Scientist programs. I'm not sure why he made this decision, probably the Republicans' general opposition to "big government," to the Johnson's administration of the "War on Poverty" and the "tax and spend" Democrats. *With the withdrawal of this program we are now paying the price with a shortage of nurses due to the scarcity of nurses with graduate degrees to teach in the Nursing Schools.* This was a big disappointment although the letter included information about possible student loans that seemed very unrealistic for me at the time. In spite of this obstacle, I decided to return to the U.S. and live in Colorado and work out my future when I got there, thinking perhaps that I could work and study for my doctorate part-time.

In many ways it was a sad time. Maracaibo was always my "first mission" and I would leave many memories behind. After final exams and graduation, my colleagues and some of the students treated me to a wonderful farewell party at a local restaurant. They presented me with a beautiful Mexican leather briefcase and made the customary complimentary speeches. I wrote out my own speech and emphasized the fact that Venezuelan nurses were now prepared to develop their own nursing model based on their own national reality. I strongly urged them to continue publishing *Perspectivas* as it was a symbol of the professionalism of the Venezuelan nurses.

I started selling or giving away most of my furniture at my apartment. I contracted with an international moving company to pack what I wanted to keep, including my collection of the *American Journal of Nursing*, several favorite books, my files and my kitchen equipment. I sold my Ford Cortina to Margarita Jimeno, one of my former students. I took with me a beautiful wall hanging designed by a famous Goajiro Indian, Luis Montiel, as well as two lovely coffee table books, one on Venezuela the other on Maracaibo. Sister Teresa Jaramillo, with whom I had worked in Hospital Coromoto and in Caripito, kindly told me that her brother Fred who lived in Aurora, a suburb of Denver, would be glad to store my belongings until I could find a permanent place to live. So all my boxes were shipped to her brother and he stored them in his garage. I flew back to Denver and stayed for about six weeks with the Lang family in Boulder until I could find a job.

CHAPTER 19

BOULDER

I began looking for a job but had to use public transportation. I thought that my proficiency in Spanish would be an asset but it seemed that most places where I applied did not consider this valuable, although there were many Spanish-speaking migrant workers in the Boulder and Denver area. A Supervisor in Boulder told me that there was a social worker in Denver, thirty miles away whom they could call on for translations! The other obstacle was that with my Master's degree employers believed I was over-educated and I wouldn't stick it out in a job for long. I had decided that medical-surgical hospital nursing in the U.S. was definitely a little too high-powered for me, so came to the conclusion that I would be more prepared to work in Public Health. This was not easy either. At interviews I was asked about my familiarity with Medicare and Medicaid requirements and regulations. As I was deficient in this, I did not qualify.

Finally after being rejected by at least thirty different organizations, I met with the assistant Director of Nursing Service at Tri-County District Health Department (Adams, Arapahoe and Douglas counties,) all close to the Denver area. Because of a big state budget cut in July they had to let several nurses go. In September the federal budget allowed them to hire more nurses, so I had shown up at just the right time and was hired as a Public Health Nurse III (grade for an experienced nurse.)

I began working at the Tri-County office in Commerce City. I took out the money from my Seaman's Bank savings account and bought a used Toyota Mark IV. When I got my first paycheck I looked for a rental. Fortunately I found a nice one-bedroom duplex, whose owner was a retired Swedish lady, Ingeborg Snyder, who lived by herself. It was on 10th St. on the "hill" in Boulder near the Flatirons and close to the University of Colorado. I saved my money to buy furniture and to get my other belongings from Fred Jaramillo's home in Aurora. During all these transactions the Lang family was more than helpful and gave me lots of information I badly needed about living in the United States. Jodie, one of the Lang girls, even took me to a local jeweler where I had my ears pierced!

I mostly attended Sunday Mass at the St. Thomas Newman Center, a center for Catholic students attending secular universities and loved the sermons and the lively young people's music. I also signed up with "Bread for the World," an interfaith group that advocated for solutions to the problem of world hunger.

My job at Tri-County consisted of helping with the various clinics held at the office and making home visits to mothers and babies, to some communicable disease patients and to the homebound elderly. I quickly learned the meaning of Medicare, Medicaid and working with the Social Services department especially in cases of child abuse or neglect. Each nurse was also assigned a Home Health Aide,

Dad in U.S. Army in France, 1919

*Portrait of Anna
Dengel, 1919
(Courtesy of Medical
Mission Sisters)*

Portrait of Mother

Severynse siblings—Mildred, Frank, Petronella, Edward (ca. 1919)

With older brother, Bob (ca. 1928)

With younger brother, Herb, 1943

Trinity College yearbook portrait, 1945

*Friend of family, Aunt Anna,
me, and Aunt Marie, 1948*

Herb, me, and Bob, 1949

Bob and Grandma, 1949

Sister Miriam, friend, me at Hospital Coromoto, Venezuela, 1951

Herb, Bella, Dad, Bob, 1949

Teaching at Hospital Coromoto, 1966

Aunt Mildred, 1960

First class of nursing students with instructors, University of Zulia, Maracaibo, me at the right, 1970

Otilia and me at bottom of Grand Canyon, 1974

Class of 1972, University of Zulia, with professors at cocktail party, me fourth from right (six students not in photo)

Ron and Karen Phillips with their five children, 1979

At my office in Alamosa, Colorado, 1976

The Lang Gang, Boulder, Colorado, 1978

Dating David, San Diego, 1986

Ready for our honeymoon, 1989

David's portrait for his book,
Imagination Factor, 1984

With David and our friend, Alice

Book signing at Lone Pine, 1997

*At Father Crowley Memorial,
Death Valley, 1997*

Herb and his wife, Anna (late 90s)

Herb and Bob (late 2000s)

With Trinity friend, Julie Wood, at the Tin Fish, Imperial Beach Pier (ca. 2006)

Book signing in Killarney, Ireland with Peggy Lyne, 2003

Exercise class in Imperial Beach, me in "Diego" shirt, 2005

With Peggy Lyne visiting Innisfallen Island, Killarney, 2008

mainly Spanish speaking, to help with giving messages, interpretations and simple nursing care. As I spoke Spanish I did all these things myself and was sometimes shocked to hear the advice that was given by some Aides on the phone to our Hispanic patients. Eventually I helped translate the instructions for our Lamaze classes into Spanish.

I enjoyed the work, especially not having to deal directly with doctors and the almost independent type of functioning. We each had our own phone and we could plan our own day's work, carry our own case load of about 100 families and determine how often we needed to visit each one. It was a friendly office where all our desks were very close together so we all knew about each other's patients (and also hear the afternoon phone instructions by many of those with children at home telling them "take the meat out of the freezer" or "turn the oven on at 350" etc.) Coffee break allowed us to share personal stories or events in our lives, celebrate a birthday and occasionally a little gripe about the bureaucracy of our health care system.

I found Boulder a wonderful place to live. When I came home from work in spring, summer and fall I often took hikes to the nearby foothills where I began my love affair with the many Rocky Mountain wildflowers I found there. In the winter I bought myself a pair of cross-country skis and started taking some simple classes and trips in the area. Once at the end of one strenuous day of skiing, I sprained my ankle and had to go to work in my hiking boots. I attended some community education programs, such as the History of Boulder with side trips to the old gold mining areas. In the Architecture of Boulder classes we took tours to see the many old Victorian era homes and the famous Boulderado Hotel. One of the homes was then being used on the *Mork and Mindy* TV program. Another class on the Botany of Boulder included a walking tour to identify the various species of trees in town. The University's foreign film program introduced me to Ingmar Bergman, Fellini and Truffault among others. At the price of only $1.00 it was almost impossible to miss seeing them.

In August of 1975 the Medical Mission Sisters were celebrating the 50th anniversary of the founding of the Society and I received an invitation to attend. The custom of not having contact with "ex'es" had long been discontinued so I decided to take my vacation time and catch up on my friends "in" and "out." I put a notice on the "ride board" at the University of Colorado in Boulder for ride sharing and received a few offers. One guy wanted to know if I had a hitch so he could take his motorcycle and another said he couldn't drive. Finally I received a call from a young geologist, Tom DeVries, a few blocks away and interviewed him. He was working in Denver and wanted to visit his family in White Plains, NY as his sister was getting married and he would drive her old car back. He seemed very courteous, so Tom shared the driving and the fuel expenses which saved both of us a lot of money. I met him at his work place in Denver about noon and we drove to Lawrence, Kansas. We didn't know there was a big football game going on, so motels were full. He offered to stay in one room with me and he could sleep on the floor, but we finally were able to find two rooms for the night.

We then drove the next day as far as Columbus, Ohio where we stayed with my Cuban friend Otilia and her parents. Otilia was now a doctor having graduated from the University of Zulia. Her parents had extra space in the basement so it was a comfortable visit. The next day we drove all the way east and across the George Washington Bridge to White Plains. It was pouring rain so I let Tom do the driving. I stayed overnight at his parents' home and drove to visit my Aunt Loretta and Aunt Anna in Madison, N.J., and my Aunt Mildred in West Orange. They all had retired and were living quite simply in small apartments, occasionally taking tour bus trips to scenic areas.

The 50th reunion of the Medical Mission Sisters was very emotional for every one, with lots of hugs and a lot of prayerful services. When we would meet someone we didn't know we would ask "Are you in or out?" As we were all in lay dress it was sometimes difficult to guess. Of course those that came with their husbands and/or kids, it was pretty obvious. We all got updated on their present status and shared a lot of old stories. I was impressed by the fact that not only had the Medical Mission Sisters expanded their work, but also that many of the former members were involved in community service in their own areas. The Medical Mission Sisters had left an indelible mark on all our lives.

On the way back west I visited some of the Sisters and former Sisters and found that even if I hadn't known the person in years past I always felt more than welcome. I visited my brother Herb and went with my Aunt Mildred to see my brother Bob and my old college roommate, Gennie, in Vermont. I visited Ann Skelton (Peace Corps friend from Maracaibo days) in Connecticut, Erika Voss in Milwaukee, Jane Blewett in Laurel, MD, Sister Marie Schmid in North Carolina and Fr. Boor in Kansas. As I had so many places for hospitality I didn't need to stay in motels, so it was a leisurely drive back to Colorado.

One day in the fall of 1975 one of our public health nurses, Marge, told me of her social worker friend who often had to go to the San Luis Valley, a six-county area in southern Colorado to help with the Handicapped Children's program there. She told me about a new position being offered by the State Health Department for a regional public health nurse consultant for the San Luis Valley. Actually the title was Nurse Planner-Coordinator, as the position would be housed with the San Luis Valley Council of Governments and with some funding coming from that group. Most of the staff had titles with "planner" or "coordinator" attached. Later I heard one County Supervisor grumbling: "We have a planner/coordinator for every toilet!" Because of the large Spanish speaking population, Marge thought I might be interested in the position. I did apply and went for an interview both at the Health Department and also at Alamosa (about 250 miles drive away) with the San Luis Valley Council of Governments, (often abbreviated to the SLV COG). I saw the great need and the challenge of the position, especially as I could start from scratch, being a new position. I was offered help to find a suitable apartment in the small town. The office would be located at Adams State College in quarters occupied by the SLV COG staff. I applied and later discovered that the only other viable candidate was a non-nurse, so I was selected to start on November 3, 1975.

CHAPTER 20

ALAMOSA AND THE SAN LUIS VALLEY

After I turned in my resignation, I made arrangements with a local moving company to help pack my belongings. As the movers were college dropouts they were pretty cheap and also allowed me to sit in the front seat of the truck while the second helper sat or lay on top of the mattress in the back. We stopped for lunch on the way and then proceeded to the one-bedroom apartment on Thomas Avenue in Alamosa. They unloaded everything in the correct place and were very helpful. Then I returned to Boulder with them to stay a few more days with a nurse colleague, Courtney Thomas, who lived in Boulder. Finally after a lovely farewell party at Tri-County and a visit to the Langs, who told me I would always be welcome when I had to come back to Denver, I was on my way to a whole new adventure.

Again I was confronted with the vote of no confidence, as I had to report to another Nurse Consultant instead of directly to the Director of Nurses. It sort of reminded me of being appointed "Acting" Superior and "Acting" Director of the Nursing School in Pindi. If higher-ups didn't consider me competent enough, they shouldn't have appointed me or told me how I could have improved to warrant an upgrade, but that never happened. I could understand this at first as I was so new to the Health Department, but I was hoping that I could be promoted to a position of Public Health Nurse Consultant II instead of a PHN Consultant I. This promotion never happened although I did request it later. The pay for a PHN Consultant I position was a lot more than I had at Tri-County so it wasn't the pay that bothered me, but the lack of confidence and the bureaucratic confusion it caused. I had to live with it as I had done in the past and I did for the next eight years, the longest position I had ever held in the Medical Mission Sisters or out on my own. In the end I believed that I had done a good job and was proud of my work.

Before I moved to the San Luis Valley I had a few days of orientation at the Colorado Department of Health especially being informed of the role of the various specialty Nurse Consultants and other departments in the Health Department such as record keeping, statistics, reports etc. There was only one other "generalist" consultant with a position like mine and she was living in Grand Junction to supervise several of the rural western counties in the vicinity. Consultants stationed at the Denver office made periodic supervisory trips related to their specialties. The counties with big cities such as Colorado Springs, Pueblo, Fort Collins, Grand Junction and Boulder had their own Health Departments so did not have generalist consultants assigned. I was the only one who actually lived in the area I supervised. This sometimes made for my having a different viewpoint from the staff in Denver since I could relate to the concerns of the rural counties that often were very different from those of the State bureaucracy.

Next I attended a whirlwind of meetings with the public health nurses from the six counties of Alamosa, Conejos, Costilla, Mineral, Rio Grande and Saguache. The total area of the region was about 7,000 square miles and a total population of about 40,000. The counties of Conejos, Costilla, Mineral and Saguache had only one public health nurse each, the other two, Alamosa and Rio Grande had two or three each. With no sanitarians or other public health officers the nurses had to do everything related to public health. They all reported to their respective County Commissioners (Supervisors) who paid their salaries, approved their budgets and made major decisions regarding public health. The County Commissioners were under a contract with the State Health Department for it to conduct the professional nurse evaluations and recommend new hires in case of a vacancy. This was to be part of my job.

I also had a contract with the SLV-COG as a member of their staff with travel and office expenses paid by them under a Health Education grant for the area. I attended regular staff meetings with the SLV-COG where I learned much about the area from the other staff—experts in transportation, labor, water and land use planning, programs for the elderly, housing, health education and general grant writing and reviews for State and Federal grants. I attended monthly meetings of the SLV-COG Board that consisted of representatives from each of the six counties and some of the major towns of the region. Their agenda often consisted of consideration of the many A-95 applications for federal grants. They always had two questions: "what will it cost my county?" and: "who will pay for the program when the grant runs out"? The SLV-COG executive director, Ron Phillips, was a master at presenting these grant applications in such a way that most of them got passed. Three of the San Luis Valley counties were also the three poorest counties in the state so any extra money coming from the government was always welcome, regardless of the county Supervisors' own conservative views. I usually attended the monthly Regional Development meetings where economic issues and plans were discussed. All of these meetings were in the evening and on my own time, so no extra pay, being a salaried employee with no overtime pay. These meetings were very educational.

I spent my first few months getting to know each nurse in her own agency, being introduced to the six groups of County Commissioners and other local non-profit or government agencies in each county. I compiled information from various regional programs, such as the Migrant Health Program, the Mental Health Services Department, the Handicapped Children's Program, The State Child Development and Evaluation Program, the various Senior Centers, the Nutrition Programs, Colorado Extension Service, School Nursing and Special Education, Comprehensive Health Planning Commission and Emergency Medical Services. Later other groups formed to set up various programs for domestic and child abuse prevention, hospice, a wellness program, alcohol and drug abuse and a food bank, all of which I contributed to with information about possible resources.

I contacted the four local hospitals and explained the public health nurses' role in relation to discharged patients and follow-up. I was a member of the San Luis Valley chapter of the Colorado Nurses Association and attended most monthly meetings. Often I was the one who informed the hospital nurses about changes that would affect their own performance, such as when Medicare announced its plans for paying for patient costs by a system called DRG's or Diagnostic Related Groups. At first they seemed indifferent to the fact that this would affect them in any way. They soon found out the reality of this change when they had to do more "paper work" and follow strict guidelines. I was truly becoming a Nurse Planner-Coordinator and I just loved the job in spite of its many difficulties, especially those related to the rural areas' low opinion of all State and Federal agencies, which included my role. It took a while for the nurses to fully accept me. Every day was different with something new to challenge me so I never got bored. This new job afforded me an opportunity to satisfy my penchant for being a pioneer.

Since I was receiving some funding from the Health Education grant, I was asked to interview and hire a Health Educator for two of the counties, develop a program for them and a system of evaluation. Two health educators began their work in Conejos and Costilla counties in January 1976. Those two counties were about 60–80% Hispanic, so we hired two Spanish speaking aides who eventually did an excellent job and were well accepted in their communities. In 1978 this program was discontinued and my travel expenses came from the Colorado Department of Health.

Vacancies in the county nurse positions were common so I was often involved in recruiting, hiring (with the County Commissioners' approval) and evaluation of the county nurses. As many of the nurses were recent graduates, I arranged for some observation experience with other more experienced PHN's. They found it especially helpful to observe a Well Baby Clinic before they instituted one on their own. The older nurses cooperated in this role and helped orient the new nurses to public health. We met as a group (all the nurses from all six counties) once a month to learn of new programs, discuss problems, make suggestions and each give a report on activities in her county. These meetings were often held at the home of a different nurse each month so it became a kind of social event with the meeting followed by a potluck and socializing. Little by little I began feeling accepted by the group and they could see the advantage of having an advocate (as I became to be) at the Health Department and with other agencies. There was a lot of work to be done, but soon I got a welcome break.

In 1976 I received an invitation to the tenth anniversary of the School of Nursing of the University of Zulia. As it happened around the

Fourth of July I took a few days off to attend and flew to Maracaibo, staying with Rosario Richemont who had been one of my students and now was a professor of Nursing at LUZ. Sister Juanita was also there along with other professors and we were treated royally. They took us to a symphony concert at the Teatro, and had a wonderful dinner with speeches. Some of the nurses who had once been my students delivered a series of professional papers. Sister Juanita and I were both given beautiful plaques acknowledging our efforts in starting the school. It was so gratifying to see so many of my former students who were now teaching other nurses. It was a wonderful event.

On my return in 1976 we were faced with the Swine Flu epidemic and the mass vaccination of the local population. This we coordinated with the Health Department in Denver and managed a great turnout of 60%, providing transportation services for those that could not get to the clinics and coordination with other agencies. Soon another challenge presented itself.

There was only one county, Alamosa, that had a Home Health Agency program and a contract with Medicare and Medicaid for reimbursement. There were at that time no private Home Health Agencies since the area was considered too small in population to be cost effective, so the public health nurses were making home visits as best they could. In June 1976 the federal Department of Health, Education and Welfare (HEW) was offering expansion grants, but the deadline was July 1st. I quickly got the application forms, consulted with the State and Federal officials, got help in writing the grant from the SLV-COG grant writers and from the Public Health nurse, Dixie Moulton, who was managing the Alamosa Home Health Agency. As this was an A-95 application, it had to go through the SLV-COG for recommendation. They quickly approved the application and on October 4, 1976 HEW informed me that we had received the only grant for Federal Region VIII as so few had applied. Eventually contracts were made with the other counties, using Alamosa as the home agency responsible for the finances and peer review etc. involved in the Medicare programs. The grant of $39,271 enabled us to hire Home Health Aides, a billing clerk, and pay for some travel and office expenses. This money was a godsend as often the County Commissioners threatened to close the

Public Health office when budget problems arose. This way we could point to the income the public health office was bringing in and paying its own way.

Other money came from the WIC program, the Development and Evaluation Program (mostly school screening tests) and the services provided to the local schools by the county PHN. Previously the PHNs were visiting the local schools for immunization clinics, vision, hearing and scoliosis screening without any remuneration. As the school districts were small they couldn't afford a school nurse, but I finally convinced them that they could pay for one-quarter of a nurse, shared with another district etc. All these various funds added together made for some County Nursing Service offices paying for their whole budget. This made everyone happy and prevented the County Supervisors from cutting the nursing programs.

The San Luis Valley Council of Government's Executive Director, Ron Phillips, was living at the time in a duplex house near the College. They had four children and expecting a fifth. Previously they had torn down the walls separating the two parts of the duplex and were living in the entire house. Ron told me he was thinking of moving to a bigger house about a half a block away. As I was now quite settled in my position in Alamosa, he asked me if I would like to move out of my apartment and purchase his house. This was a generous offer that seemed like an ideal situation for me as the income from the other half of the duplex would help pay for my mortgage. I had been saving money at the local Credit Union and got a generous loan for the down payment and I assumed Ron's loan at a much lower rate than was current at the time. Ron offered to put the walls up again and return it to its original situation. Each duplex had two bedrooms and its own garage with the yards separated by a fence. It had a nice backyard with the grass already planted. In August 1977 I closed the deal easily and moved in. Ron showed me how to run the furnace and in general care for the property. This was my first house in the U.S.! I soon found renters for the other half of the duplex, so everything worked out well.

I had a sprinkler system put in on both front and back of both sections of the duplex. The next summer I spent my vacation digging up the sod and making a vegetable garden. A friend of mine, Sue Ward, had a friend who owned sheep and she arranged for him to come and put down some of the sheep manure in the garden. Because the elevation of the San Luis Valley was 7,500 feet, the season was short, from mid May to mid August. I managed to find short-season vegetable seeds. The house was about a block away from the Rio Grande and the soil was old river-bottom and full of earthworms, so everything thrived. I had a good crop of corn, sugar snap peas, beans, beets, carrots, lettuce, radishes, zucchini, spinach and tomatoes. Rhubarb had already been growing along the fence. Some of this I shared with friends, especially with Ron's family. His youngest boy, Scott, would come over and help me plant the "baby corn."

For the extra bedroom I bought a small cot and some other furniture and sewed my own drapes and bedspread for the room. Eventually I was able to provide hospitality to visiting friends and also to two young women who were with the "Up with People" singing group when they were in Alamosa on tour. Later a young Spanish woman from the same group stayed with me. There were also foreign students at the Adams State College who asked for lodging and paid me a minimal rent. Hoa, a Vietnamese girl whose father had owned a restaurant in Vietnam, fixed some tasty dishes for us. She stayed about three months and referred a Brazilian friend, Sayonara, who also stayed for a few months in 1980. I was so fortunate to have her living with me at the time, as I had to go into the hospital for a hysterectomy (for early endometrial cancer.) She would visit me at the hospital, bring me my mail and later help me out around the house while I was recovering. I later had an American graduate student who was spending time with the Migrant Health Program who stayed about two months. Hoa eventually moved to Houston, and Sayonara went to Dallas and later back to Brazil. Over time I had various renters of the duplex, the last being a local school teacher, Pam Herrman. She told me that if I ever wanted to move, she would be interested in buying the house.

In July 1978 I was assigned as consultant to an additional four counties in Region 13. The public health offices were located in Leadville, Lake County; Canon City in Fremont County; Buena Vista and

Salida in Chaffee County; and Westcliffe in Custer County. This assignment did not include a pay raise or an assistant, just more work for the same salary. These places ranged from 100 to 150 miles away so I often got home late in the evening. Each month I spent from two to eight days on visits to these locations. These trips afforded me a real opportunity to see more of Colorado up close. After I left the offices at 4 p.m., I often had a chance to make side trips to the many scenic areas in the mountains. The Wet Mountains, a part of the Sangre de Cristo Range, west of Westcliffe, were exceptionally beautiful as was the Arkansas River valley with the Royal Gorge near Canon City.

I established monthly meetings of the Region 13 group and again we met at the nurses' homes. Because I did not live in that area, I was not as personally aware of the problems nor of the political implications involved in many decisions, so had to rely more on the nurses that had worked there for several years. For both Region 8 and Region 13 I had to send in a monthly report of my activities to the Director of Nurses in Denver with a copy of Region 8 report to the Director of the SLV-COG. Region 13 was a little more stable area with low turnover of nurses so the problems were minimal. When I would go to meetings in Region 13 the nurses asked me to bring a 100 lb. bag of the famous San Luis Valley potatoes—at $7.00 for a hundred pound bag they were just thrilled and each nurse bought her own share to take home. I sometimes would drive on the county roads in Conejos County and pick up the potatoes that bounced from the uncovered trucks as they were on their way to the storage facilities. This way I often had a free very fresh potato to enjoy. Wild asparagus often grew next to the fences throughout the county so about every February the locals went out picking.

I attended the County Nurses of Colorado annual meetings (those in the rural counties without a Health Department) and began seeing the need for a County Nurses Newsletter with contributions from each rural county. The SLV-COG staff helped with the layout and copying and each county had a nurse assigned to report on events and new programs in her respective county. This quarterly newsletter was well received and when I left, one of the nurses took over the responsibility as editor.

We were approached by the University of Colorado School Of Nursing and another local Denver school to provide some clinical experience for their students in rural public health. I was appointed as Clinical Assistant Professor and coordinated the activities of these undergraduate and graduate nurse students. The Migrant Health Program also had graduate students who came to the San Luis Valley.

The Colorado Department of Health Nursing Consultants and heads of other departments often asked our San Luis Valley to be the site for many pilot projects, so there was always plenty of work. The specialist consultants would come to the San Luis Valley for educational in-services, but sometimes would cancel appointments as there was a snowstorm in Denver. (They did, however, expect me to be in Denver, a 250-mile drive, for the scheduled Staff meetings, regardless of the snow.) I remember once in May I got stuck in Colorado Springs overnight as an unexpected wet spring snowstorm arrived and the roads were closed for a while. It still took me about six hours to get back to Alamosa, driving very carefully over the 10,000-foot high La Veta Pass. I must have had a great guardian angel as there were many whiteouts and ground fog to contend with over the mountain passes and I somehow survived by following at a distance the truck lights in front of me. Also my wonderful American Motors Eagle car with permanent four-wheel drive helped negotiate the snowy or icy roads and I didn't need snow tires or chains.

In 1979 I was a member of a panel for the Colorado Rural Health conference which discussed problems of recruitment of health professionals in rural areas. The Colorado Department of Health had us all working on Quality Assurance, Community Assessment Tools, Primary Care Nursing, Community Health Nursing Standards and revision of our daily statistics of each nurse's activities for time-cost studies. These "dailies" were the bane of the public health nurses who called them "the damned dailies." However, I did point out to them that they could give a better report to their County Commissioners if they could identify all they had contributed to their county including the income they brought in. Eventually I made my own community assessment tool or a county profile for each of the ten counties.

These profiles consisted of a demographic overview with a summary of the health resources of the county and the activities of the County Nursing Services. These proved useful especially for orientation of new nurses and for new Colorado Department of Health consultants. It also gave bragging rights to the County Commissioners around election time.

Off Duty Here and Afar

Social life in Alamosa was at a minimum, but I managed to find some interesting things to do. The college occasionally put on some reasonably good plays and concerts that I enjoyed. I took a course at the college on the History of the San Luis Valley, and became interested in some of the out-of-the-way places. When I was traveling on the county roads I would find old Catholic churches, abandoned post offices and Penitentes' "moradas" or meeting places, most of them now unused and began taking photos of these and other historic buildings. I joined the San Luis Valley Historical Society and found out that the town of San Luis in Costilla County was the oldest town in Colorado and Our Lady of Guadalupe Catholic Church in Antonito, Conejos County was the oldest Catholic Church in Colorado. There had been various settlers in the area, from Mormons and Dutch Reformed in Conejos County, to Swedes in Rio Grande County, and Spanish and Mexican settlements in all the counties. I began especially documenting the history of a little settlement in Conejos County, Las Sauces, (the Willows) which still had some very interesting buildings and stories. Hardly any of the San Luis Valley natives even knew about Las Sauces or other out-of-the-way places.

I attended Sacred Heart Church in Alamosa and Sister Angelo, one of the Sisters on the staff was in charge of programs for the elderly. She asked us to "adopt" a senior that lived alone and needed some company. I "adopted" Amalia Trujillo, an eighty-year old single lady who lived in Senior Housing nearby. She spoke a little English but we mostly conversed in Spanish. She had never married as she was caring for her sick mother for many years. She invited me to

Sunday dinner that I thought gave her some independence and the opportunity to give as well as receive. She had a very small income as she had a pension from working as a cook at a small school in Conejos County, but she had the common sense to prepare meals she liked, regardless of the cost. So we would sit down to a lovely lamb chop dinner (her family always had sheep and a vegetable garden) and potatoes and vegetables. Her favorite dessert was "hot ice cream" which she had heated slightly.

She was one of the descendants of the old Spaniards who colonized the area in the sixteen hundreds. She still spoke the ancient Cervantes style Spanish of that century, using words such as "tunica" for "dress," whereas the more modern Spanish used the word "vestido." I used to love it when she would have a little problem with her oven and maybe the potatoes were burnt and she would exclaim in her "Spanglish," "Oh shite!" I took her on a few rides to visit favorite areas in Conejos County especially the old Hot Creek School, now abandoned, where she once worked. She was quite aware of her advancing age and consulted with Sister Angelo regarding her death, buying a coffin in advance and settling her affairs. She later decided to move into a care facility out of the San Luis Valley and died shortly after in 1981. I missed her and my Sunday meals with her, but new interests came to fill up my weekends, such as archaeology.

The Rio Grande, which begins in the high country of Mineral County, is also the site of many petroglyphs. A group of people consisting of history buffs—Ruth Coleman, a retired school teacher; Diane Machado, a young photographer; Sharon Barnes, a woman who was getting her Masters in History and her son Randy; Armenio Lujan, a young man who was a columnist for a local paper; Ian McDonald, a local writer, a couple of others and myself would go on impromptu trips to find more petroglyphs. We did find them and helped Sharon use the photographs for her Master's thesis on the San Luis Valley petroglyphs. Once we had to report to the Forest Service about one petroglyph that vandals were beginning to remove from the site. They had to remove the large rock completely before the vandals would and put it in a museum. We tried not to publicize the site of these petroglyphs in order to protect them.

During the years I spent in Colorado I had the opportunity to visit the many gold mining towns and other tourist sites. I visited Rocky Mountain National Park, Mesa Verde ruins, Taos and other towns of Northern New Mexico. The Great Sand Dunes National Monument was only about 30 miles from Alamosa, so it was a favorite spot to visit with its 700ft-high dunes surrounded by the majestic Sangre de Cristos at 14,000 feet. I often saw many deer there and even pronghorn antelope grazing in the meadows. Once I noticed a deer licking some remnants of my Coke on the nearby picnic table, but unfortunately my camera was in the car so never got to take his picture. Every year in late spring I was happy to see the snowmelt from the nearby peaks streaming down to the dunes in a strange pulsating stream that seemed like little tidal flows. *The "Monument" is now a National Park.*

In 1976 I finally realized my dream of seeing the Grand Canyon. My Cuban friend, Otilia, was living and working as a Family Practice Doctor in Wisconsin. She and I planned months ahead and stayed at the El Tovar Lodge at the rim and hiked down the South Rim. We stayed overnight at Phantom Ranch, where we stayed in a cabin for women that held eight bunk beds. We also enjoyed a hearty group supper at the Mess Hall and an evening guided walk down Bright Angel Creek. As it happened to be full moon, we awoke early and began hiking up the canyon in the moonlight, which made it an even more beautiful experience. The only time I was a little frightened was when I had to choose between walking on the cliff side with the flying bats or the edge of the trail close to the canyon. This was my first encounter with the moon flower or datura plant and its elegant white trumpet flower. *Later when I moved to the California desert, I discovered that these flowers were abundant as weeds along the roadsides.* The nighttime hike allowed us to enjoy the cool weather before the sun came up. Towards the rim, we would stop about every twenty steps to rest but never sitting down or talking to save our breath. By nine o'clock we made it to the top and we celebrated the event with a champagne lunch. I still remember the Canyon fondly any time I notice the typical smell of the willow bushes and arrowweed that grow near rivers.

Later when I lived in Desert Hot Springs I took a trip with Father Ned Reidy and other parishioners of the Newman Center to the western end of the Canyon, at the Havasupai Indian Reservation. The hike down to the canyon from Peach Springs, Arizona was much easier than the South Rim or North Rim and we marveled at three beautiful waterfalls, took a dip in the pool below them and admired the many wildflowers in bloom. We stayed overnight at the simple motel there where I shared a room with a family and a bed with their two young girls.

In 1977 my friend Sarah Ann O'Gara, a former Medical Mission Sister living in California, and I planned a trip after Labor Day and hiked down the North Rim of Grand Canyon, staying overnight at one of the cabins on the Rim. The North Rim was quieter than the South Rim with fewer tourists and the trail a little longer. We hiked down and stayed overnight at Phantom Ranch. Although not aware of it in our planning the trip, there was a bright full moon so we arose early and hiked out. This trip cemented my life-long love of the Canyon.

I joined a group called Single Again and we would take trips to the Forest Service areas to cut down Christmas trees, cross-country ski in the area or hear a lecture on a topic of interest to all. I met some nice people at these events and also at the occasional potlucks but never managed to have a date. I felt very lonely and wanted at least to have a boy friend, if not a marriage partner, so made various efforts to contact eligible men. As a woman in her fifties, it was not going to be easy. I enrolled in weekly Fred Astaire dance classes held in Colorado Springs, but no one special showed up for me.

In 1982 I put an ad for singles in *The Mother Earth News* and corresponded with several men. Some were turned off by the fact that I had never married and had been a Sister at one time. One interesting man from South Carolina wrote and invited me to visit him in Cortez, Colorado as he was doing some archaeological research there. He took me to see some of the sites in the Four Corners area. He spoke a lot about planning a trip to visit the Mayan ruins in the Yucatan and invited me to go with him. I made my plans for the winter of '82. He had brought some thoughtful gifts for me, such as roses in a pretty vase, chocolates, a gold chain and two glasses for a champagne toast to our meeting. It was all very romantic for me as I had never been treated like this before. Later he talked to me on the phone and told me he wouldn't be able to make the trip to the Yucatan as his godfather was sick and he had obligations to the Defense Department that he couldn't postpone. I met him in New Orleans for a day where he took me to listen to the Preservation Band there and gave me some photos he had taken of Mayan ruins in the Yucatan. He promised to keep in contact with me.

In November I went by myself to the Yucatan, stayed in the Casa de Balaam Hotel in Mérida and took bus tours to the various Mayan sites, Chichen Itza, Uxmal, Tulum and the beach at Playa del Carmen. For this trip I stayed at a small motel to get the early morning bus to Playa del Carmen, but didn't want to take my entire luggage. I asked the manager if he could store some of my stuff for a couple of days. When I returned I asked for my luggage and he went near the desk to a little open space beneath the stairs with no doors, where my suitcase and open shopping bags were kept. I was duly impressed by the honesty of the people as anyone could have just stolen all or any of my possessions. Not an object was missing.

As I spoke Spanish I was able to glean a lot more information than most tourists and I had read several books on the Maya. I met some friendly Americans and occasionally joined with them on the tours. I had an opportunity to attend the Cuban Ballet Group at the beautiful theater where they had one evening performance at a low price for the less well-off—the "noche popular." I was impressed by the fact that the theater was completely full and everyone so well behaved. I visited the local Nursing School and had an interesting visit with the Director of the School. Among other things I discovered she had no qualms about smuggling in medical supplies from nearby Belize. I loved the Mayan people and it was such a thrill to see people with the typical Mayan features and the women wearing the beautiful "huipil," the typical dress worn by the Mayan women.

When I returned, my archaeologist friend still wrote but I could tell he had other plans. Finally in June he called and said he was going to get married to a nurse who cared for him when he had a back injury. I wasn't in love with him but still it was a big disappointment to me as I had enjoyed his company. So that was the end of the romance.

I had made a "Search Weekend" with one of the assistant pastors at the church in Alamosa, Father Tony Hanebrink, and made a private retreat in 1977 with him. This was one of the first times since I had left the convent that I had confronted some of my faults, problems and need for spiritual guidance. He himself was going through some questioning of his vocation and told me about how he had been helped by the "Healing of Memories" which was popular at the time. A few months later Tony decided to leave the priesthood, took a job locally with a Day Care center but eventually moved to Ogden, Utah where he became a mental health counselor and two years later married a divorced lady, Diana, with two young boys. He was able to find a priest who was willing to marry him in the Catholic Church as his laicization from Rome took too long in coming. It still is hard for me to cope with the Church's stand on priest celibacy and also the fact that most ex-priests would give anything to be able to say Mass and minister to a congregation. I visited him a few years later and found him to be well established in his job, his church and his community and happy with being a father to two teen-age boys and married to Diana. One thing Tony remarked that probably had some relevance to my ever-single state was: "You can take the woman out of the convent, but you can't take the convent out of the woman." Perhaps the fact that my female role models were mainly women who had never married, including my aunts, may have been a factor in my finding it difficult to attract a partner.

In 1980 I took another trip back east and found out later, that this was the last time, (as well as the first since Bob's ordination in 1949,) that the three of us Jollett children were together, when we visited my Aunts Anna and Loretta in Madison. It was at this time I realized how far apart I had become from my two brothers as far as their views on the Church and the world were concerned. Bob was really an old time conservative on the role of the Church in modern society and had become a Canadian citizen. Herb, much influenced by his time in the Navy, was a little less conservative in regard to the Church but a committed Republican. They had not changed much since my childhood and adolescence but I had. Vatican II had not had much impact on either of my brothers. In fact my priest brother would have preferred to return to pre-Vatican II days. *My Dad had always been a union member and a staunch Democrat and I have always been a Democrat since returning to the U.S. Of course my time in the Medical Mission Sisters and the foreign missions had a lot to do with our different viewpoints on both the Church and politics.* We managed however, to argue politely, agree to disagree and have a pleasant visit. I was glad I had made that visit as my Aunt Loretta died a few months later, leaving my Aunt Anna alone in her apartment. My brother Herb would visit her frequently to help put in her air-conditioner etc. so she was not left without help.

By the beginning of 1983 I began seeing "the handwriting on the wall" that the State of Colorado Legislature and a Republican Governor were making large budget cuts everywhere. Ron Phillips had left in 1979 and moved to Oklahoma and the San Luis Valley Council of Governments was disbanded in 1982. A few people who had specially funded programs stayed in the office. I was told by the Health Department to find another site for my office. I was able to make an arrangement with Adams State College to stay where I was for a while. I was notified that the State Health Department was going to cut my position due to budget cutbacks from the State Legislature. I tried to understand the rationale behind their decision, as there were many other places they could have made cuts, but I guess I was too far away from Headquarters for them to worry about any repercussions. Maybe it made them uncomfortable having an employee so far from their control.

The County nurses in both Region 8 and 13 expressed their dismay at the decision but to no avail. I was offered another consultant position with the Health Facilities Department but I declined as it would mean snooping and policing the Nursing Homes in the State (not to my liking) and I no longer felt that my loyalty to the State was appreciated. This meant that I would not be eligible for unemployment insurance. I went to the County Commissioners and asked to buy the old Selectric typewriter that I used, which they allowed me to do. I had a lot of work informing everyone that I would no longer be available, and that any consulting would be done out of the Denver office. I cleaned up my files and took everything important to the Denver office where I had a little farewell party. I was disappointed that none of the other consultants interceded for my position, but my guess was that there were a lot of political issues at stake and no one wanted to buck the establishment. There were no job opportunities for me in the San Luis Valley so I decided to leave the area.

The County Nurses of the San Luis Valley gave me a beautiful farewell party and the gift of a photo album with pictures of the nurses at the various meetings we had. They also gave me a lovely pottery bowl and vase. My last day as Nurse Consultant was June 30, 1983.

CHAPTER 21

ON THE ROAD AGAIN

I was lucky to sell my house quickly to my duplex renter, Pam Herrman. As we both had our accounts at the San Luis Valley Federal Savings and Loan, the whole process took us about one-half hour. After living in the house about six years, it was hard to leave it, but fortunately the price of real estate had gone up considerably and the proceeds from the sale tided me over for the next eight months when I didn't have a job. One of the nurses from Alamosa County, Roxie Rauch, offered to put me up at her house for a few days, so I could pack my furniture. I had kept in contact with a friend, Dr. Erika Voss, a former Medical Mission Sister who had been with me in Karachi, who kindly flew in from Milwaukee to help me with the packing and then drive with me back to her home in Milwaukee. Another local friend, Sue Ward, offered to pick up my mail at the Post Office and forward it to different addresses as I toured the country. With the help of some guys from the Single Again group I put my furniture and other belongings in a 10 x 10 unit at the U-Lock-It storage facility in Alamosa. I gave the key to Sue Ward so she could make the arrangements with a moving company to send the contents to me whenever I found a permanent home.

I began thinking during those last months that I would eventually like to retire somewhere in the Southwest, possibly Arizona, New Mexico or California. I wasn't sure where, but I did want it to be a warmer place than Alamosa, "The Land of the Cool Sunshine." I packed my American Eagle with a couple of suitcases with some clothes, and a bunch of maps of the Southwest area. The 1979 issue of the AARP magazine featured an article about San Diego with an appealing photo of the Alcazar Gardens and the Museum of Man at Balboa Park and other sites in San Diego. This made me think about San Diego, but I wasn't sure yet of where I wanted to live. So, off I went on a tour that took the next couple of months.

As Erika had never been to Colorado, we took the scenic route through Aspen and then to Boulder to say goodbye to my dear friends, the Langs. Then we drove on to Rocky Mountain National Park, north to Cheyenne and Fort Laramie, through South Dakota to the Black Hills and Mt. Rushmore and the stone monument in progress honoring Crazy Horse. On Highway I-90 we saw several billboards advertising Wall Drug and its "free ice water." As there was not much else on the road we decided to find out what this place was like. There were many souvenirs, a whole room full of postcards of all kinds and just about anything a traveling tourist would want. And yes, we did need to get the free ice water, as it was quite hot in July.

Another interesting spot was the Pipestone National Monument in Minnesota where the Sioux Indians used to quarry soft pink stone for their peace pipes and other uses. The roads in the Plains States offered a series of farm fields, grain silos and then a large farmhouse with its barns. When we got further east we enjoyed the beautiful wooded hills and lakes and then the dairy farms of Wisconsin. We stopped first in Madison and had a visit with Otilia who had a family practice and a regular field clinic among migrant workers in Wild Rose. Later I took a side trip to the University of Wisconsin's Stephen's Point where they had established a Lifestyle Improvement Center and developed lifestyle assessment questionnaires and educational programs on wellness (at that time a fairly new concept.) I had already been exposed to some of these concepts in Alamosa when I attended a workshop on Holistic Health for Nurses and found the concepts quite challenging.

We finally arrived in Milwaukee where I stayed with Erika for a few days. She was working at a local community clinic as a family practice physician. We had a great picnic lunch on Lake Michigan with her sister and I picked up a bag full of very smooth stones from the Lake. *These proved of immense help when I later published my magazine and these stones prevented the desert winds from blowing them away when at an outdoor event.* I thanked her for all her help and company on the trip and drove the rest of the journey alone.

On July 15th I left Madison via Rockford, Illinois and Indianapolis on my way to Cincinnati. It was very hot and humid and as I was now driving alone and was getting tired, I finally decided in Remington, Indiana to stop at the Day's Inn. After lunch, siesta and shower I was able to keep on driving until I arrived in Cincinnati about 8 p.m. I stayed with Isabelle Healy, another former Medical Mission Sister who was working as Supervisor of a Home Repair Project for the Elderly on contract with the city of Cincinnati. We attended a Greek Festival and then Isabelle borrowed a typewriter from her next door neighbor so I began writing circular letters to friends called "Joan's Journeys." *I still have carbon copies of these letters. They help me a lot in remembering the details of the trip. The first was dated July 17th and the last one is August 25th. For the last letter I used my old Selectric typewriter which I took out of storage in Alamosa.*

From Cincinnati I visited the fascinating Mound City (now called Hopewell Cultural Park) near Chillicothe, Ohio. This is an ancient mound site of primitive Indians. From here I drove on to Grafton, West Virginia, the home of Anna Jarvis, who first suggested we celebrate Mother's Day. West Virginia's mountain country was very beautiful and I picked a few wildflowers to put into my wildflower press that I had brought along with me. I then drove over the Skyline Drive through the Shenandoah Mountains and on to Laurel, Maryland. There I stopped to visit another former Medical Mission Sister, Jane Blewett, and drove her to New Jersey where she had to give a talk the next day.

Once in New Jersey, I visited my Aunt Anna in Madison and then my Aunt Mildred in West Orange. We drove together to Vermont where we visited my old college roommate, Gennie, who lived in the little town of Craftsbury. Mildred and I went on to Waterloo, Canada where my brother Bob was assigned. We returned to New Jersey via Vermont, Massachusetts and New York and then I said goodbye to Mildred.

I drove later to see my brother Herb who had retired a few years earlier and was living with his wife, Anna, in Netcong, NJ. His wife was originally from Brooklyn so they often took trips there so she could visit her relatives. I visited the Medical Mission Sisters' Motherhouse in Fox Chase, Philadelphia and had a nostalgic visit with many old friends and just to have a few days rest before continuing my travels. Sister Sheila McGinnis was active in holistic health modalities, so I had a nice chat with her as I was planning on attending the American Holistic Nurses Association in Springfield, Missouri. I was interested in all aspects of this new view of health and medicine.

On my way back west I stopped in Baltimore to visit my dear friend, Sister Mary Louise, who had been in the Novitiate with me. She was active in an organization called Alliance for Justice. We toured the Baltimore Harbor and later out to Fort McHenry of Star Spangled Banner fame. She took me to Hausner's Restaurant which had a very wide selection of foods, and tons, and I mean tons, of art works—paintings, sculptures, statues, vases etc. on every square inch of wall and floor space available or in glass cabinets. The family that owned it had collected all of these—it would have taken hours just to look at everything. It was a very popular place. Nearby we visited the Babe Ruth Museum as he was born in that section of Baltimore and raised in a Catholic orphanage.

My next stop was North Carolina and the Smoky Mountain Park that was just beautiful with many deer sightings and lots of wildflowers. The non-stop chirps of the cicadas and the tree frogs started in the evening and continued until sunrise in Gatlinburg where I spent the night. When I arrived in Gatlinburg at 10:30 P.M. the night life was in full swing with everyone out on the street. I enjoyed the mountain crafts at the Appalachian Craft Center in Cookeville, Tennessee. The mountains rose above me in a series of ever fading shades with rushing rivers below. I crossed over from Memphis to Arkansas and stayed the night at Blytheville. The countryside here was mainly cotton and soybeans and an Airforce base in Blytheville. I had been 13 hours on the road but as the weather was reasonable, it wasn't too hard staying awake.

From there I drove to Springfield, Missouri where I arrived on time for the opening of the American Holistic Nurses Association meeting at 1:30 p.m. This meeting lasted from Wednesday to Sunday noon. I stayed with other nurses at the college dorm and went out for Chinese dinner one night. I was impressed by the number of nurses who were going into private practice in holistic health or who are incorporating holistic nursing concepts in their classes in Nursing Schools or in hospital continuing education programs. Many nurses were like me—in transition and looking for new approaches to health care and opportunities in nursing. Everyone in the different group sessions was very supportive of each other. *Later, I realized that try as I might, I never could learn to visualize, or meditate and was still often too skeptical to accept all the new modalities, so never got further than Public Health Nursing. However, I remained committed to preventive health care.*

In Enid, Oklahoma I stopped to visit Lee Oldham, a nurse who used to work in Alamosa Public Health. She was now a Wellness Consultant at the local hospital with plans for a fitness center at the local hospital and a cardiac rehabilitation center. I soon found out how big Texas really is. I passed through some woodsy sections near Huntsville and Lexington and then on to Port Arthur where I visited with another former Public Health Nurse from Alamosa, Laurel Patterson. She was working as Infection Control Nurse in a small hospital but also did Utilization Reviews, Quality Assurance and Financial Audits etc. So little by little, I was getting a broad spectrum of all the possibilities for future opportunities in Nursing. I visited Searama in Galveston and then on to San Antonio to visit another former Public Health Nurse from Costilla County, Martha Buls. She and I went for lunch at the Café del Rio on the beautiful San Antonio River. Here I discovered that the maitre'd was a Venezuelan so we had a nice chat. He also quickly took off the reserved sign on a choice table next to the river.

I stayed the night in San Antonio and later visited the famous Carlsbad Caverns. From here I went through the Guadalupe Mountains and on through El Paso and Las Cruces to Socorro, New Mexico. Here I stayed the weekend with Marcy Bachler Wolf, a former Medical Mission Sister who had been in Maracaibo. She was married to an ex-priest and had three lovely children. She was working in a Mental Health Center for the Zuni Indians and her husband was consultant for the Navajo education system. We went to the annual fiesta for the San Miguel church that is over 300 years old. We visited the Bosque del Apache Wildlife Refuge with the sandhill cranes who had adopted the endangered all-white whooping cranes with their seven-foot span of wings and long necks. The first time I saw them in the wildlife refuges in Alamosa, I thought they were sheep as they had their heads down while they were grazing. Like me perhaps, they were migrating to strange new places and needed to stay, as I was doing, with old acquaintances to feel safe and comforted.

Finally after all these touristy and visiting friends' spots I arrived back in Alamosa where I stayed with Roxie Rauch, visited another Public Health nurse, Shirley Walker, in Monte Vista and took care of some business including getting my Selectric typewriter out of storage. I had planned a side trip to Dinosaur National Monument (one of the few places in Colorado that I had yet to visit). On the way I stopped at Pitkin where I hooked up with some people whose names had been give to me at the Holistic Nurses Conference. I was only able to meet with a friend of these—she was the owner and manager of the Pitkin Hotel that she was renovating and hoped to have seminars there as well. As I was talking to her, she put me to work, fixing ham sandwiches, helping to serve breakfast to two guests, etc. as she was pretty busy. Everything was quite laid back and I had an informative chat with her.

When I got to Fruita in western Colorado I discovered what I guessed everyone else knew, that Douglas Pass to Rangely was closed, so that if I wanted to get to Dinosaur Monument I would have to go to Price, Utah which was quite far out of my way. So I scrapped that idea and kept going till it got to be evening and I decided to stay in Thompson, Utah. It is a <u>very</u> small town with a very simple motel. However it is a stop on the Amtrak line between Denver and Salt Lake—I saw the train going through one hour later and all night there must have been at least six freight trains going through. Ordinarily I don't notice those noises but each train was preceded by the clanging of the warning bells and I was a half a block away from the tracks! Next morning at the "Cook Tent Eats—Suds and Soda" place I heard about a petroglyph site about 3 miles out of town up Sego Canyon where there had previously been coal mining activity. I did manage to find them—they were actually mostly pictographs (colored paintings) of animals and shaman figures on the canyon rocks.

This town of Thompson was very desolate but in talking to the restaurant owners —they had come from Minnesota, had lived in Aspen and Grand Junction but didn't like it there—so leased this place and seemed happy. I had learned on this trip that no matter how miserable a place may appear to the outsider, there are always people who find something they like there and call it home. I heard him say to a customer that he had to work 16 hours a day and seven days a week to make a go of it—but he seemed happy as he drove home on his bicycle. His food was good too. He told me not to miss Dead Horse Point State Park so that was my next stop.

The story goes that in the old days the cowboys would corral wild mustangs here as their only escape was through a 30-yard piece of land controlled by fencing. Mustangs were then roped and broken with the better ones sold or kept for personal use. Unwanted culls or "broomtails" were left behind to find their way off the Point. According to one legend, a band of broomtails was left corralled on the Point. The gate was supposedly left open so the wild horses could return to the open range. For some unknown reason, the mustangs remained on the Point. There they died of thirst within sight of the Colorado River, 2,000 feet below! This area is near Canyonlands National Park but instead I went to the Arches National Park (Edward Abbey territory) and spent some time there. I stopped later at Natural Bridges

National Monument and headed towards Capital Reef about 9 p.m. The moon was just coming up over the Colorado River near Lake Powell and it was a stunning view. I arrived into the small town of Torrey and stayed at the Rim Rock Motel. By morning I had decided I did not want to see any more canyons and opted to skip Capital Reef this time around, so headed out through Dixie National Forest which offered a woodsy alternative to the canyons. I lay down my ground cover and took my much-needed siesta looking up through the pine trees to the bright blue skies above me.

In spite of my previous resolution not to visit any more canyons, I couldn't resist a quick view of Bryce Canyon and was very impressed. I stayed that night in Beaver, Utah and in the morning discovered that my power steering fluid was leaking. It was Sunday so no repair shops or parts shops were open. At the gas station they filled it up but told me I should try going to Cedar City as they had an American Motors dealer there and I could probably get it fixed on Monday. That was a bit off my itinerary, but no other big city nearby. I found the little Catholic Church there (in a renovated private house) and went to Mass. I made reservations at the local Best Western and then took a side trip to Cedar Breaks National Monument and Brian Head Peak. I took along a can of transmission fluid, just in case, and discovered how difficult driving could be without power steering. The trip was really worthwhile—a combination of high mountain country with wildflowers in abundance and views of the canyons in the distance. The next day I stopped at the American Motors dealer only to find out they had been closed for over a year! I was able to get the power steering fixed at the nearby Chrysler dealer and then was on my way.

In Nevada I crossed one small mountain range after another on Highway 50, often called the Loneliest Highway in the World. I felt right at home, as it seemed to be made for one of the loneliest persons in the world. I arrived in Fallon, which was my first contact with casino gambling even in the wee hours of the morning.

Soon I was back on Highway 50 after going around beautiful Lake Tahoe and finally arrived in Sacramento. Here I stayed with my friend Sarah Ann O'Gara, who was working as a medical record

administrator for the California Health Department. I hadn't seen
her since our hike down Grand Canyon. I spent a few days with her
and knew I was finally on the last leg of my trip.

My last comments in my "Joan's Journal" were:

I have traveled over 10,000 miles in 49 days and visited 27 states, D.C. and
Canada and have found each place has its own claim to fame, e.g. Baltimore
for Babe Ruth; Beaver, Utah, birthplace of Butch Cassidy; Grafton, West
Virginia where Mother's Day was first celebrated and even Port Bolivar,
Texas where a little store called Zeke's Place had a sign on the outside which
read "Famous For Nothing"! There were many signs that read "The————
Capital of the World." *You can fill in the blank.*

There are so many wonderful places to see in the U.S that we often don't
realize that in our quest for 'faraway places.' I found that small joys are important e.g. the Dairy Queen sign on a hot day; finding that the next street is the
one I'd been desperately looking for; a nice wide bench in a picnic area where
I could lay down for a few minutes for my siesta and above all living "one day
at a time" and not planning too far ahead. If one planned trip didn't work out,
then usually something even better would turn up.

CHAPTER 22

OCEAN BEACH, CALIFORNIA

Driving down Highway 5 through the agricultural areas of the
Central Valley was an eye-opener. California was indeed the vegetable and fruit garden of the country with acres of olive, pistachio,
almond, grapevines and citrus trees, strawberry fields and all kinds
of vegetables. To the east were the magnificent snow-capped peaks
of the Sierra Nevada. I stopped on the way to visit the historic Fort
Tejon, which was where the Camel Corps had its headquarters in
the late 19th century. Then driving down the steep Grapevine (part
of highway 5) I suddenly came into Southern California. I got a big
thrill when I began seeing signs such as "Cardiff-by-the-Sea" and
"Beaches" along the way.

I finally arrived in San Diego on September 8th and as I had previously arranged, I stayed for a while with the Medical Mission Sisters who had a house in the Golden Hill area. Sister Betty Dougherty, who had been with me in Pindi and Karachi, was now semi-retired and working with a Hospice program. She was a great hostess and the other Sisters were very kind to me. She made suggestions as to where I might find an apartment. By now it was obvious to me that San Diego was where I wanted to live and work and then retire. At first I looked in the classified ads for rentals and was almost ready to settle for a dingy place inland. Finally Sister Betty mentioned that she thought rates in Ocean Beach, a neighborhood in San Diego, would be reasonable. This sounded like a good idea. As I did not yet have a job, I had to do some fast talking to convince the landlord that I would be able to pay the rent which I did with a Travelers check. On October 4th I moved in to a nice little one-bedroom apartment on Narragansett Avenue about two blocks from the beach and the Ocean Beach Pier. A borrowed cot, a chair and a card table were sufficient at first. Then I wrote to Sue Ward to please arrange to have my furniture taken out of storage in Alamosa and shipped to Ocean Beach.

Four days later my furniture arrived and I was so relieved to finally settle in to my own place with my own address and my own phone and my "stuff." It was a happy day when after three months on the road I could sleep in my own bed. I finally got my $8,000 check from the Mt. Carmel Credit Union in Alamosa and was able to open a local account. I spent my time trying to figure out how to get around the city and a lot of time thinking of what I might want to do now. I tried to get an interpreter job in the hospitals but they only used an occasional volunteer or counted on the housekeeping personnel to help translate for Spanish speaking patients when needed. Driving in a big city was also a challenge. I really didn't want a job in nursing but didn't have much luck in finding anything related to my talents. I did help at a Cancer Clinic translating a few hours a week, but they didn't call me very often so that petered out.

I attended several lectures on Holistic Health and attended a nurses group called Well Within with a focus on preventive health and alternative modalities. I even had a Rolfing session and one on the Bates method of Eye Training. I became friends with that instructor, Mary Margaret Huber. Sadly, later she came down with breast cancer but refused any of the modern medicine therapeutic measures and was hoping that the Hawaiian Kahuna methods would cure her. Unfortunately, about a year later her daughter told me the cancer had metastasized to the bones and she died shortly after. This reinforced my reluctance to rely solely on alternative medicine approaches.

Early on, I met someone on a walk downtown that told me about Walkabout International so I joined the group which is all volunteers who walk all over San Diego County at different hours. They get their information on upcoming walks by a monthly newsletter. This was one way to find my way around the city, where the off ramps led to many of the interesting parts of San Diego. *Now that I have returned to San Diego County I still do the Walkabouts.*

I finally received my $15,000 from the sale of my house in Alamosa and put most of it in a six-month savings account, which at that time was offering an interest of 9.85%. I kept some of it to live on and managed to do so until March of 1984.

In October I drove up to see the Torrey Pines State Reserve and there met one of the docents who told me they were starting a new course for docents in November, so I signed up for that. I was asked later to write up an article for their newsletter on why I became a docent. I wrote:

After I left my home in Colorado in July of 1983 I started traveling to see many beautiful places. As I was driving along I let my mind wonder about what kinds of things I would like to do when I finished my travels. Without any conscious effort a strong desire came to me to somehow be able to share this beauty with others. Shortly after I arrived in San Diego I visited Torrey Pines State Reserve and fell in love with it. With its single species of tree, the Torrey pine, the Reserve is like an elegant jewel set as a single stone surrounded by various other smaller gems that enhance its beauty, but also have their own special wonder. I enjoyed the regular meetings too with the other docents. When I heard from June Warburton of the opportunity of being a docent, it sounded exactly like what I wanted, with the chance to learn more about the various plants, animals and rocks and how together with the wind, sea and climate they all fit together so harmoniously to form the delicate and unique ecology of Torrey Pine State Reserve. Here I met some wildflower friends I knew in Colorado and elsewhere but also some completely new ones. It's nice to get acquainted with them and know them by name. I am hoping that being a docent will keep me closely in tune with nature, constantly renew my spirit, and let me share this special place with other nature lovers.

The above words still rang true later when I became a docent at Big Morongo Reserve in Morongo Valley in the desert and at the County Park in Idyllwild. They still hold true today now that I am in Imperial Beach with an even different type of beauty.

Still looking for work I contacted Intrex, a language translation company, and was paid $20 for every 1,000 words translated. I did several jobs for them translating from Spanish to English. They didn't consider my Spanish "native" enough for me to translate from English to Spanish. However, I did a few small jobs such as discharge instructions for patients at the University of California San Diego Hospital, etc.

Intrex also paid me for translating for a patient in Grossmont Hospital. He was a young Uruguayan who had severe injuries from a motorcycle accident. He had completed his time in rehabilitation. As he came from a wealthy family, he had a physiotherapist from Uruguay come to the States to learn the follow-up measures needed for his full recovery. The patient knew English but the physiotherapist did not. My task consisted of translating the P.T. instructions to the Uruguayan P.T. This was not as easy as I thought as there were many technical terms. I did get some help from the patient himself.

Later I contacted some nurses at San Diego State University and ended up accompanying a team of nurses to the Hospital de Niños (Children's Hospital) in Tijuana, Mexico. The Pediatric Nursing Instructor gave a class for the graduate nurses there and needed a translator. This was very interesting and quite a challenge. I had to first translate every paragraph the instructor was saying for the students. Then if they had any questions I translated them back to the instructor and again with the answers back to the students. The topics were related to the Growth and Development of the Child so were not too difficult to translate. The nurses were very studious, although some of them fell asleep in class as they had just come off night duty. Some were very tired, as they had to work two shifts to earn a living for their families. I didn't have to do the driving, as the head of the program, Mary Ann Small, a former Peace Corps volunteer in Brazil, was the driver. Each class lasted three hours and was held for about ten weeks. They paid me $15 an hour.

As a result of this experience I became involved in binational nursing meetings that discussed transcultural issues of interest to both the U.S. and Mexico. I learned great respect for the hard-working Mexican women. One of the nurses invited me to visit her at her home in Tijuana and I accepted the invitation taking a bus to get to her house in the La Mesa area of Tijuana, where I enjoyed a tasty soup (sopa de nopales-cactus pad soup) with her family.

Still looking for a job, I thought I might be able to work for a travel agency, especially as I knew Spanish. I had no previous experience in computers so when I went to a class to learn the required Sabin computer system, I discovered a "floater" in my eye and it made reading the cursor on the green background of the computer screen very difficult so I discontinued that. *Was the floater a little warning that this kind of work was not meant for me?*

I must have applied to over 20 different places for a job but was either over-educated or lacked certain talents, such as computer skills and my application was rejected or I found that what they offered wasn't very interesting. I began to realize that I would have to settle for a job in public health nursing. I had applied for a position with the County Public Health Services but had to wait several months for the California Board of Nursing to give me a PHN certificate which really only required that I have a Bachelor's degree in Nursing—California's bureaucracy was almost as bad as Venezuela's.

Meanwhile I heard about a position opening in Mid City at a Community Clinic for an RN Dispatcher in their clinic. The job required an orientation by the clinic Pharmacist and then dispensing medicines on my own for the clinic patients. The clinic doctor had to check each pill bottle and compare it to the prescription and initial it. As I had done considerable work in Venezuela in the Pharmacy in Caripito this was pretty easy. It was a four-day-a-week position so I didn't have to work on Fridays. This was in March 1984 and my first real paying job since I left Colorado in July of '83, so I was happy to have a regular income again.

Without a regular job I found this period a lot of fun exploring a new and vibrant city, but I was also feeling very lonely especially in the evenings and at holiday times. I was pretty desperate to make friends. I so wanted to belong to someone. I even found myself going through my telephone roster and calling people I knew just to have some meaningful human contact. *Little Jumping Joan was still "always alone."* I was also looking for men friends for dating and possible marriage. I did attend one group for Catholic Singles but found it depressing. Those attending were mostly widowed or single women and very few men. The few men at one evening supper all congregated together in one corner. The competition would have been fierce so the whole scenario seemed hopeless. When they did announce that one couple had gotten married it sounded like some-one had won the Jackpot in Vegas. The male president was heard saying that a person could only be complete if they married. This comment and the general atmosphere turned me off to staying with the group, so I stopped going to those meetings.

Later I joined other singles groups and matchmaking services and had several dates. Most of the guys were nice enough but some didn't like the fact that I had never been married. Others were retired and wanted someone who would not be working. Others I rejected because of their very conservative political views. I soon learned that men wanted to date women who were younger so I was limited in choices. Women outnumbered men in the older age group.

Little by little I settled down into Ocean Beach which was a friendly town and with the Pier and the beach so close, I always had a place to go when I felt down in the dumps. The Sacred Heart Catholic Church was also within walking distance, and the library and the stores on Newport Avenue were only two blocks away.

Although actually a part of the city of San Diego, Ocean Beach had its own neighborhood character which was due to its history of retired navy families and the hippies of the sixties. They even still had a People's Store that was pretty much run by volunteers with organic food and other items. This strange combination united once to protest a developer's plan to build a high rise hotel on the beach. Ocean Beach won out on this and even today has never had any building taller than three stories. *Years later I have met persons who said they had lived in San Diego and as newcomers many of them started out renting an apartment in O.B. as it was fondly called. You couldn't go any further west than Highway 8 so that is where they stopped. Even on travels around California it did my heart good to see the elegant seagull sticker on the car's back window with a big O.B. in it. You knew you could talk to the owners and have a friendly and nostalgic conversation.*

I found two good neighbors in the complex. Next door was Eleanor Garrison, a retired lady who was a lot of fun to talk to. She died a few years later. The other was a young woman, Barb Hughes, who was working as a para-legal. She and I had some lively conversations especially about politics. A couple of times we went out together to see a play at Horton Plaza or to the beach. She later married and moved to northern California. In 1986 I met Ramona Anderson on the bus going to Quartzsite, Arizona for the "Hands across America" event. I was surprised to find out she lived only a few blocks away in a beautiful condo on the beach. We became friends and I visited her occasionally in Laguna Niguel where she later lived. Several years passed and she moved to Yakima, Washington. *I must say that one disadvantage of living in California is that the population is very mobile, often moving away, making it difficult to make long lasting friendships.*

I was working at the Pharmacy at Mid City and one day in June, Jean Granquist, the Nursing Supervisor for the County Public Health service in East San Diego, came by to orient a new public health nurse to the resources of the community. After a few introductory remarks, she asked me about my background. When I told her of my public health nursing experience she said she thought she could get me a job with San Diego County. My PHN certificate had finally arrived after several inquiries to Sacramento. After an application process and an interview I was hired to work as a PHN II (a nurse with previous public health experience) in the Chula Vista (southern part of San Diego county) office located on 2nd and Fig St.

San Diego County Nursing

This was an eight to five job with all the benefits of the County system including health insurance and generous pensions. It also paid well. The office covered the whole South Bay area and had about nine PHN's, each with her own desk, phone and district case load.

The position was very similar to the one I had at Tri-County District Health Department in Denver. We each planned our visits on our own but also had to be available for working in Well Baby, Family Planning, Prenatal and Immunization clinics. These latter were very well attended and the lines formed outside the clinic for a block. Some of the home visits were for tuberculosis and venereal disease control and follow-up. The rest were for prenatal and postpartum patients especially the young mothers that needed the most help in parenting skills. As in other bureaucracies we had staff meetings regularly and frequent in-service education programs and had to adapt to whatever was the newest trend. In some ways I was relieved not to have the responsibilities that I had as Nursing Consultant for the Colorado Department of Health. The really difficult cases were those of domestic violence or child abuse.

Occasionally something new would come up, e.g. when there was a case of contaminated cheese or watermelon. We were all assigned to make visits to all the restaurants in our area and have them throw out all their Mexican cheese (the culprit cheese did not come from Mexico but California) and soak it in Clorox so no one would use it. We called ourselves the "Cheese Busters." Later watermelons also had to be destroyed. This was really a job for the sanitarians but they were overwhelmed so asked for the PHN's help. As at Tri-County we enjoyed our coffee breaks, birthdays and other celebrations and it was quite a pleasant place to work.

In September of '85 I was transferred to East San Diego office on 52nd and University (back to Jumping Joan again!) This area served a different population but had similar programs. There were many Southeast Asian refugees living in the area. The staff too was quite diverse with Filipino, African-American, Hispanic, Spanish and Vietnamese PHN's as well as a Laotian aide.

Case Management for the Elderly

In February 1987 I was transferred back to the South Bay Health Center but in a special program for case management for the elderly. By the end of the year I was transferred to the Area Agency on Aging with a contract they had with the Public Health Services. The office was in the City Heights area and I worked with a social worker, Liz Dunasky, and an aide. This was very interesting work and we were able to help a lot of seniors stay in their own homes by referring them to various community helping services. We often made joint visits and decided which one of us would carry the case permanently. If the problems were mainly social, Liz would take the case; if they were more medical I would take the case.

With this arrangement we were able to consult each other when there was a problem. Eventually the program had one other public health nurse, Lucille Bub, working with another social worker. Liz, the aide, Diane, and I shared a small office. I would attend general meetings that discussed issues of providing services to seniors so learned a whole new field of public health.

One of my colleagues from the South Bay office asked me to write down my thoughts describing the role of a case manager for the elderly. I wrote the following article for her:

A case manager for the elderly has to be:

A Sherlock Holmes—who did what, and when and why and putting the jigsaw puzzle together. Ready for anything: situations where people live, their relationships, what they eat, their values, what they will give up and what they won't—some examples: a client who eats, by choice, only toasted waffles and syrup, ice cream and dry cereal; a client who has very substantial savings yet won't spend anything on needed services such as a homemaker or a hospital bed; clients who are "adopted" by neighbors as if they were their own relatives.

Willing to sit on the only available chair, the commode; willing to convince a person that the "rainy day" he's been saving for is NOW; aware that some changes are for the better, such as moving to a downstairs apartment, getting home-delivered meals, having a live-in housekeeper etc.; aware that sometimes a Board and Care placement or a Skilled Nursing Facility placement is not the end of the world or a disgrace to the family.

It means:

Taking time to establish rapport and trust with the client before being able to help him sort out all the various helping people he may have encountered.

Helping clients understand the maze of government programs which can be very confusing, frustrating and full of terms they don't understand.

The frustration of knowing that often the information a client receives is sometimes too late to be useful, e.g. giving away resources to family members thus making them ineligible for certain programs.

Often being satisfied with a less than ideal home situation—especially in the person of the caregiver. Oftentimes, if that person were not there, the available alternatives are few.

Helping the older person face the reality of his physical, financial limitations and those of government agencies, family members and other support persons. Yet, helping them not to lose hope and making the most of what they have of what is available.

Never assuming that relatives will help out or act in a very caring way OR that they won't; that just because a person dresses poorly or has poor home furnishings that he is poor; or that just because a person dresses well and has elegant furnishings that he is rich.

Taking a look into the fridge to see what's there and what's not; giving and getting a hug at the end of a visit; rounding up all the medicines in the home and making some sense out of them so they will be helpful to the client.

Some frustrations:

Calling other agencies, getting recorded messages, being put on endless hold, transfers and told to call back later, leaving a message knowing they will probably return it when you are out in the field, and that when you return theirs, they will be out in the field.

To see family members especially sons and daughters who not only don't come to the assistance of the client, but seldom visit, phone or write. That old disagreements and grudges have often allowed this situation to occur, causing a devastating loneliness and depression.

When relatives do everything humanly possible for the client, and yet the client complains that they don't do enough and want them to be at their beck and call, not considering the many responsibilities they may have.

When doctors don't tell their patients what they need to know to stay healthy, don't listen to their concerns and complaints, or attribute everything to "old age."

Of having to be patient with people who have savings who are indignant that they can't get on Medi-Cal or SSI when they have saved all their life and now have to spend their life savings on medical expenses, whereas they see others who are less careful and hardworking get lots of help from the government.

Of having a client who is confused, disoriented and definitely not mentally capable of caring for himself adequately, but the system has judged him mentally competent, so therefore deprived of needed help.

The loneliness of those who have alienated relatives, friends and neighbors and insist on living alone and yet need socialization so desperately.

Some satisfactions:

Getting and giving a hug at the end of a visit; seeing everything fall into place when needed services are found and utilized by the client.

Of seeing a home that has been a "disaster" turn into a neat and homey place after a homemaker has done a good job.

Of knowing that a client is much safer now that he has a medical alert bracelet and someone to check on him frequently, grab bars in the shower, a wheelchair ramp, home delivered meals or someone to help with transportation.

Of knowing that the client can call back when a crisis occurs and he will be listened to.

<u>To summarize:</u>

Being a case manager is a Jack-of-all-trades kind of job that brings out experiences, resources and education that can all be utilized to the benefit of the client, along with an alert attitude, a caring and sensitive concern and innovative ideas to help a client live a healthier, happier life.

CHAPTER 23

MEETING DAVID

I had signed up for different dating services in San Diego and had a few dates but they didn't work out for me. Finally remembering my ad in Alamosa through "The Mother Earth News" I encountered Andrea Bray and her little newsletter for single seniors, and I paid to put in an ad. Here it is: "Affectionate, romantic, adaptable young lady of 59 is a good listener, politically liberal, self-supporting professional with varied interests. Seeking an educated, non-smoking, caring man with sense of humor for shared times and a possible permanent relationship. #92955.)" She interviewed me at my apartment as she tried to match up people she had interviewed and found one that seemed to have possibilities. One of the ads she pointed out to me was: "Very caring person with active inner child... health professional, 64, 5'5", 134 lbs., into biking, beaches, desert. Like quiet times, natural foods, massage... enjoy sharing what's going on in my life and I'm learning to say what I want and don't want. Would like to meet an independent and colorful lady who appreciates the lighter side of life and love. Encinitas. #92354." I told her I had been a Catholic Sister several years ago, so she thought this candidate whom she had also interviewed might be a good match. She checked out with him and soon I made an appointment to meet David Brooks.

He chose to come to my apartment in Ocean Beach. He wore a white embroidered loose muslin blouse hinting he was probably a New Age type of person. He had a kindly courteous way about him, so I was definitely interested. He didn't seem to be turned off by my having been a Sister. We chatted a while as he told me about his career and what he was doing. When he told me he had taken special courses in therapeutic massage, Touch for Health and Trager therapy, I became interested and he offered to give me a foot massage. It certainly was a good way to connect with me. He was five years older than I. He had been an artist since the age of five and was now working in San Diego at Neyenesch Printers Company.

Over time I learned details of his life. David had been born in Kansas City, of non-practicing Jewish parents of Russian and Polish descent. As a high school student he worked as a delivery boy for Walgreen's Drug Store using his bicycle. His family moved to Chicago and in his last year of high school attended the Newark Fine Arts High School in New Jersey and stayed with an aunt there as his mother had recently been divorced and remarried. From this second marriage his mother had a daughter, Ethel, who later lived in Beverly Hills after her marriage to a businessman. He spent six months attending Art classes at a local Junior College. His first job was as a window dresser in the Ladies Wear Department of a department store in Chicago and became a supervisor of that department. At the age of 21 he joined the Army two days after Pearl Harbor. After some training in drafting at Fort Belvoir he was assigned to the South Pacific for four years as a Tech. 5 clerk, mapmaker and cameraman in the Corps of Engineers. Like many veterans David said little about his experiences in World War II. He did reveal later that he had tried unsuccessfully to commit suicide by taking an overdose of Aspirin. When he returned he was very much an anti-war veteran.

After the War he returned to Chicago. He had various jobs as a newspaper reporter, a radio news announcer and was involved in Labor Union activism and the peace movement. He attended the University of Chicago under the G.I Bill of Rights and received a Bachelor of Arts degree in Philosophy in 1951. He married a classmate, Dorothy Komerska in 1948 and lived in Veterans housing. They had a son Danny and later moved to California. In 1962 the couple filed for divorce. From 1960 to 1963 he attended San Francisco State College with a Master of Arts in Humanities. At one time he had an art gallery in Berkeley, another later in Santa Cruz and one on Haight Street in San Francisco. He taught Cultural History and Philosophy at a couple of Community colleges, one in Florida and the other in Bremerton, Washington. He spent about a year and a half in the 70s backpacking in Europe and Asia visiting major museums in the European cities. He was on a spiritual search and became interested in eastern religions, especially Buddhism. When he ran out of money, he spent about a year in Iran teaching English to the oil workers during the Shah of Iran's regime. He also spent about six months doing art work in Puerta Vallarta, Mexico.

Sometime in the seventies he got word that his son Danny had committed suicide while in the Army in Washington State. This tragic incident stayed with him for the rest of his life. He attended a grief workshop with Elizabeth Kubler Ross, but the Fourth of July was always a sad day for him (the day of Danny's death.) He was also active in alternative medicine in his free time, having attended many lectures and training sessions including one from Dr. Milton Trager whose method of massage was gentler than the traditional Swedish massage modalities. In 1984 he wrote and published a book called *Imagination Factor* based on some of his lectures in Santa Cruz on getting in touch with the "inner child" by use of the imagination.

When I met him he was living in Encinitas and taking a course to be a minister in the Church of Religious Science. I later went to his group's ordination ceremony at La Jolla Cove and attended a couple of his simple services in Encinitas. A few years later he stopped practicing as a minister or attending services of the Church of Religious Science. He had a business in Encinitas as a Wellness counselor discussing nutrition, stress reduction measures and other healthy lifestyles with his clients.

We dated a while and when his roommate in Encinitas left he moved in with me in November of '84. We had a serious relationship and thought we would marry. So he went to the local priest in Ocean Beach to apply for an annulment from his previous marriage that ended in divorce. When this was denied, I began to have second thoughts as I did not want to marry outside the Catholic Church. I did love him for his great qualities, his spirituality, his integrity and how he treated me. We also had common political beliefs and a commitment to a simple life style. He definitely was in love with me, but had to accept the decision when I asked him to leave in June of 1985. This was difficult for both of us. I did see him a couple of times later after he moved to the Hillcrest area. I went with him to Joshua Tree National Monument in November but I could see that our relationship was ended. He then moved to the small town of Desert Hot Springs in the Coachella Valley.

During the time I lived with David in Ocean Beach I had several out of town visitors including three nurses I had worked with in Maracaibo at the University of Zulia. One was Rosario Richemont, one of my former students, now teaching Medical-Surgical Nursing at the University. I had kept in touch with her by mail and occasionally a phone call. Another colleague was Francisca Estrada who later became the Director of the School of Nursing; and another was my former student, Alba Villasmil Guiria, who was also teaching. She was about six months pregnant and came with her husband. They all enjoyed David who correctly predicted that Alba's baby would be a girl. We went to see the historic sailing ship, The Star of India, and later had a champagne brunch at the Casa de Zorro in Balboa Park. I caught up on news from Venezuela—the last I was to get for a while, although occasionally I would phone Rosario.

In 1985 I started seeing a psychologist, Mary Gilligan Wong, herself a former nun, who helped me deal with my breakup with David and other concerns I had. I also attended some group meetings she held for women that were very helpful. I dated some other men but none who wanted to make a permanent commitment. I was proud of myself when I started going to Vacation Village in Mission Bay for their single mixer dances and was able to meet someone on my own without benefit of a matchmaking service. I wasn't too good at flirting but I learned what I had to. I met Leonard Cancilla that way and we dated for a while. He was an easy going pleasant companion, but I was not in love with him. We went to Catalina and several sites in San Diego and neither of us wanted to get married so it was just a dating relationship.

CHAPTER 24

TRAVEL AND OTHER ACTIVITIES

In December I took time off to go with the San Diego Natural History Museum on a trip to Costa Rica. There were 18 in our group with two naturalists. I loved the country and we learned about the natural environment there, visiting cloud forests, rain forests, volcanoes and the beach. We saw ringtails, monkeys, and sloths in the trees and many species of tropical birds. A highlight of this trip was in Monte Verde where the trail signs dealt with generalities about the cloud forest. On the #2 trail sign it described the Quetzalcoatl bird. What a pleasant surprise when we looked up and there in the tree perched the famous and spectacular Quetzalcoatl bird with its long colorful tail. We saw it also in flight. Other birds we saw from the lodge were the motmots and the toucans. When traveling in the bus we noticed the wild impatiens plants growing in the roadside ditches, mostly of a brick red color. *Now I have a large pot on my little porch and as it's on the north side, it sports a beautiful brick red impatiens which loves the shade.*

One thing that impressed me was the fact that Costa Rica did not have an Army but only Civil Guards. This made for a peaceful environment but also gave the country a lot more money to spend on education and the environment. We now see the result of that in the fact that, unlike other Central-American countries, they have never gone to war. We spent Christmas up in Monte Verde where there was an American community founded by the Quakers and then New Years we were back in San Jose and found a disco where we celebrated the new year. We also had a chance to see the jade and gold objects in the city's museum.

San Diego State University was offering a Master's program in Cross-Cultural Nursing, so I applied and was accepted. The only course I took was Anthropology as later I realized that my Master's program credits from Penn were too old. I did a study called "Pregnancy Beliefs in the Mexican-American Community of San Diego" I enjoyed doing this as I believed it might add to our knowledge of how to deal with our Hispanic patients. I got an A on the paper and tried sharing it with various agencies but it wasn't considered important.

My priest brother, Bob, visited me a couple of times as he had been asked to be a chaplain for the Carnival Cruise lines and because the ship left from San Diego he was able to get his way paid. He is a big bicycle fan so had a good time trying some of the more scenic areas like the Coronado Strand.

In 1987 I drove back East to visit family and friends. When I visited my Aunt Mildred she was living in a care facility in Tom's River, New Jersey close to my twin cousins, Ruth and Lillian, where they were available if she needed any help. I hadn't seen them since they were pre-teens in Brooklyn. Mildred was showing signs of forgetting things and had several health problems. The twins informed me that she had left me a War Bond. She had bought one each for the three of us during the War. It was a bitter/sweet memory for me of how much she cared for us. Bob drove back with me and stayed about two weeks. I could never get my brother Herb to visit as he said his wife was afraid of flying.

I heard of a program called Beyond War, a peace group, and attended several of their meetings. We stood in Balboa Park asking people to sign petitions for global peace especially with Russia. Their philosophy was that if we could change the mentality of 20% of the population, needed change would occur. Actually it was about this time that "perestroika" and "glasnost" were popular slogans and soon we saw the collapse of the Soviet Union, so that was an encouraging note.

When I was living back in Alamosa I had an idea for a new product, but as Alamosa was a small town I never pursued it. When I arrived in California I found an ad in the newspaper for a person, Larry Kerby, who would help people with developing new products and patent information. My idea was called "See-Salt" and was just regular salt with a food coloring for visibility. My rationale was that many people oversalted their food because they couldn't see it well. This was true especially for older people. People rarely over-peppered their food because the pepper was clearly visible. Common food items such as eggs and potatoes were often oversalted because of their white color. Some people who were on salt-restricted diets were unwilling to give up salt completely. Some were unwilling to use the salt substitutes on the market. However, if they could actually see clearly how much salt they were using at least they could lower their salt intake. My proposal was to use a red vegetable coloring so it would be acceptable to all.

I contacted Larry Kerby and had a meeting with him. I had written up my rationale for the product and ideas for marketing to doctors and other health professionals. He seemed very interested and he agreed to help me with production and marketing with a 50/50 share of the income from the product. I paid him some money and he contracted with chemists to produce two or three different types of red salt. The one with rhatany root seemed to be the most appropriate. I used to anxiously scan the grocery shelves to see if anyone else had had the same idea. Then I gave him $2,000 to continue with other production costs. For some reason he never followed through and I was unable to contact him again. Unfortunately I never got my $2,000 back. Once I met someone who knew him and who lived in his neighborhood. He knew him pretty well and told me to forget the whole thing with the comment: "You can't get blood out of a turnip." This was another one of those lessons in life I needed to learn. *I still occasionally look for a similar product in the stores but never see any. If any of my readers wish to follow through on this idea, be my guest!* Recently, I decided to make some See-Salt for myself by adding red food coloring to one salt shaker to use on my food, especially eggs and potatoes. I'm sure it helped a little to decrease my salt intake.

My other idea was to organize a system for visitors to San Diego to have contacts with other like-minded people. For example, the spouses of people from other locations who were attending business conferences had already seen the major attractions and were bored with their stay. My system would be called Hobby Match Services or HMS. Hotel concierges, motel managers and others could have a list of people they could contact to see if they would like to meet another person with the same hobby or interest. An example would be for someone interested in gardening would be matched up with another person with the same interest. Another could be for railroad buffs to be matched up etc. I had a long list of hobbies and interests that could be put on these lists. I offered to help with contacting at least two or three people from each category who would have to be available in case of the absence of one person. The concierge or other person would contact the volunteer and ask if they were willing to meet with the visitor. If so, the visitor was given the phone number of the volunteer. They could make their own arrangement for a meeting place. Sometimes it might be just a regular meeting of for example, the Garden Club, or a trip to special places like old historic cemeteries, or a visit to the person's home to see their doll collection. I did not try this idea with any entrepreneurial consultant but submitted it to various tourist agencies, hotels and chambers of commerce. *My idea never really took off but later when I was in the desert I redid my proposal and hoped with so many advances in computer use I would be able to convince people to use it. I presented it to the Palm Springs Convention and Visitor's Center and got a promise to consider it. However, there was a high turnover of staff at the center so there was never good follow-up. I still think it would be a good idea. I wasn't asking for any money but just thought I could help people enjoy their stays better.* Another lesson learned?

In July of 1988 I had decided it was time to stop renting and get my own place so I found a one bedroom condominium on W. Point Loma Blvd. in Ocean Beach. I borrowed $10,000 from Leonard Cancilla for the down payment and paid him $1,000 monthly at 10% interest. My loan was easily approved and I soon moved in. It wasn't as close to the beach but not too far away.

CHAPTER 25

DAVID AND ME

One day in October 1988 I received a call at work from the Sister who works with the diocesan Catholic Marriage Tribunal that handles annulment cases and she told me after further research into his case, that David could now get an annulment. She had discovered that his first wife had been a Catholic but because she married outside the church, that marriage was declared invalid so David could now get married. (David had never mentioned that his wife had been raised a Catholic but never practiced it as an adult.) This kind of shook me up and I had to do some deep thinking. By this time David had moved to Desert Hot Springs near Palm Springs. On reading a page in his book, *Imagination Factor* about the ideal mate, I came to the conclusion that I still wanted to be with him. I contacted him to tell him the news and that I really had missed him and hoped we could renew our relationship. A few weeks later he invited me to visit him in Desert Hot Springs and I stayed a few days. He had bought a new two-bedroom house with a garage and a yard. He was working in Desert Hot Springs at the Two Bunch Palms Spa where he gave Trager massage sessions.

At the Christmas holidays I visited him in Desert Hot Springs and after discussing our options, we were formally engaged at a delicious dinner at the Two Bunch Palms Spa. During the meal he gave me a beautiful diamond engagement ring (we both had picked it out at a Pawn Shop in Indio) along with some other beautiful gifts including a Heart-to-Heart Bear that has a heartbeat if it is held tightly, *(the bear now sits in my rocking chair and strangely his heart still beats when held.)* We made plans to marry soon but I wanted to stay working for the County in San Diego until at least July so I could qualify for a county pension.

I had two bridal showers, one at South Bay Health Center and the other at the Area Agency on Aging. One of the Filipino nurses at South Bay helped with the wedding booklet that I had planned. As we were both older we did not have to go through the six months preparation period required of younger couples in the Catholic Church. On January 28, 1989 we were married in the Ocean Beach Sacred Heart Church at a simple wedding with a reception in the vestibule of the church where we greeted the friends who attended. My bridesmaid was my friend from Sacramento, Sarah Ann O'Gara and David's best man was Lorenzo, a friend he had roomed with in San Diego. Liz Dunasky helped with my wedding bouquet and flowers for the bridesmaid. (I told her she was like my godmother.) Some of the Medical Mission Sisters came and one of them, Sister Jeanette McDermott, read one of the readings, Lucille Bub read the other. Sister Sheila McGinnis had come for a conference from Philadelphia and took photos at the ceremony and later sent me the pictures. Sarah Ann gave us a gift certificate for a professional photographer in Ocean Beach, which we used later.

The hymns I had chosen were "The Wedding Song," and "Morning Has Broken" and at the recessional "Let There be Peace on Earth". *When I first started to list the hymns, I wrote that they included "Amazing Grace" and "The Ode to Joy". Where did these come from? They were included in my funeral plans I had made in Alamosa along with my purchase of a burial plot and gravestone. I had also purchased a plot when I arrived in San Diego. I never wanted to burden others with these details. Both of these plots were later sold back to the cemeteries.* A young woman from the parish with a very beautiful voice sang all the hymns. We then went back to my condo, changed clothes and began our honeymoon.

We had decided to take an automobile trip to Baja California. I offered to do the driving. We took our favorite tapes to play in the car and a few books we could read together. Our first night we spent at the Las Rosas Hotel right on the beach a little north of the city of Ensenada. The dinner was exceptional with a very good jazz band playing. The next morning we spent some time in the Jacuzzi and listened to the piano player.

Then we headed for Agua Caliente on Highway 3. We didn't stop as we had gotten off to a late start, so kept on to the little town of Ojos Negros—way out in the hills. The AAA map had a symbol that we could get gas there but the gas station was closed. Someone told us to go up the road a bit and a man was selling gas at his house.

The instructions were not too clear, so on the outskirts of town we stopped at a house. The lady said to go back to the street the church was on and then three blocks. We did so and a man working in his yard told us to go across the street. A lady there had her young son bring out an open 20-liter drum and siphoned gas into our car. We drove back to Ensenada where we had duplicate keys made so that both David and I could have a set. We also filled up our tank.

We then set out for Estero Beach and on the way we stopped to see La Bufadora, or the intriguing blowhole that splashed everyone at the lookout point as it was high tide. At the Estero Beach Resort we rented a little duplex cottage and walked on the beach and had supper at the restaurant. We visited the little "Museo Nicolas Silva" on the grounds. It had an interesting Mayan collection and cactus and seashells.

The next morning after another beach walk we set out for San Quintin arriving in time for sunset. We had no reservations so stayed at the modest "Motel Chavez" on the outskirts of town. We found out that these small places usually did not have heat so we pulled out our own quilt from the car. On the road at The Costa Azul restaurant David splurged on a huge plate of crab claws. *As honeymoons go, it was a beautiful experience. I found out how much I had expected of David, however, one evening I pulled the blanket as I turned over and he shouted angrily "You took the covers from me!" I felt rejected as I had not intended to cause him discomfort. How could someone who loved me shout at me? I started crying and couldn't stop. David said he had a hard time when women cried and didn't know what to do. He did continue to provide me with Kleenex as I continued sobbing. I remembered that we had both said in our wedding prayer that we would "pledge to each other the gifts of admiration, appreciation and acceptance." I learned that the acceptance part was the hardest for both of us. It took us both a while to fully live out our marriage prayer. We were both pretty independent people. He did promise me, that no matter what he said or because of disagreements, he would never leave me. That calmed me down, as being rejected was one of my biggest fears.*

We continued our travels with a side trip to the ruins of San Fernando mission and on through the Vizcaino Desert. We stopped at Cataviña with its exotic desert plants such as cardon cactus, elephant trees, and the strange boojum tree which looks like a huge upside down carrot (in Spanish called "cirio) and many other better known cacti. We stayed at the Hotel La Pinta in Cataviña where I found a $20 bill in the public restroom! In the morning we looked for the nearby petroglyphs but were unable to find them so continued on to El Rosario and Punta Prieta where we bought some food for a picnic supper. We drove down a dirt road to a small fishing village, Rosallilito, where we camped out on the beach, using our sleeping bag as it was quite chilly. The stars here were spectacular as there were no city lights anywhere and the crescent moon didn't show up until morning.

The next day we headed for Guerrero Negro where we finally got our tourist cards signed (the post at Meneadero was closed). We went to the big marsh and watched the shore birds and the salt production facilities. We stayed at a little room at the Hotel El Morro for two nights as we had plans to take a trip in a tourist motor boat on the Laguna Guerrero Negro to see the famous whales. We watched them blowing and spying so were not disappointed.

Our next stop was the lovely old mission town of San Ignacio founded in 1728 by the Jesuits with many flourishing date palms that had been planted in 1730. Their descendants can be seen everywhere and provide an abundant harvest for the people today. We drove south to Mulegé on the Sea of Cortez where we stayed at a small guest house, Casa de Huespedes Nachita, with the bathroom in a small adjacent building. We visited the very interesting old stone church of Mulegé. In the evening we attended a Carnival Dance but the Carnival Queen didn't arrive until about 10:45 p.m. We watched the dancers and listened to the live band for a while but had to leave early as we were tired. The dance went on until about 2 a.m. After breakfast and a festive Mass the next morning there was a little presentation in the plaza by the local school children.

We drove south to the old mission town of Loreto founded in 1697 on the Sea of Cortez. Loreto mission is the oldest Jesuit mission still existing in Baja California. The sign (in Spanish) reads "Head and Mother of the Missions of Lower and Upper California." Loreto had been the capital of both Baja and Alta California for over 100 years. The first Jesuit mission in Baja was founded in 1683 north of Loreto at San Bruno by Father Francisco Kino but had to be abandoned because of lack of a potable water supply. Sunday was quiet, but we had a delicious fish taco from a street vendor, (this was the kind of taco that inspired Rubio's restaurant's favorite item.) We drove around town and stopped for a drink at the elegant Hotel Mision de Loreto. When we arrived back at Mulegé the Carnival car parade was in full swing so we joined in with the crowd. We spent the next night again at the Nachita. We were now more or less on our way back home, as Loreto was as far south as we went on the trip.

We stayed at the Cielito Lindo Motel in San Quintín Bay and then on towards Ensenada. We took a detour to Colonia Vicente Guerrero as there was an LVN (Licensed Vocational Nurse) from the Chula Vista public health office, Sandy Sterling, who used to go to the clinic and orphanage there. We brought with us some Tempra we had bought in San Quintín as she had requested and gave it to the clinic. She herself did not show up but it was an interesting visit.

We made another attempt to get to Agua Caliente, five miles off highway 3. The manager gave us the key to the one private hot tub and rented us a room at the motel that had about 14 rooms, none of them occupied but ours. There was no electricity and the restaurant was closed so we ate our snacks. I read Rev. Matthew Fox's book *Cosmic Christ* out loud by candlelight. Although David was not a Catholic he did relate to Fox's creation spirituality message which had a touch of New Age and eastern religion in it. Later we soaked in the hot tub. We walked around the grounds and found a small shrine to the Virgin of Guadalupe up on a nearby hill with candles and flowers and a basket for donations where David deposited his extra Mexican coins. I thanked Our Lady of Guadalupe for the great hospitality that the Mexican people had shown us on this our first trip together to Mexico.

We crossed over the border at Otay Mesa. We had travelled over 1800 miles in 12 days. I enjoyed every minute of it, even the little mishaps, but David was happy to be back in San Diego again. I spent the weekend writing thank you notes for our wedding gifts. Soon after, David left for his home in Desert Hot Springs, while I went back to work.

On my return to the Area Agency on Aging I continued using my maiden name. I checked with San Diego County and found out I could retire with exactly five years completed in the beginning of July, but the pension would only begin when I turned sixty-five (1990.) In the meantime, David came from Desert Hot Springs to visit me most of the weekends from February to July. He also wrote me a few romantic letters which made me very happy and phoned frequently. Once he left a message on my phone recorder which I didn't erase but recorded it. He read a poem he had found on a small card: "I love you, not only for what you are, But for what I am when I am with you. I love you, not only for what you have made of yourself, But for what you are making of me. I love you for passing over all my foolish and weak traits that you can't help but see. I love you, for drawing out into the light my beauty that no one else had looked quite far enough to find. I love you." I thanked him for the message and realized I could have sent him the same message as it expressed how I felt about him. I never told him that years before I had read the entire poem and had copied it in a notebook. He kept the card and I found it later in one of his cookbooks. It now is on my fridge, a poignant reminder of his love.

When July approached I put an ad in the newspaper and sold the condo to a local nurse at a profit. As soon as I had cleaned up the condo I packed my "stuff" and was on my way to join David in Desert Hot Springs.

CHAPTER 26

OUR HOME IN DESERT HOT SPRINGS

David's house was brand new, very well built and practical with a wonderful southern exposure that helped warm the house in winter and cool it in summer. He had qualified for a subsidized house loan with the Farmer's Home Administration so the mortgage was quite low. Later we had to readjust the payments because of my additional income. We had a window air conditioner in the bedroom and a swamp cooler (also called an evaporative cooler) for the rest of the house. With the money I had made on the sale of the condo I helped pay to have the front and backyard landscaped with ornamental rock and planted with bushes, flowers and a sprinkler system. We built a large covered patio on the back of the house that later proved a great boon for both of us where we often had our meals and eventually became David's art studio with his favorite north light.

David had already made three wooden vegetable grow-boxes so we soon started planting a wonderful garden with crops planted in February and then again in September. We had to contend with the extreme desert heat of the summer and the almost constant winds which would sometimes kill the little sprouting plants. Most of the time, however, the garden was pretty successful so we enjoyed eating the plentiful crop and sometimes sharing it with others. We even shared our huge 8-foot sunflowers with the many finches that had to stand upside down to get at the seeds from the nodding sunflower heads. We were not prepared for the huge amount of bok choy, as we discovered that just one leaf could make a meal, so in later seasons we limited that crop. One year we also planted hollyhocks that thrived but when we pulled them up later we discovered they had thick 6-foot roots!

We hung a hummingbird feeder on the patio close to the Cape honeysuckle vine. The hummingbirds often entertained us with their feisty personalities. In the dense part of the vine a mockingbird made her nest two years in a row. The mother bird was very territorial and aggressively fought off even the ravens and roadrunners, but wisely left the hummingbirds alone. The roadrunners loved the little lizards in the vegetable garden, and were fun to watch as their tales bobbed up and down. Their pitiful cry when they were courting contrasted with their usual harsh voice. Mourning doves were also common and seasonally we would see migrating birds such as Bullock's orioles and red-shafted flickers—both very easy to identify. Once a Cooper's hawk was seen sitting on the fence and most of the small birds disappeared for a while. The birdbath was much used by the birds for a drink, but the starlings just loved to bathe in it and splash around like kids. We had a pretty high cedar fence that David had built around the backyard, so we never saw any rabbits that might sample the vegetables, but there were plenty in the surrounding open lots, as were the desert quail that needed the bushes for safety.

We planted a mesquite tree that soon produced the edible pods so valued by the Cahuilla Indians. I picked them off the ground, asked David to grind them up in the Vitamix, sifted them and then stored the flour to make delicious high-protein pancakes. A few years later the mesquite tree that I could see from my window served as a model for the logo for my publishing company.

In mid July of 1989 David made arrangements to rent a 22-foot RV that we hitched up to his old Coupe de Ville Cadillac. We learned from the rental agency how to manage the utilities etc. and off we went. We shared the driving, although I asked David to squeeze into the gas stations and other tight spots. David's beautiful Border collie, Misty, accompanied us on this trip. However, a sad thing happened in Desert Center about 50 miles from our home. David tied her up to a caboose next to the restaurant there. She was not there when we came out. We looked all over for her and reported the loss to the local police, but she was nowhere to be found. This was a very sad time for David as Misty was very special to him. We continued our journey without Misty. This trip served as a second honeymoon for us to see some of the Southwest sites and also for David to meet some of my friends.

We traveled through Arizona, Colorado, Utah and Nevada for over five weeks staying at campgrounds. David met Roxie, Courtney, Harriet and other nurses from Colorado. We also stopped in to see my friend Larry Mayer, now married with kids in Alamosa and up to Fort Collins to touch bases with Ron and Karen Phillips. I showed David where I had lived in Alamosa next to the Rio Grande and a quick trip to my favorite getaway—the Great Sand Dunes National Monument *(it is now a National Park.)* We also visited some former Medical Mission Sisters, Phyllis Martin in Pagosa Springs, Colorado and Betty Mantey in Ignacio, Colorado. In Ogden, Utah we stayed with Tony Hanebrink and his wife Diane. In Prescott, Arizona we enjoyed a friendly visit with Lorrain Dauvilliers, a friend of David's and a former French policeman who had lived across the street from David in Desert Hot Springs and was happily re-married after his wife's death.

We both enjoyed Canyon de Chelly and Monument Valley with its fascinating Indian heritage. This whole trip enabled David to get acquainted with many of my friends and he enjoyed meeting them and they all appreciated the visit. It was wonderful for me and I was very happy to be able to share some of my past life with him. Shortly after this trip David sold his Cadillac. About 1994 he bought a used Mazda truck with a camper shell. He kept this for the next three years.

Once settled in Desert Hot Springs we had a big garage sale as we merged our furniture and belongings. I also changed my name to Joan Brooks and settled in to be a married woman. *(This change had an additional bonus in that later when I was writing, my new name was now understood more readily than Joan Jollett without needing to spell it out.)* In December we had a house warming party where the 38 guests were friends of his and co-workers from Two Bunch Palms and some people from the Newman Center. We received a few lovely gifts at this party and I got acquainted with his friends.

Community Involvement and Trips

When I was in San Diego I had attended a conference on Creation Spirituality given by the Reverend Matthew Fox, a Dominican priest. His main theme was *Original Blessing* (the name of his book) that counteracted the emphasis on original sin and the dualistic trends in much of Catholic spirituality. His theory was that all creation was one and he called it "panentheism" (not pantheism) or everything created in God. I had heard about this book from my friend Jane Blewett and of course bought his book and later several of his other books, (David and I read one of them "The Cosmic Christ" on our honeymoon.) At this conference a Father Ned Reidy from Palm Desert was there along with a nurse, Kathy McCarthy, both of whom worked at the Christ of the Desert Newman Center in Palm Desert.

In September I started going to Mass at the Newman Center although it was a half-hour's drive from Desert Hot Springs. It was a small chapel that had practically been built by donations and labor of some of the local Catholics who wanted a friendlier and more participatory type of liturgy and spirituality. A shared Gospel homily was usual and we did not use Missalettes (prayer books with the Mass prayers) but listened carefully to what was read. The hymns were well chosen. On special feast days a group of women dancers enhanced the service. At the Children's Mass the children were invited to sit on the floor around the altar. The interaction with the children in discussing the Gospel of the day gave us some unusual insights. The hymns at these Masses were appropriate for the lively children. I remember hearing one 10-year old boy whispering to his mother "can we come here all the time?"

I often attended workshops there and book discussions. Recovery programs for those addicted to alcohol and drugs were available. One disappointment for me was that I was never successful in introducing some of Sister Miriam Therese's scripture songs to the congregation, in spite of giving tapes to several different choir directors and the priests. David sometimes accompanied me especially to the Healing Masses said by Father Bill Faiella, a jolly Italian-American who often cooked his specialties for the refreshments served sometimes between Masses at the Emmanuel House next to the chapel. Emmanuel House was dedicated mostly to bereavement outreach. Occasionally I had to attend Mass at St. Elizabeth's church in Desert Hot Springs when I had some other engagement on a Sunday. This was a beautiful church and almost always filled to capacity but I loved the smaller more intimate space of the Newman Center.

In the last few years I was in the desert, a group of us that attended the 11:15 Mass decided to eat out afterwards as a social get together. We ended up calling ourselves "The B.S. group" as we almost always ate at Baker's Square. The group would count from about 4 to 15 depending on the priorities of the group. Brother Carl Sternberg, a Holy Cross brother in charge of Spiritual Life Ministries, usually attended, so we had many lively discussions, stories and of course, jokes.

For the Millennium Brother Carl and his committee planned a big event for peace and spirituality. This interfaith event included talks by various ministers and a rabbi. Maya Angelou attended and gave a very inspiring speech on compassion. Demetria Martinez who is a staff writer on mostly Hispanic topics for the *National Catholic Reporter* (a national weekly Catholic newspaper owned and run by lay Catholics) also attended and we joined hands as she stood next to me in the chain of prayer.

That same year Fr. Ned Reidy and Kathy McCarthy both left the Newman Center and the Roman Catholic Church in protest of the Church's stand on women's ordination and other issues. Kathy invited those of us at the Newman Center to her ordination as a priest by a Bishop of the Ecumenical Catholic Church. It was held in St. Margaret's Episcopal Church in Palm Desert and out of friendship most of us attended. A small number of the Newman Center parishioners then attended services at Father Ned's small church but I decided to stay with the Newman Center and hope that changes would eventually come. Some even went to either service or both, whichever was most convenient.

Father Jack McGinnis took over as our pastor. He was a recovered alcoholic and was very active in giving workshops and retreats all over the West. He especially loved the children and they loved him. The Children's Masses were beautiful and appealed to everyone. He wrote his own spiritual songs that he sang accompanied by his guitar. Later he began a project of "Kids for Peace" with a program for children to study peace and non-violence. We still had Father Bill Faiella who was running Emmanuel House. An Irish priest who worked as a counselor for Catholic Charities assisted in some of the services.

It wasn't long before I got involved in a group called The Desert Council for Aging and offered to help put together a resource booklet for the elderly. This involved visiting various agencies to compile information. (*Now most of that information is probably on computers.*) Through this agency I met Lois Jackman, who had post polio syndrome and walked with a cane. She and her husband wanted to open a store in Cathedral City that would provide a friendly non-medical appearing place where those with various handicaps could find what they needed to remain independent. They picked the name "Yes I Can" for their enterprise. The store was set up with the objects placed in the various "rooms" for example, bathroom equipment in a "bathroom," kitchen aids in a "kitchen" etc. As she was new to the area I shared with her my resource booklet and helped her contact various agencies and persons in the health field for her publicity. The business was advertised on TV and radio and soon was very successful. A few years later they opened another "Yes I Can" store in La Quinta. By this time she often had to use a wheelchair, but continued working and was an inspiration for me and for all who came to her store.

I signed up for a lecture on archaeology at the College of the Desert in Palm Desert and was persuaded by the instructor, Anne Duffield, to accompany her and others on a weekend tour at the Desert Studies Center in Zzyzx in the Mojave Desert. This had once been a spiritual and health center near Soda Lake off of highway 15. As we entered the compound we saw the sign at the entrance that Dr. Springer had erected to greet his clients, "The Boulevard of Dreams." Anne took us to visit petroglyph sites near the Cinder Cones and we attended some lectures on archaeology. After this trip I was hooked, and joined the Coachella Valley Archaeological Society, (CVAS) which met in Palm Springs monthly.

I was a member of this organization for the next 15 years and served as secretary for some of that time. We occasionally took trips to local archaeological sites, such as Corn Springs, Joshua Tree National Monument, the Old Lake Cahuilla Fish Traps, and the Indian Canyons in Palm Springs. Guest speakers presented slide shows on Egypt, The Mayan Ruins, The Lost City of Ubar and the Old Incense Road in the Middle East, Greece, etc. The monthly newsletter added to our knowledge as did an annual Symposium with several invited speakers, often with many of the local Cahuilla Indians speaking of their history and traditions. (Slowly I was getting bonded to the desert which at first I thought was barren and uninteresting.)

I learned more about the desert by attending the scheduled hikes by the Palm Springs Desert Museum. These leisurely hikes led by trained guides with pertinent information on the native plants of the area, the animals, birds, local history and geology emphasized the role of earthquakes in the formation of the landscape. While in the desert we experienced two major earthquakes, 7.2 and 7.4, centered about 50 miles from Desert Hot Springs—the only damage was to a bathroom mirror which detached itself from the wall but did not break as it leaned on the sink faucets. A few objects did fall off the top shelf of a bookcase. Later we removed one shelf of that brick and board bookcase to make it more stable and safe. We also assembled an "earthquake kit" in case of a more severe emergency. *Now living at the beach, the earthquake kit serves as a tsunami kit.*

I soon learned of another picturesque area about 10 miles from Desert Hot Springs. The Big Morongo Preserve is unique in that it is a riparian habitat, due to the underground water that bubbles up from the runoff of the San Gorgonio Mountains and is trapped by impervious layers formed by previous earthquake action. The Preserve offered docent training so I signed up for that with Debbie LaMonica, Mike Smiley and Ann Clarke. Mike was already knowledgeable about birds and reptiles so we learned from him as well as from the instructors. We gave scheduled walks mostly for elementary school children. I liked to point out to the children that this was the Indians' "supermarket" with salt grass for salt, yerba mansa seeds for pepper, mesquite beans and wild rabbits for food; cottonwood tree bark for mattresses and diapers; reeds, grasses and palm fronds for their dwellings and baskets. The little water striders and the frogs fascinated the boys, while the girls' favored the wildflowers and butterflies. When I asked them after the walk what they liked the most, they often responded: "the mud," a rare sight for those in the high desert.

In 1992 an arson fire in part of the Preserve charred many of the mesquite and cottonwood trees. However, we all had a lesson in Mother Nature's therapeutics. With more sunlight, native plants such as the moonflower (datura plant) and the wild rhubarb now flourished. The dead branches left in place provided shelter for the wood rats, insects and birds. To help me bone up on the plants and animals I discovered the wonderful *Desert Magazine* (the last issue was in 1985) and spent hours in the library writing down where the information could be found that would help me. I also started to buy back issues of the magazine at swap meets and estate sales so I could eventually have my own collection.

In May 1990 I drove to the San Jose area to visit my friend, Jane Blewett, who was attending a conference there and on the way back visited the Kern River Reserve and Sequoia National Park. California was so full of interesting places to visit and so many botanical bounties and fascinating history. Over time I made trips with Elderhostel to places of natural beauty—Ventura and the Channel Islands, Catalina Island, Yosemite National Park, Death Valley National Park where we hiked in five different canyons and Big Bear Lake east of San Bernardino. I also made a trip to Sacramento to visit my friend Sarah Ann O'Gara and went as far north as Klamath where I stayed at the Hostelling International house (formerly Youth Hostel) close to the beach and explored the various sites in the California Redwoods. On this same trip I took the "Skunk Train" out of Fort Bragg which traversed through the redwoods and on to Willits and back. At Fort Bragg I stayed at a charming old house called Jughandle Inn that had been recommended by the clerk at the Klamath hostel. Here I had a cozy comfortable private room and at the time there were only a couple of other guests. The institution is dedicated to programs that reflect their commitment to preserving the local environment. (Jughandle is the name of the nearby creek.)

Over time on various trips with David or alone I had stayed at the Youth Hostels in Santa Monica, San Pedro, Merced, San Luis Obispo, Santa Cruz, Cambria, San Francisco, Independence, Klamath, Tecopa and back in San Diego at Point Loma. All had their own individual character. The only one I didn't care for was the one at San Pedro—a former army barracks and no character. At an average cost of between $15 and $24 a night it sure helped us save money. Many of the foreign students would often share their country's cuisine with the other hostellers so I enjoyed that too. On one occasion one of the younger people asked David: "Are you somebody?" He strung them along for quite a while and enjoyed the whole episode, leaving them still guessing. On another trip by myself (to get away from the desert heat) I visited most of the California missions, each one with a unique atmosphere.

In the fall of 1990 I bought a used mobile home at the Idyllwild Trailer Park for $10,000. Idyllwild is a small mountain town near Mt. San Jacinto at about 5,000 feet where we could escape the desert heat in a friendly little town. An hour's drive from Desert Hot Springs took us along a very scenic road. There were many forested trails in the vicinity where I could hike and explore. A resident family of three raccoons under the mobile home deck entertained us and we drove carefully to avoid the many squirrels on the road. Acorn woodpeckers drilled numerous holes in the local pine trees to store their acorns. I visited the Idyllwild County Visitor Center just out of town and eventually signed up as a volunteer, mostly at the desk answering questions. I met some friendly people there, especially another volunteer, Diane Robertson, who eventually moved to Palm Springs. Later I met her again at the Palm Springs Writer's Guild meetings.

As I had not yet completed my "quarters" making me eligible for Social Security, I had to keep working. There were no vacancies in Public Health so I tried out for a position with Eisenhower Home Care. After a month I discovered it was too "high tech" and by mutual agreement I was let go. I then found a job as a Health Care Supervisor with a local agency, Health Concepts, in Palm Desert. They provided nurses, home health aides and homemakers to private clients. My task included making the initial assessment and helping the family or caregiver make the decision as to what services would be needed. I enjoyed the work and stayed there from February to May of 1991.

In May I was assigned a young patient with an advanced case of Lou Gehrig's disease. He was on a respirator. A special LVN (licensed vocational nurse) who had cared for him in Sacramento supervised his care. He was a lawyer and living with his well-to-do parents. When the LVN left, I told my Supervisor that I no longer felt I could be responsible for his care as I hadn't worked with respirator cases, so turned in my resignation. As I still needed a few more months of work for Social Security benefits, I asked her to call me for any cases at the LVN level and I would work on an hourly basis at that salary. By March of 1992 I had filled in enough hours to apply for my own Social Security and also Medicare. I was now fully "retired."

David and I had a weekly "date" at home. With either éclairs or cream puffs as a "treat" and coffee with brandy, we listened together for about an hour to tapes of blues and old time jazz. David had heard many of the old jazz players when he lived in Chicago, and was very knowledgeable about most of the players and had an extensive collection. I learned a lot from him how to appreciate all kinds of music (as well as all kinds of art.) Soon I was to be busy with new projects but we never missed our "dates."

CHAPTER 27

AMERICAN DESERT MAGAZINE

I still spent hours in the library jotting down the *Desert* magazine information when one day I said to myself: "someone should try publishing this magazine again." When that "someone" didn't turn up, I decided it just might be me. I spent a lot of time in the winter of 1991 planning and familiarizing myself with the magazine. I went for a week in the dead of winter (so I wouldn't be tempted to go out) in the Idyllwild trailer by myself with some old issues of the magazine and outlined my plans.

I spent the next nine months learning about publishing, printing, marketing and everything I could about the entire business of magazine publishing. I had picked the title of *American Desert* magazine as I didn't want any copyright problems with the *Desert* magazine although the company had gone into bankruptcy. Unfortunately I couldn't find their old subscriber list. Finding good articles about the desert was relatively easy, but finding advertisers was difficult. I visited one of the former printers, Joe Mullenax with Desert Printing and he mentioned Doug Bunn who had once been Art Director for the old *Palm Springs Villager* magazine (now *Palm Springs Life*.) I met with Doug and he helped me understand the business and I signed a contract with him to produce a cover, a logo, a media kit and help with the page layout. We worked together at his kitchen table and sometimes on our patio. I set up a little office in our second bedroom and David kindly gave me his old office desk where I worked.

I met with several other people for advice and suggestions including Charles Shelton, one of the former publishers of *Desert* magazine and Karen Sausman, founder and director of The Living Desert in Palm Desert and Dennis Casebier of the Friends of the Mojave Road in Goffs. They all stressed the importance of advertising. I subscribed to the magazine for magazines, *Folio*. I requested writer's guidelines from similar magazines, and their advertising rate sheets for ideas and format for pricing ads. I still had only my trusty old Selectric II typewriter.

I soon discovered that the local printers were far too expensive for my budget so heard about American Web based in Yorba Linda, in Orange County, California with their main printing press in Denver. Printers outside of California were probably cheaper but I wanted a company that had local representatives that I could meet personally. They sent out a customer representative who was very helpful and answered my many questions. I analyzed the old magazine and used it as a model for format and content. I applied for a fictitious business name or as it is commonly called, a DBA (Doing Business As.) I decided to apply as an individual owner rather than a corporation as that was too costly. I applied for a Home Occupancy Business License in Desert Hot Springs and had to notify by mail every property owner within 300 feet of every side of our house...about 50 owners' names which I obtained from the County Assessor's office. I also had to appear before the City Planning Commission. Our next door neighbor, an elderly woman, objected to what she thought would be hordes of cars and visitors to our home. I listened to her at the hearing and held my breath. Later my application was approved as I had explained that most of my business would be by mail or phone.

I paid for a post office box number and bulk rate postage, had my own business phone, FAX and a separate business account in Wells Fargo Bank. Later I paid for a toll-free number and the setup for taking credit card orders. Bob Larsen, a printer's broker, arranged for the printing of my stationery and helped Doug with designing beautiful ivory colored business cards. I also had special gift cards and envelopes made to send to those receiving a gift subscription. I applied for an ISSN number and registered with the Library of Congress and had to send them two copies of each issue. A UPC barcode was sent to American Web to be printed on the magazine so it could be sold by retailers and on the newsstands.

I drew up lists of possible places where I could sell the magazine. I was very disappointed to discover that the National Parks, including Joshua Tree, Anza-Borrego Desert and Death Valley (all "desert" parks) could not carry "commercial" magazines. I'm sure I would have sold many at these sites and probably could have increased my subscriber list. American Web referred me to a regional distributor, Russ Warner, who would sell to the wholesalers, who would sell to the newsstands and stores. I would receive 40% of the net sales of copies actually sold; the wholesalers received 20%, the retailers 30% and Russ 10%. If I sold directly to a retailer I would receive 60% of the price. Only about 20% of the books sent to retailers sold, so it wasn't as profitable as it might sound. Russ later proved to be a valuable friend. He often didn't get paid for up to five or six months after the sale and I often had to wait for months to be paid, although sometimes he sent me an advance payment when I asked. The magazine also included a prepaid insert envelope for a subscription. This was done by Bob Larsen's company and sent to American Web.

I began doing some detective work trying to find writers who had contributed to the old *Desert* magazine. I spent a lot of time on the phone and in the library on research. I began visiting typical desert sites, such as Death Valley, petroglyph sites, Joshua Tree National Monument, the Eastern Mojave Desert, Anza Borrego Desert State Park, and other places often mentioned in articles in the old magazine. I joined the Friends of the Mojave Road based out of Goffs off Highway 66, the Mojave River Valley Museum in Barstow, The Mohahve Historical Society in Victorville, the Death Valley Natural History Association, The Shadow Mountain Gem and Mineral Society and visited the Palm Springs Historical Society. I was fortunate to get small free notices in their newsletters to tell their members of my plans. These were the best sources for my subscriber list. I mailed out promotional letters to anyone I could think of as a possible subscriber including my own Christmas list (I wrote a "Christmas in July" letter.) David kindly helped with folding, stuffing and stamping envelopes. My antennae were up for good leads on new subscribers and also for new stories or new twists on old ones.

I planned to have each issue contain one article on plants, one on animals, one on geology or gemstones, one historical article or ghost town story, one on Native American culture, one on a desert personality, several book reviews, small news items, letters to the editors, an editorial and hopefully some ads. In later issues I added a "Kid's Corner" written by Cheryl Jeffrey's son Paul. The entire focus had to be on the desert with no "travelogue" articles, poetry or fiction. The cover would be in 4-color and always a desert scene. I finally decided on a bi-monthly magazine priced at $18 a year with individual copies at $3.95. I had hoped the magazine would be out for the end of 1992. I had decided on a print run of 10,000 copies. Some copies were mailed directly to Russ and others ended up in stacked boxes in our garage. I got pretty good at carrying the heavy boxes of 150 magazines to wherever needed.

When I went to the local *Senior Lifestyle* newspaper I was given the name of one of their ad agents named Ted Pal. I met with him along with Doug and we discussed how we would operate. He would be getting a 25% commission on each ad. We met with him several times, but he seemed to have the idea that only a full-page ad or maybe a half page would be worth his trouble. Doug had designed a beautiful "media kit" to present to prospective advertisers. On my own I obtained a few classified ads from people I knew, but I thought Ted would be able to do better with his experience. After many meetings where he talked a lot about a "data base" it finally became clear to me that he wouldn't get any ads. I tried many other people who offered to help but they never followed through. I had counted on a minimum of a few pages of ads, but everyone I talked to complained that their budgets were spent out, or the California economy in 1992 was pretty dismal, or they would wait until I had a higher readership. I realized that my readership did not appeal to those who had the money. I even did a few complimentary ads, hoping that maybe after the second issue they would pay for an ad. That never happened. Only American Web helped with a free back cover, the cost of which they deducted from my bill.

With my own savings and a few early subscriptions I had received, the first issue came out in November of 1992. What a thrill! It had a beautiful front cover of the Palm Canyons that I had obtained free from the Palm Springs Convention Center and a back cover by American Web with a picture of Mark Twain and his ideas on humor. The front inside cover was a color photo of the old *Desert* magazine headquarters in Palm Desert. It was now LG's Steakhouse, so I had Doug airbrush the photo with an accompanying blurb headline: "Two Great Traditions, Good Food and Good Reading." Later we tried to contact the owner again to pay for an ad but to no avail. The inside back cover had a full-page ad for the Friends of the Mojave Road for membership in their group.

Cheryl Jeffrey from the Coachella Valley Archaeological Society contributed an article on the Cahuilla Indians. Mike Smiley, my colleague as a docent at the Big Morongo Reserve, wrote one on the desert tortoise. Dennis Casebier of the Friends of the Mojave Road told the story of the old Goff's schoolhouse that wouldn't die. An English lady, Pat Rimington, whom I had met at the Joshua Tree National Monument, described the history of homesteading in the high desert. Another CVAS member, Al Pennington, wrote a lost treasure story and Katie Barrows, a naturalist that had taught us at Big Morongo Reserve, described the strategies for survival of desert plants. A friend of Katie's, John Purcell, provided a profile of Gary Paul Nabhan who wrote several desert books including his most popular, *The Desert Smells like Rain* and was the founder of Native Seed/Search in Arizona. Glenn Vargas had written for the old *Desert* magazine and he sent me two articles, one on geodes and the other about the flash flood he and his wife encountered on their trip to get married in Quartzsite. A local historian, Francis J. Johnston, referred to me by the Friends of the Mojave Road, wrote a fascinating article on the mysterious murder of Herman Ehrenberg at Dos Palmas near the Salton Sea. A local Sierra Club leader, Bern Schwenn, wrote a beautiful description of the old Indian trails in the Coachella Valley complete with maps. I usually requested the authors to include their photos or slides as well as maps when appropriate.

The first issue had five book reviews and a cartoon by a Desert Hot Springs artist, Buzz Gambill. Later I also had some cartoons by Jim Willoughby of Arizona. My editorial explained how I came to publish the magazine and a map of the four western deserts. Five small classified ads helped a little and a column of three ads did too, but I had to work harder! I paid the authors only three cents a word and three copies of the magazine. They seemed happy to get published and that was all I could afford. I paid more for the photos that I usually returned to them. Occasionally I used my own photos or those from the National Park Service that only requested that I include their source. Two of the covers were by Jon Stewart who wrote several books on desert wildflowers. (I had to pay for these as he was a professional photographer.) Another cover was a gift from the desert artist, Bill Bender, and one from the National Park Service. My first editorial read:

At last, I am happy to tell you of a dream come true! Some years ago when I left Colorado, I turned eastward and then, like the pioneers of old, ever westward until the road ended at the Pacific Ocean (literally at Highway 8 and Ocean Beach.) I spent many hours alone on this long, three-month journey, and viewed one beautiful landscape after another. A question kept haunting me. 'What do I *really* want to do?' I felt this vague urge to share with others some aspects of the beauty and history of our wonderful country; so much of it unnoticed, unappreciated and unsung.

I had to earn my living at an eight-to-five job, but I often spent weekends exploring the surrounding region. One month after I arrived in California, I became a volunteer at Torrey Pines State Reserve near La Jolla and derived some satisfaction leading nature walks on the trails through the chaparral and on the cliffs overlooking the sea. Some time later I married, moved to the desert and stopped working.

At first, this was a difficult time as I missed the ocean and the bright greenery; but gradually I began to look around at my new desert home and found it intriguing with its own more subtle beauty and mystery. Again I became "bonded" to the area by volunteering at the Big Morongo Preserve. I began to do some reading to learn more about the plants, animals and history of the desert. Among the most informative and fun-to-read articles were those in the old Desert magazine. How I wished there were more! I said to myself: "Why doesn't someone publish the magazine again?" Friends remarked to me that they would like to see a magazine on the desert again. This vague wishing went on for a while until one day it dawned on me: "Why don't you?" So, I decided to do it. The dream began to be fulfilled nine months ago...the usual time for a baby to develop and then see the light of day...when I began seriously taking on the task of publishing American Desert in the tradition of the old Desert magazine. It has been a labor of love and more fun than I've had in a long time. I've had much to learn and in the learning, I have gone down many a blind alley, but I have had help along the way from many people who believed in my dream.

Now, I am asking your participation, dear reader, to keep this dream a vibrant and enduring reality. I welcome your comments, suggestions and, of course subscriptions and advertising as well. I invite you to send in your desert stories and photos. You are all a necessary part of my dream. Let's share the dream together in our enjoyment and love of the great American Desert.

When I received the first copies I invited some friends and those who had helped to a small party at our house to celebrate with me the re-incarnation of the old *Desert* magazine. All seemed happy to see the results of my efforts.

Other aspects of the business included setting up a subscriber list, printed address labels, keeping a ledger of income and expenses, paying California sales taxes which required having a Resale Certificate, and paying annual income taxes. I kept a scrapbook of activities and reviews and my own personal notes of contacts by phone or interviews for future reference. I received many "queries" from eager writers as I had advertised in the *Writer's Market* magazine. I answered their requests for writer's guidelines and if I had to refuse a manuscript, I gave them a reason and suggestions where they could possibly publish their articles.

The readers received the first issue with enthusiasm. By November of 1993 I had received subscriptions from desert lovers in 44 of the

United States and five foreign countries. My final subscription list was about 1250. I also sold copies to about 30 public libraries. I went the rounds of the Coachella Valley hotels, motels and museums and sold to about 35 different gift shops in their establishments. I had less luck with book stores, such as Barnes and Noble and Brentano's as they said they had to go through a distributor. I usually referred them to Russ but never sold any in the area.

By the second issue, and definitely by the third, I was discovering the huge cost of magazine publishing. Although I was the only employee (unpaid) of the business, I had to pay my contractors, Doug Bunn, Betty Wallin and Bob Larsen and later Nicolette Sundberg. Printing, especially 4-color was very expensive. Doug Bunn, an old-school Art Director, had to send his copy to Desert Printing for typesetting which meant I also had to pay them. He wasn't familiar with the computer and the more modern pre-press system. By the third issue I contracted with *Desert Business Journal* and they did the pre-press after Doug turned in the "boards." They were difficult to deal with and overcharged me so I wasn't very happy with them. I had met Nicolette Sundberg through a previous contact at a Small Business Administration conference and she told me she could do pre-press for magazines as she was doing one for "Art Scene" and had done several for the real estate business. She was not an artist, so I kept Doug on as retainer to help with drawings and other art work. Nicolette worked well with American Web sending the galleys on a Zipdisk and helped me find a good photo service locally at a discount. She helped me put out the 4th and 5th issues without any problems. I paid her by the page at a very reasonable price.

The second and third issues came out quite well and I made the payments on time. I had plenty of manuscripts I could publish, but by the fourth issue I cut the 4-color pages to 8 instead of 16 in order to save money. I also changed to a cheaper paper. As I constantly needed more money, I decided to take out three of my annuities which came to over $11,000. *This decision gave me a much smaller income than I could have for my retirement, but at the time I was willing to make the necessary sacrifices.* I had a total of seven credit cards that enabled me to borrow advances when I needed to.

As time went on and the needed ads still weren't coming in, I sold the mobile home in Idyllwild at a loss for $7,000. I also sold my Ford Tempo and turned it in for a much cheaper older Monte Carlo so that helped a little. My old cross-country skis and ski boots were the next to go which I sold in Idyllwild at the same price I had paid for them in Boulder. Other small items such as some clothes and binoculars I managed to sell at consignment shops or pawn shops. In June of 1993 I noted I had $21 in my business checking account. I was making only the minimum payment on my credit cards. I even got a special list of about 20 local philanthropists, including Walter Annenberg, who appreciated the natural beauty of the desert and mailed each a special letter requesting financial help. I never received even a negative reply or inquiry from any of them. I asked my brother Herb if he could help with a loan but he was concerned about his wife's income if he should pass away. Both my brothers told me "you'll either go bankrupt or be on welfare."

The fourth issue had a very peculiar problem that gave me a lot of trouble. The monthly code number on the UPC barcode was "04" when it should have been "06" so the distributors returned them at my expense. I had checked the bluelines (the last proofs before printing) and missed that error because I was thinking the "04" was for my 4th issue, but the numbers referred to the month of the year and should have been "06" for June. This error did not affect my subscribers' issues or my local retailers. I gave 1,000 copies of the second issue to one of the booths at the Gem and Mineral Show in Quartzsite in order to publicize the magazine among the visiting rock hounds. It had an article about opals so I thought it would catch their attention. Promotion and complimentary copies amounted to another 2,500 free copies. There was no way that subscription prices would ever cover the costs of printing and related costs unless I had substantial ad revenue.

About March I started looking for either an investor or a co-publisher and then later for someone to take over the publishing. I must have contacted over 20 magazine publishers with similar interests but they all seemed to be having economic problems as well. In June 1993 I found Ed Brand's name in "The Publishers Representatives

Directory" and signed a contract with him to help with advertising. Unfortunately it was too little too late as I did not have the funds to continue. When I had to break my one-year contract with him, the penalty was for $5,000. I paid him back in small monthly payments for the next ten months.

Before we printed the fifth issue, Russ Warner had told me I needed a more readable logo for the title and also some cover lines or blurbs on the front cover to indicate to the newsstand customers what was inside. The original logo was very artistic but for some people was hard to read so with help from Nicolette I came up with the Hobo font for that issue and found a front cover picture with enough space to put the blurbs on the front cover. This might have helped a little if I could have continued publishing, but I had hit rock bottom. I was unable to publish any more issues so I sent new subscribers back issues as best I could and told others I was no longer publishing at this time and returned any checks for renewals.

In March of 1994 I had met Ray Shadwick, an advertising sales-man who heard of my plight and thought he could take over the publishing and I could stay on as editor. We set up a legal contract whereby he took over the rights to the magazine. In May of 1995 I resigned as editor as he had not yet come up with a real plan. I still had the rights to the old copies and the income from their sales. By December 1995 I turned over the subscription list to him. He never followed through to this day.

I finally realized that this was really the end of my dream to resur-rect the magazine of the desert. It took me about the next two years to pay off all the credit card debt, but at least I never went bankrupt. It was a huge disappointment to me and my subscribers and friends. The magazine business is very difficult. I often read in *Folio* maga-zine that a certain magazine folded up because they had less then 50% ads. I think if I could have obtained even 5 pages of ads, or about 10% I would have been able to make it. It was like when we used to play Pinochle in college. After our team lost we always managed to say "if I only had..." I learned many lessons from this venture, including how to bounce back from failure; how to live more simply and later discovered that the whole experience had many benefits

I could not even imagine at the time. As the magazine had been listed in *Writer's Market* I received many free copies of desert related books for possible review. I kept most of the books as they were very interesting and informative. I think that by this time I could say I had really "bonded" to the desert. I had also enjoyed the project immensely.

Several of the old *Desert* readers had asked me about whether anyone was ever going to index the articles from *Desert* magazine. As before, I asked myself the question and decided I could do it with some help. I had already tried once to copy the content pages from magazines that were at the San Bernardino City Library, but this did not constitute an index. After a few false leads I discovered one of my subscribers, Tom Budlong, was also a computer expert and wanted to help. At first we had a few other collaborators but eventually decided it was best if just the two of us did the work. I went to visit him in Los Angeles in August of 1994 and we came to an agreement on what we wanted in the index and how we would share the costs and income (50% each.) The California Room Librarian at the San Bernardino City Library, Chris Shovey, suggested we make a separate category for maps as she always had readers, mostly rock hounds, requesting maps. The map section ended up being 11 pages of three columns each and was much appreciated by all. Tom found specialized software and came to our house to show me how to input the information on disks for each issue. At this time I did not have a computer so David let me use his. Each issue took about an hour and a half to input all the needed information. Sometimes it took a little longer as I started reading the whole article. Then I would send Tom the finished disks and he would eventually combine them with the ones he did and made a master disk to be put in book form in alphabetical order.

We shopped around for a publisher and were fortunate to find the Arthur H. Clark Company in Spokane, Washington. They published many popular western books so we thought it a good deal. Tom did most of the negotiations with them and we were promised an 80% royalty on the list price (which might be lower than the actual price of the book.) We were doing all the promotion, thus the generous royalty. It ended up being a 525-page hard cover book,

8 ½ x 11 with an old prospector with his burro as the logo on the cover. It covered 534 issues including my own five *American Desert* issues. We included an introduction on how to use the book, a note by each of us, a grid with the dates of all the published issues, a short history of the various publishers of the magazine over time and a brief biography of the founder, Randall Henderson. We decided together with the publishers that $65 would be a reasonable price for the book and we requested they print 500 copies. Tom kindly took care of all the bookkeeping involved and dutifully sent me a check when the books started selling.

It took us almost three years (the same three years that I was working on *Desert Padre*) before the book saw the light of day in October of 1997. We were both very pleased with the result, and so were the readers. *Since then the book has sold out and now is a collectible on Amazon.com. Recently a member of E Clampus Vitis, Neal Samson, contracted with Tom and me to reprint the Index and has since been published under his own name. He paid us a royalty of $7,000 which we shared equally for all the books at once, so that was an added bonus. From the trials of my experience with "American Desert" magazine I soon learned the truth of an old proverb: "When God closes one door, He opens another."*

CHAPTER 28

DESERT PADRE

Meanwhile back at the ranch—David had bought a Mazda pickup truck with a camper shell and in July 1994 we decided to take a road trip to visit the Eastern Sierra of California, mostly following Highway 395. Neither of us had visited that area before. As I usually do before taking a trip, I checked out the maps and found three places along the way that caught my attention. The first one was "Father Crowley Memorial" on Highway 14 near Inyokern, the second was the "Father Crowley Vista Point" on Highway 190 which leads to Death Valley and the third was Crowley Lake 30 miles north of the town of Bishop and close to Mammoth Lakes. We set up our tents in the forest west of the town of Independence to enjoy the natural beauties of the Sierra. We visited the Eastern California Museum in town and I discovered a panel of photographs and clippings regarding Father Crowley. What really intrigued me was a small typewritten note that stated that Irving Stone, the famous biographer/novelist, had written an article entitled *Desert Padre* about Father Crowley in the May 1944 issue of the *Saturday Evening Post*. Given the popularity and prestige of both Stone and the Post I came to the conclusion that Father Crowley must be a very interesting man.

When I returned home I called Bill Michael, the curator of the Museum, and asked him to send me a copy of the article if he had one. He obliged and then I was hooked as it seemed like a story that needed to be retold in more detail. Reinforcement came when I found another article entitled "Padre of the Desert" in the old *Desert* magazine by Margaret Phillips, wife of the photographer in the town of Bishop who had taken Father Crowley's last photograph. As I was still in the mode of publisher/editor, I thought it would make a nice article for a magazine.

This was how it all started. Like Topsy, it just "grew." I spent the next three years doing my research on his life, learning the publishing industry, writing the book and putting money in a savings account every month so I would be ready when printing time came. My next venture was to accept an invitation by Deacon Burns of the Santa Rosa Church in Lone Pine, Father Crowley's parish in the Sierra. The church was celebrating its 75th anniversary and had invited many parishioners and other old timers to a big dinner. I met with one of Father Crowley's nephews (his brother Frank's son, Frank.) He was there with one of his young daughters. Several old timers had little stories to tell me of the Padre (a name he gave himself and was used by everyone who knew him.) I even had a nice conversation with Irene Brichaga who had been his secretary in both Fresno and Lone Pine. As the Padre had died in 1940 it was not always easy to find people who remembered him.

Later I visited one of the parishioner's homes and she showed me some clippings in a scrapbook of newspaper photographs and also some human-interest columns written by the Padre himself. Frank Crowley had some articles kept in scrapbooks too but no one had a complete set of these "Sage and Tumbleweed" columns written by Father Crowley under the pseudonym of "Inyokel." I knew these would be a treasure trove. Frank Crowley gave me the name of Bishop Harry Clinch, the retired Bishop of Monterey-Fresno who had known Father Crowley when the former was just a high school student in Fresno. He told me to contact the Archives department of the Fresno diocese to see if they still had the bound copies of the old *Central California Register* (the diocesan newspaper) where Father Crowley's articles were first printed. I drove up to Fresno to talk to Fr. Perry Kavookjian who was the Chancellor of the diocese, director of the Newman Center and also the diocesan archivist. He took me to the room where the archives were stored and eventually we found the issues from 1934 to 1940.

At first Father Perry copied some few articles for me but then wrote to say he was just too busy. I talked him in to letting me come up and pick up the seven volumes and took them home promising to take care of them and return them when finished. I took the large bound volumes one by one to Kinko's and copied every "Sage and Tumbleweed" article (about 200.) This was not always easy as some of them were in the "gutter" of the binding and impossible to copy, so I resorted to writing those few words at the ends of each line by hand. When they were all copied, I carefully wrote the date on each column or continuation page and filed them in chronological order. When I had the *Central California Register* volumes I also checked the various news items for anything that gave me a clue to what was happening in Father Crowley's area and times. Later I filed these columns differently by topic as I started putting the book together. I hate to admit it, but it was actually about nine months before I could return the volumes to Fresno. I didn't report to them that while copying at Kinko's, one of the volumes slipped to the floor and cracked the dry binding. I had to pay $50 for a professional rebinding job.

When I did visit Fresno again I received permission to have access to Father Crowley's personnel file where I found copies of his application to the seminary and other personal information and letters.

Bishop Steinbock of the Fresno diocese gave me written permission to reprint these columns and other information garnered from Father Crowley's files. Father Perry also gave me a 1993 copy of the Catholic Directory (which covers the whole United States) and the latest copy of the Fresno diocesan directory. These two volumes helped when I tried to contact priests and others who may have known the Padre.

References were made in the files to an article the young John Crowley had written in the Catholic weekly magazine, *America*, about how he had decided to enter the seminary. I figured the best place I could find old copies of *America* was at the Catholic University of San Diego. I had to look very carefully as it turned out there was no title to it and no author, so I went methodically through the 1914 and 1915 issues. In the education section of the September 5, 1914 issue was an article "Autobiography of a Student's Soul" but it was unsigned. All the indications as to the author pointed to John Crowley. It was quite a long article and gave me much material for the book.

Another hint came in one of his columns where he mentioned the financial help he had received from the Catholic Extension Society. Knowing he would probably have written a nice thank you note, I called their magazine editor and asked them to see if they had anything about a California church they had helped in the period of about 1919 to 1924. They did some research although they did not have an index for their articles. The one entitled "In the Footsteps of Junipero—By a California Missionary" was also unsigned but definitely told the story of his little church in Lone Pine with a few photographs. This article was dated April 1922 and gave me the information I needed for his early years in Lone Pine.

I contacted Monsignor Francis Weber, the Catholic historian for California. He told me that Father Crowley had written an article entitled "Inyo, County of Contrasts" for the Los Angeles diocesan newspaper, *The Tidings,* dated August 8, 1924. This elaborated in a different way his work in Lone Pine.

I found out from Frank Crowley that Father John Crowley's youngest brother George had been a Jesuit priest teaching at Los Angeles High School and later lived at the Jesuit community house in Los Gatos, California. I called the Jesuit archivist there, Brother

Tom Marshall, who had personally known Father George before his death. He gave me some information and a copy of an unpublished manuscript, entitled *Desert Padre* that Father George had written about 1950 that was a fictionalized story written for young boys who might consider becoming priests. Throughout the book he introduced "Father Considine" with some of the incidents from the Crowley family life. (The Considine family was definitely the Crowleys.)

As Father Crowley had been pastor also of the Death Valley area, I thought it might help if I attended the fourth Death Valley History Conference held in February 1995 at the Death Valley Visitor Center. Here I met Lou Pracchia from Ridgecrest who mentioned he had been thinking of writing the life of Father Crowley. He had some papers given him by Father George whom he had met a few years before his death. He was President of the Upper Mojave Historical Society and also a member of the Ridgecrest Knights of Columbus, whose branch was named "The Father John J. Crowley Council." Some time after this meeting I was able to visit him in Ridgecrest and he shared with me some photos and especially an unpublished "Sage and Tumbleweed" column that described something that had puzzled me—what was the mysterious illness that afflicted Father Crowley in 1933? The column was the key and helped a lot as I had been thinking he might have had either tuberculosis or a nervous breakdown. His illness was neither of these (you'll have to read the book to find out the rest of the story.)

Father Crowley had three Sisters who became nuns so I contacted the Sisters of Mercy in Burlingame, California and was fortunate to get a short obituary from 1988 of two of his Sisters, Alice and Pauline, as Sister Petra and Sister Paula. This provided more family stories and a lovely poem written by John Crowley for his two young sisters.

Then I decided to see what information I could glean from his Alma Mater, Holy Cross College in Worcester, Mass. The archivist there kindly copied several issues of the *Holy Cross Purple* monthly magazine and the 1915 Yearbook, *The Purple Patcher*, which added greatly to my story of the young John Crowley. I asked them to send me a good copy of his yearbook photograph. I contacted his seminary, St. Mary's in Baltimore, for information on his seminary days.

I wrote to the Worcester Public Library and the two local Worcester newspapers that gave me more small items to add to my store.

I made an appointment with the Eastern California Museum and obtained letters and other information on Father Crowley, Ralph Merritt and the Inyo Associates as well as permission to use some of their photos. (This was now beginning to shape up as a book and not an article.) Another place I contacted was the Laws Museum in the town of Bishop. The Library there was Father Crowley's old church in Bishop. At first I had to go to the city of Bishop Library to obtain microfiche copies of the old *Inyo Register* and the *Inyo Independent* in hopes of finding news items I could use. This was very tedious work but fortunately the bound copies eventually ended up in the Laws Museum so I could access the material there which proved invaluable. They also had some very good photos that I used. I found more information from the county library in Independence and the small branch library in Lone Pine.

When I attended the 4th Death Valley History Conference in February of 1995 I networked with many desert historians and others who gave me good leads as to where to find more information. Blair Davenport, the curator of the Death Valley National Park, found some very useful material for me about the time that Father Crowley was chaplain for the CCC (Civilian Conservation Corps) at Death Valley. She also gave me a copy of a photo of the Padre at Shorty Harris' grave in Death Valley. Here I contacted Steve Esteves' daughter, Pauline Esteves. Steve was a Basque stone mason and had married a Timbisha-Shoshone woman and their daughter was Pauline. Steve had helped build Father Crowley's cabin at Whitney Portal. (He also did most of the beautiful stonework at Furnace Creek Inn at Death Valley.) I interviewed Pauline and she took me to see her father's grave on top of a small hill near Furnace Creek where other Timbisha-Shoshone Indians were also buried. (This site is usually off limits to the general public.) Pauline is still an activist in issues concerning her Indian tribe.

I met Ted Faye who has since produced a couple of excellent videos on Death Valley and he referred me to Ted Goodwin, the son of the former Superintendent of Death Valley who had been a close friend of Father Crowley's. He told me the two were very good friends and he remembers seeing the light on in his father's room late into the night when the Padre was visiting.

Another museum, The Maturango Museum in Ridgecrest had some items about Father Crowley and some photos as well. Their interest arose mostly because of the fact that he died close to Ridgecrest and that the local Council of the Knights of Columbus was named after him. The Knights also took care of the memorial cross where Father Crowley died and later even the monument on the road to Death Valley, both of which had been frequently vandalized.

Once I realized how much information the local museums had, I thought maybe the Searles Historical Society and Museum in Trona might have something. There I met George Pipkin's daughter, Margaret Brush. Her father had written a book, *Pete Aguereberry* with a whole chapter on Pete's contact with Father Crowley. Pete had been a famous Basque prospector in Death Valley and at one time a partner of Shorty Harris (a whole other story with a Father Crowley connection!)

Later the Mojave River Valley Museum in Barstow provided me with some photos of Father Crowley's parish church in that town. I also visited Randsburg, another one of his earlier parishes, and picked up a few items of interest and spoke to some local residents who remembered him. Randsburg still has the only church left where Father Crowley was the pastor—all the others have been torn down or moved to other sites.

I searched just about everywhere for more information. I investigated every name mentioned in the "Sage and Tumbleweed" columns and I tried to contact that person or at least a relative. I obtained an Eastern Sierra phone book that helped in this task. Many people said they didn't know Father Crowley but then gave me the name of someone who did.

I took a trip to Pasadena to meet with Sr. Petra Berg, (she had been referred to me by Bishop Clinch) who had helped Father Crowley with catechism classes in the summer. Her father had known Father Crowley as he had been contracted for heating projects at his parish and at the Dow Hotel in Lone Pine. One of her brothers sent me a paper written by their father recounting his meetings with the Padre. Sr. Petra gave me other names, all of whom helped fill in the picture. One was Irene Gage Sundberg who had also helped Father Crowley with the summer school catechism classes, so I visited her in Pauma Valley in northern San Diego County. She told me the story of how Father Crowley had helped her get through the tough days of Nursing School at Mercy Hospital in San Diego. She gave me a photo of Father Crowley and a postcard that had the architectural plan for the Padre's dream of the All Souls Memorial, a church he had hoped to build in Death Valley that would honor all those who lost their life in Death Valley.

Pauline Aigner, (her father in-law owned a repair garage in Lone Pine) who had lived in Lone Pine during the Padre's time, gave me the name of Claire Dueker, a doctor's wife who had lived for a while in the rectory apartments that the couple rented from the Padre. She lived in Washington State but sent me a beautiful letter with many reminiscences of the Padre.

Jim Price had written articles about the Yuma and the Clifton train depots for my now defunct *American Desert* magazine. I discovered that his mother and father were school teachers in Lone Pine and had also boarded at the little apartments at the rectory. His mother had written an article for the old *Album* magazine about the "Wedding of the Waters" with photographs she had taken with her new little Brownie camera. This event of October 1937 which was organized by Father Crowley was also reported on in his "Sage and Tumbleweed" columns and in local newspapers and magazines.

I contacted Msgr. Pointek in Tehachapi and he provided interesting details about Father Crowley as he had once been pastor in the town of Bishop. He had listened to his inspiring sermons at the Cathedral when the Padre was in Fresno.

I went to the County Clerk's office in Independence and requested copies of Father Crowley's probate file. Arlene Grider kindly found it and also gave me a copy of the beautiful poems about the Padre written by a local poet, David S. Bromley.

Through a letter to the editor I saw in *The Album* I contacted Marian Brooks who used to own a cabin at Whitney Portal and who was familiar with Father Crowley's cabin near hers. She gave me an old photo of the cabin and some names and phone numbers and eventually I was able to meet Eric Jessen from Laguna Beach. His father had a cabin at Whitney Portal and Eric took me to a friend's cabin that used to be owned by the Padre. I was very touched that his little stone altar was still intact, although the cabin had burned down (at least the wood part of it) back in 1953 when George Palmer Putnam's widow was living there. This of course, led me to reading a couple of Putnam's books where he mentions the cabin when he first bought it and also another book that told again the story of Steve Esteves and Father Crowley. (Putnam, the famous publisher, had once been the husband of Amelia Earhart.)

The present day Dow Villa Hotel is where I often stayed in Lone Pine. When I was soaking in their outdoor Jacuzzi, I realized that this land and the adjoining motel were the former location of Santa Rosa Church, Father Crowley's parish.

The owners, Lynne Bunn and Jeanne Willey kindly let me reprint the panoramic photograph that was hanging in their lobby, dating from the thirties and included the old hotel and the church.

I was interested in finding out more about a close friend of the Padre, Ruth Cornwall Woodman, who had been the New York script writer for the old radio *Death Valley Days* sponsored by Pacific Coast Borax of Twenty Mule Team fame. Father Crowley had made several suggestions for her to look into a desert story or interview a person involved in the history of Death Valley. I discovered from a reference in Richard Lingenfelter's book, *Death Valley and the Amargosa* that the collection of her papers was in the Special Collections Library at the University of Oregon in Eugene. I was able to obtain a few scripts, correspondence and later a copy of an unpublished article she had written about the Padre for the *Reader's Digest*, "My Most Unforgettable Character." I also made contact with a friend of her son, Bill. Bill and Art Rath had put out three booklets about Death Valley that I found at the Death Valley Visitor

Center. As Art informed me that his friend Bill had died suddenly in December of 1995, I was not able to contact him directly.

Sooner or later I knew I would have to tackle the Los Angeles Department of Water and Power story which was probably the most difficult chapter to write. I did contact their P.R. person, Chris Plakos and Dave Babb who was a local writer, but eventually had to resort to reading several books on the L.A./Owens Valley history and their water problems. The best objective book I could find was *Water and Power* by Dr. William Kahrl who generously let me quote from his book.

Pat Roberts from Lone Pine was the daughter of the local pharmacist, Ben Baker, who used to supply the Padre with free medicines for the poor people in Death Valley and elsewhere. Pat gave me the name of LaVonne Foust Harrison who contributed a touching story about her childhood in Cartago and a visit in the hospital from the kind Padre when she had broken a leg playing baseball. Pat generously loaned me her empty mobile home for three nights when I was in Lone Pine. I met many other people from Lone Pine, Independence and Bishop that gave me bits of information that added to my store. These contacts and others from different areas are mentioned in the acknowledgment section of my book, *Desert Padre*.

I copied articles from various books, magazines, newspapers and newsletters to give me a better idea of his standing in the local community. I ate, slept and dreamed about the Padre. *If I had been hooked up to the Internet at the time I probably would not have had to do so much detective work, but then I had a lot of fun, met or talked to a lot of great folks on the phone and I loved doing the research.*

You may guess that I had begun to keep notebooks similar to the ones I had with my *American Desert* magazine. Eventually there were over 1,200 pages of research notes and phone calls regarding *Desert Padre* and a whole new set of files. Later I kept a large scrapbook with newspaper clippings of reviews and book signings and other events related to Father Crowley and the book. *Many copies of my resource material, including copies of the photos have been donated to the Eastern California Museum in Independence.*

Simultaneously with my research I also studied book publishing, and bought the book *Complete Guide to Self-Publishing* by Marilyn and Tom Ross and found it very useful. I also gave a lot of thought to the future marketing of the book. I applied for another DBA, this time Mesquite Press, the name of my own publishing company. (Sitting at my desk and looking out the window, the little mesquite tree was my inspiration.) David contributed the pen drawing of the mesquite tree that is on the cover. I had special forms printed for those who wished a copy of the book for possible review.

I realized how little I really knew about book publishing, so in October 1996 I contracted with Marilyn and Tom Ross especially for them to find me a reasonable and competent printer, a cover artist and help with a marketing strategy. I did not contract for editing or proof reading or distribution of the book. I had heard of Marilyn from the COSMEP organization that helped writers and publishers and had recently gone out of business. She later founded two organizations, "Small Press Association of North America" (SPAN) and "About Books" which was her consulting firm. This arrangement was not cheap but I thought it best to go to the experts. I met them personally at a Writer's Conference they gave in Palm Springs. In September 1997 I attended one of their SPAN workshops held in Berkeley that offered many useful ideas on marketing. *During one conversation I discovered that Marilyn Ross had once worked in the small town of Saguache, Colorado, a town I used to visit frequently in my consultant role with the Colorado Department of Health... small world! Now in Imperial Beach and a volunteer at the Tijuana River Estuary I met Debby Good, one of the Park rangers who once lived in Saguache when she was a young mother. Very small world!*

I again worked with Nicolette Sundberg who kindly lent me her old Mac Plus computer and printer. She signed a contract to work at $12.50 an hour and I trusted her to keep careful record of her time spent. Painstakingly, I inputted all the text that ended up being 401 pages when it became a book. I put these on disks that I gave to Nicolette who transferred them to her more modern computer. She and I worked together on typeface, fonts, page layout, chapters, headings and many other details. Much of what I had wanted I found in certain books in the library, for example, I used Richard Lingenfelter's book as a model for my notes and bibliography format. I got ideas for the format for the table of contents from other books I had looked at in the library. With a combination of three different maps and some computer magic Nicolette put together a useful map at the beginning of the book which depicted the Padre's territory.

I did not ask her to do editing or proof reading, but decided to do it myself. This meant spending about 30 minutes at a time and going over each page until they were all done. (I found that more than 30 minutes would result in boredom and inattention to mistakes.) I must have repeated this process about 30 times so as not to miss any typos or other errors. I used the dictionary and *The Chicago Manual of Style* to check punctuation, capitalizations, indexing, notes etc. I am proud to report that so far I have not found any typos.

I asked five people to take a look at the first draft and they gave me some helpful suggestions. These were: Willma Gore, who writes children's books and gives classes on creative writing, pointed out some grammatical errors; Alice Bell, a friend who had written an article for the *American Desert* magazine, addressed issues of reader interest; Phil Brigandi, a historian I had met at Death Valley, checked some of the historical material; Kathy Barnes at the Eastern California Museum made some suggestions about the Owens Valley and Ann Marie Cousineau, a newspaper reporter, helped me avoid long sentences and extra words (like this one, for example.) Of course, I was fortunate that much of the book consisted of Father Crowley's own words so I did not need to edit those, just proof read.

I got permission from Irving Stone's widow to use a few phrases from his article for which I had to pay a fee of $250. (She originally quoted the price of $500 and after I told her I was a new publisher she lowered the price.) Fortunately, other authors just gave permission without asking for payment. Nicolette helped me arrange the photos I wished to use in the book, some of which I had to pay for. One was a photo I had seen on a calendar (Bishop Clinch had told me about it) on display at Simonian Farms in Clovis. This featured many historical photos of Fresno County. One showed Father Crowley at the Fresno train station greeting Babe Ruth and Lou Gehrig in 1927. They had come for an exhibition fund-raising game for the Fresno diocese. When I inquired about the photo I was told I would have to go to the Image Group, a professional photography company that had bought all of Claude Laval's work. The negatives were still unsorted in numerous drawers but they promised to look for the photo. Eventually they found the negative. *Several years later they even found the person, still living, who as a young boy was pictured with the baseball handed to him by Babe Ruth!*

With a little detective work I discovered that Charles Shelton, who had been a publisher of the old *Desert* magazine, had taken a photo of Father Crowley saying Mass on the top of Mt. Whitney. It had been published in the *L.A. Times* in a report on a photo contest. The photo won a prize for the most unusual photograph. As I had met him before, I visited him in a board and care facility in Palm Desert and he was happy to find out that the photo he took as a journalism student at USC in 1934 was now being used. He had no idea at the time of the identity of the priest or the server. I told him the priest was Father Crowley, or the Desert Padre, and the young man serving the Padre in the photo was a young seminarian, now Bishop Clinch, also in a residential facility. When I told Bishop Clinch about the photographer, the two of them had a friendly phone conversation. Most of the other photos were from the various museum collections and I only had to pay for the cost of duplicating them. Nicolette had the great idea to run the Padre's drawings of the "Wedding of the Waters" at the foot of each photo page. These drawings were also used on the bookmarks I had printed.

Early on I asked Bishop Clinch to write an introduction to the book. He was getting on in years and his eyesight was poor but he hand wrote a couple of first drafts. I felt badly about rejecting his first effort, but he had written a nice summary of the Padre's life, so I had to tell him that was MY job. I asked him to please write about his first encounter with the Padre and the effect he had on his life. He very humbly and willingly changed it to the beautiful story that is now the introduction. When I talked to him on the phone, he said

"I'm down on my knees praying I'll live long enough to see the book in print." He sent me an envelope marked "Morale Booster" and inside was a check for $1,000. I was very touched and of course, put the money to good use.

Only after the book was printed did I actually meet him in Santa Cruz. He was happy to chat a while with David and me and told us a few other stories about his younger days as a priest and some of the more comical and outrageous aspects of the Crowley family get-togethers. I found him to be a very warm and simple man. He told me he used to be a Harley-Davidson motorcyclist, so later on a trip to Bridgeport when the group was having a rally, I bought him one of their patches. He was so pleased and told me how he used to enjoy riding and other sports. He actually bought about 20 books for his friends and relatives (another morale booster.)

I asked Alice Bell help me set up the Index. A little advice to writers—do the page numbers for the Index at the very last minute, as a minor change in the book format requires changing the page numbers. I made this mistake so we did it all over again. The index is ten pages of two columns each, so it was a chore. Doing it alone would have been even more of a chore.

Finally the sequence of the chapters enfolded as I wrote and my plan for the book was complete. I only included the columns that I thought would be of interest to the general reader. The "front matter" consisted of the map, the title page, the copyright page, a poem by David S. Bromley, Table of Contents, Introduction, Foreword, Preface and Notes to Readers. The "back matter" contained the Notes, Bibliography, Acknowledgments and Index. At Marilyn Ross' suggestion I added an order form just before the back cover.

I sent Marilyn Ross my pencil drawing sketch of how I wanted the cover to look. Although not an artist, I wanted to make sure the title was easy to read at a distance both for the front cover and the spine. I sent her a copy of the photo of Father Crowley that most people were already familiar with and decided on the title of *Desert Padre: The Life and Writings of Father John J. Crowley, 1891–1940.* (I wanted to make sure the readers understood it was about a modern "Padre" and not one of the eighteenth century missionaries.) I decided to include the little logo for Mesquite Press on the back cover along with the "Sage and Tumbleweed" logo and a small photo of myself with a short bio and a review of the book. The bar code and price of the book also had to be included. The category of "Biography/American History" appeared on the top left corner. Marilyn Ross had a professional cover artist do two different draft covers and I chose the one that Marilyn recommended with brown, tan and green colors. I also made some minor changes on the format of the back cover. (Later I realized I should have had some pre-publication reviews or comments from well-known persons to add to the prestige of the book, but....) I decided on a trade paperback or soft cover as a hard cover would be much more expensive, both for me and for many of the potential buyers.

After the pre-press disks were completed and all the photos were lined up with captions and credits and put on one 8-page signature, we sent everything to Marilyn Ross. She contracted with a well-known book printer, Bookcrafters, now known as Sheridan Books, based in Michigan. I included a hard copy along with the disks. I set the price at $19.95 that was a little lower than the price of most books that size, but I wanted to make the book accessible to all. I decided on a print run of 3,000. (I had a print overrun, so the total was actually 3,192 copies.)

It was a few months later in July 1997 that we received the first copy of *Desert Padre* and I was thrilled with how it turned out. SPAN offered its members a 58% discount for shipping with one of their vendors, which definitely saved me a good deal of money. I ended up renting a small storage facility and met the trucker there where he kindly helped me store the 111 boxes of books, 28 copies in each box. Each box weighed about 43 pounds—easy enough to put in the car, but more difficult to get out. (This was one of my main types of exercise during this busy period.)

Publicity and Promotion

As I had already received some checks for the book, I was kept busy signing each book, adding a bookmark, stuffing it in a bubble envelope, using my special mailing label and mailing it on to the individual. David again helped me pack the books. I kept a ledger of each purchaser, made out an invoice and also a "purchaser form" that included information on how the person heard about the book and any other pertinent information that might prove useful later. Individual books cost me $1.58 to mail at first and later $1.78. I was kept very busy mailing copies and also working on contacting potential retailers. At the end of six months I had sold 851 copies and my income was a little over $11,000. Of course I now had to pay some of that for the California sales tax and postage, but it was very different from the situation with my magazine. Once I had paid the printer and all the pre-press expenses, the rest was relatively smooth sailing. This time I was able to pay off my credit cards in one year.

Other expenses were organization dues as I belonged to SPAN and then joined the Publishers Marketing Association (PMA) and later the San Diego Publishers Alliance. Another benefit of the SPAN membership was a big discount for a subscription to *Publishers Weekly* and their free monthly magazine *SPAN Connection*. PMA also published a helpful free monthly magazine. Attending publisher's conferences was important so I went to one by SPAN in Los Angeles and one in San Diego by PMA. Here the topics were mostly on how to save money and tips for marketing books. Networking with others with similar problems and solutions was very stimulating. My publishing company was listed in the annual directories put out by both SPAN and PMA. The book was also listed in *Books in Print*. I attended the California Library Association annual Trade Show. It wasn't too successful as far as selling books, but I learned how the system worked and met interesting people.

I advertised in several magazines and newspapers but discovered they were not bringing in the readers. The notices in the small newsletters fared better and of course, meeting with interested groups was even better. Over time I sold copies to about 50 retailers, 15 museums and historical societies, 30 libraries and 16 wholesalers. Not all continued to order after an initial sale but when I turned over the distribution in March 2003 to Community Printing and Publishing located in Bishop there were still 55 retailers and wholesalers on the list. I sold to retailers at a 40% discount and to wholesalers at a 55%

discount, standard for the industry. I made the decision not to offer any discounts to individuals. Sometimes I gave a book to someone who really wanted it and couldn't afford it.

Another opportunity for me arose with Amazon.com. Their Amazon advantage.com program was offering a 55% discount on each book sold on their website. Their website allowed a book review by a well-known book reviewer, a photo of the book, author biography, short description of the book and even a reader's book review. This was not very lucrative but it did help to publicize my book and had enough sales to find it helpful. They also paid every month for the previous month sales, which was nicer than my experience with wholesalers of my magazine. Now they are also selling used books of *Desert Padre* at various low prices. (So, dear readers, if you want a cheap book, just try Amazon!)

I had postcards made of the book cover with information on the reverse side. A simple bookmark with the quotation taken from the monument to the Desert Padre at the "Father Crowley Vista Point" on Highway 190, added to the publicity portfolio. I collected the photos I had used in the book and others and made a slide show of about 75 slides. I did not have a specific script but adapted what I would say to my specific audience. I started two months after the book came out with my first book signing and slide shows—the first at Mountain High Video and Books in Bishop and the next day at the Dow Hotel in Lone Pine. The Dow even advertised on their marquee "Desert Padre-Sunday 2–5 pm. Meet author." Several members of the Berg family attended as well as others who had contributed information for the book. The local newspaper, the *Inyo Register*, covered these two events. I sold 57 books at these two signings so was off to a good start. I always gave out the postcards and my business cards.

A few weeks later I rented a table at the Lone Pine Film Festival and sold 28 books there. I had made a large poster showing events in Father Crowley's life and films mentioned in his "Sage and Tumbleweed" columns. It was a welcome treat to meet a Hopalong Cassidy "look-alike" and then show him Hopalong's picture with Father Crowley. The "look-alike" wore the same outfit, gun and holster as in the photo taken in 1937! It didn't hurt to have a little basket of individually wrapped candy on the table. I also had bought attractive bookstands and signs with the price of the book in case people hesitated to ask. My custom was to sign "Enjoy" and then my name. However, if the customer wanted a special message I gladly wrote that. These three events were just the first of many more slide shows, talks and book signings all over southern California, the Sierra region and Death Valley. I was even invited to a few public schools to give a talk to the students on writing and how to do research on their favorite person. I didn't have much luck with Catholic churches but I did give a talk at a Presbyterian Church in Palm Desert that was very well received. Unfortunately, Catholic bookstores were not very interested in buying the book, as they would ask me, "Was he a saint?" When I had to say "no," they decided it wouldn't sell. I did sell to a few Catholic bookstores but none reordered. One kindly bookstore owner told me honestly "Catholics don't read." That really depressed me.

I wrote up a promotion letter mailed to about 500 individuals and retailers just before Christmas inviting the recipients to buy the book as a wonderful Christmas gift. I did mention previously that my failed *American Desert* magazine had some unexpected rewards. One was my old subscriber list, as I reasoned that anything with the word "desert" in it would get their attention, so I wrote a special P.R. letter to about 800 of them, some with an attached hand-written note. This mailing had about a 6% return, a good percentage for direct mailing. Later I paid for a list of all the Catholic seminaries in the United States and sent a letter especially written for them. I also sent a special letter to every Catholic Bishop in California with a few responses.

I had one unexpected and interesting experience. A man wrote me inquiring on the cost of 20 books to be used as gifts at Christmas time and the cost of the postage. I dutifully took 20 books to the Post Office and got the total cost. I wrote to him with the information and asked if he wanted me to autograph the books. He wrote back, a little disappointed that I did not offer him a discount and wrote "no need to autograph the books, you're not the famous one." I thanked him for his order and refrained from writing him that most people would love to have a book signed by the author and that unfortunately "the famous one," Father Crowley, was presently unable to sign the book. I cried all the way to the bank as he ended up buying another four copies!

I continued with various forms of book promotion and attended publishing conferences. In 1999 I joined the San Diego Publishers Alliance that held meetings once a month in San Diego. I enjoyed the networking of the group and always learned something useful. In 1998 I was asked to give the "Author's Breakfast" at Stovepipe Wells for the Death Valley '49ers annual rendezvous. A year later I presented a paper and slide show (along with 14 other authors) at the Fifth Death Valley History Conference. I gave a summary of the Desert Padre's life but focused mostly on his connections with Death Valley. The proceedings were published later. Since then I have attended two more Death Valley History Conferences. It seems that the stories will never be fully told as something new and fascinating turns up each time.

In September of 1998 I got a call from Harry Pallenberg, research assistant for Huell Howser's TV program called *California's Gold* that played on California public television station KCET. They had been researching a story about gourds and their different artistic uses. They heard of Jeanette Whitehair who was painting gourds in the Lone Pine area. She referred Huell Howser's researchers to the Eastern California Museum where the gourd that was used for the "Wedding of the Waters" (a chapter in my book) was displayed. Bill Michael, the curator told them about how Father Crowley had used this gourd for the "Wedding of the Waters" event that celebrated the realignment of the Death Valley Highway 190 from Lone Pine to Death Valley. They had contacted various other persons who in some way were connected to that event in 1937 and I was asked to be a resource person. I gave them the names of some contacts and more information.

We all showed up in Lone Pine for a three-day weekend for the actual filming of the television program. There I met the cast of characters: Cheyenne Casado who carried the gourd from the waters up near Mt. Whitney to Whitney Portal; Gabe Fogarty, the grandson of a Lone Pine rancher Russ Spainhower who had known Father Crowley, carried the gourd from Whitney Portal down to Lone Pine;

Governor Merriam's granddaughter, Florence Cross in the stage-coach; Hopalong Cassidy's widow, Grace Boyd at the bank vault; a descendant of the Breen family of the Donner Party, Barbara Boyd, in the ox cart; Ted Goodwin, the son of T.R. Goodwin, former Superintendent of Death Valley National Monument in the plane; Chester (Bill) Best, the son of a former superintendent of the talc mill at Keeler; Mr. Brewer, the owner of a vintage '38 Ford Lincoln Zephyr; Myron Alexander who was a railroad buff at the old train in Independence; Ray Powell, a local Korean War pilot; and Slim Hernandez, an old timer at Keeler. Bill Michael was also involved as a resource person and a few other local people, such as Petrina Rich, Joy Anderson and Burl McElroy who remembered the celebration.

We started out at Whitney Portal where the filming started, then down to the town of Lone Pine. From there we went out towards Keeler on Highway 36 to the Dolomite Road where the wind blew ferociously, but provided an authentic picture of the obstacles for stagecoaches, covered wagons and mule teams. We stopped at Keeler to feature the train station. As there were no more trains here we had to detour to the historic Slim Princess train at Dehy Park in Independence where the railroad buffs blew the whistle for us and clanged the bell. We then drove to the new part of Highway 190, stopping at the Darwin Cutoff where the '38 Ford Lincoln Zephyr drove by cutting the ribbon across the highway. (The original version included sharpshooters from the Los Angeles Police Department shooting the ribbon instead of cutting it.) We continued on to Stovepipe Wells where Huell Howser, Ted Goodwin and the pilot flew over Badwater and emptied the gourd. It was a reenactment of the original event as much as possible.

Working with Huell Howser was not like filming for a Hollywood movie. We had no script nor even any idea of the kind of questions he might ask, so I spent some time re-reading the chapter on the "Wedding of the Waters" in my book so I would be prepared to answer any questions. At Panamint Springs we were all treated to a nice lunch and when the filming was completed, a pizza party back in Lone Pine. I spent some time in the motel talking to Grace Boyd and she was very grateful for the copy of the photo of Father Crowley with Hopalong at the bank. It was one she had never seen before. The Donner Party descendant, Barbara Boyd, invited me to visit her at her home in San Juan Bautista, which I did a few months later. We had all enjoyed the occasion and everything went quite smoothly.

Huell Howser was soliciting sponsorship for the video as the three-day event had been quite costly. It took until February of 2000 before U.S. Borax offered to sponsor it with a short commercial at the beginning of the video. I was offered two complimentary copies and it has been shown on Public Television occasionally. As it turned out to be a one-hour video, it is not shown as often as some of his "California Gold" series as the other programs are usually only a half-hour. *Recently I discovered that the town of Peapack, New Jersey and the name I called my toy drawer as a child was an old Indian name meaning "marriage of the waters." In some strange way Peapack previewed the "Wedding of the Waters." On a trip to Lone Pine in the summer of 2010 I was surprised and pleased to learn that civic minded citizens of the town had planned and executed a beautiful mural on the side of the El Dorado Bank picturing the Wedding of the Waters. There were about twelve local artists who painted the different episodes and others who helped raise the money for the mural. I was fortunate to be present for the dedication.*

Another spin-off of the publicity about the Desert Padre was that the town of Bishop was in the process of painting murals on the walls at various locations in the town. These murals depicted images of the old pioneers, the sheepherders, the ranchers, and other well known personalities or events from the early days. The Bishop Mural Society decided on putting one up to honor Father Crowley. I got in touch with the artist, John Knowlton, and shared as many photos as I could of the Padre. It took a while but eventually it was completed on the side wall of Z's Flower Shop in Bishop on Church Street just opposite the local Joseph's Bi-Rite Supermarket. The flower shop is just off Main Street on the west side and the mural can easily be seen if coming from the north of town. Incidentally the owner of the flower shop had once been a waitress at the old Kitty Lee restaurant in Bishop where the Inyo Associates used to meet and she knew Father Crowley. It was very tastefully done and even included his two dogs, Cuff and Trey.

The Santa Rosa Church in Lone Pine dedicated the Parish Hall to the Padre with a sign above the entrance—"Father Crowley Parish Hall." An alumnus of Holy Cross College, Bill Webster of Bakersfield, heard of the book and wrote a very nice 9-page article on the Desert Padre with photos for the Holy Cross Alumni magazine. Later, on this same theme, I'll tell you how his home-town of Killarney, Ireland honored him.

As I kept attending writers and publishing workshops and meetings, I found many were interested in the fact that I had self-published my book and wanted more information on the process. I wrote a concise little 16-page booklet entitled *Self-Publishing Basics* which I offered for sale at $5.00 each. I tried to focus on the business aspects of self-publishing, rather than the writing aspect. I usually was asked to give a short talk on the subject so it was not difficult to sell the booklet. I think it was helpful for some writers. Nowadays, it's a lot easier as we have Print-on-Demand or P.O.D. which makes self-publishing a lot easier and cheaper than regular trade printing as the number of copies printed can be very small and economical and then more copies can be ordered as needed. It seems especially useful for those writing memoirs, family histories or business manuals that need to be updated frequently.

CHAPTER 29

HOME FRONT

When we still had the Mazda camper in 1993 we took a trip to Afton Canyon off Highway 15 on the road to Nevada. It was in conjunction with the annual meeting of the Desert Protective Council. In the evening around the campfire we watched the little kangaroo rats beginning their night of foraging. They seemed quite tame as they scampered about on the ground before us. I was thrilled to see the bed of the Mojave River abundantly filled with desert willow trees in full bloom.

David and I took a trip in the camper to San Felipe on the Sea of Cortez in Baja California in June of 1994. Our next door Mexican neighbors introduced us to one of the married sons who lived in Mexicali but worked most of the time in California. He offered to put us up overnight so we could have a break on the way. His wife gave up the only bedroom for us and treated us to a real hearty Mexican breakfast. The two small children called us "abuelito and abuelita" or grandfather and grandmother. The bathroom was an outside privy. The road from Mexicali to San Felipe is well-paved but narrow and passed through interesting territory—the Laguna Salada, the delta of the Colorado River and the San Pedro Mártir mountains to the west. We had no reservations but drove around and finally found a nice seaside campground, Playa Laura, with a raised deck where we could put our stuff. Actually we ended up using our sleeping bag on the sandy beach.

The next couple of nights we stayed at Ruben's Trailer Park. Restrooms were provided and all the restaurants and shops were within walking distance. What a treat to have grilled shrimp coming straight from the sea and huge glasses of freshly squeezed orange juice at Rosita's, the last restaurant on the "malecon" or seaside street. As opposed to the fairly cold Pacific waters, the Sea of Cortez is much warmer and easier to enjoy the swimming there. San Felipe has one of the highest tides except for the Bay of Fundy, so at low tide we had to walk a long way to even get wet. We had purposely picked June as it was just after the Memorial Day holiday weekend when the college students love to take a Mexican break and the place is overcrowded.

We returned on the highway that crosses the San Pedro Mártir Mountains and past Ensenada and crossed the border at Tijuana. David loved San Felipe so we took another trip in December of 1998 but this time we no longer had the Mazda camper so we stayed in a small motel near the beach. Unknowingly, we found ourselves there for the weekend of the Mexican patronal feast of Our Lady of Guadalupe so I had a chance to watch the festivities next to the local church. They had constructed a very high wooden tower that they used to set off fireworks. It was called a "castillo" or castle. Lots of noise, lots of home-grown music and lots of food too!

That weekend we drove south past Santa María and on to Puertecitos over a very rough and rocky road. (David always said: "Joan never saw a dirt road she didn't like," —a true statement.) Many Americans had vacation places along the way and at one small restaurant I bought a painting from a local American woman that depicted the Sea and the San Felipe lighthouse high on a promontory with a palm tree below. We went again to San Felipe for a few days in April of 2003. Another time I had the opportunity to visit San Felipe alone on a promotional tour of El Dorado, an American enclave just north of San Felipe. I was tempted to buy a lot there as they were priced quite low, but somehow just living with only Americans didn't appeal to me if I were thinking of having a place in Mexico.

In September 1994 I had made a trip to Lone Pine regarding my research on Father Crowley and when I arrived home, David was in the hospital with Valley Fever (also known as San Joaquin fever or coccidiomycosis). Fortunately his doctor was a good diagnostician and soon had him quickly on the road to recovery.

David had made friends several years ago in Sri Lanka with an Austrian couple, Nino and Isabel and their young daughter Julia. They paid us a visit in 1995 so we took them to see some of the special places in the desert such as the Living Desert in Palm Desert and the Indian Canyons. Another friend, Alexandra, a French woman from Paris whom David had met in San Francisco, visited us the year before. She was teaching English with the Berlitz people in Paris. Both these European friends invited us many times to visit them but we never did. That same year one of my classmates, Julie Wood, from Trinity College came by with her husband Bill and we visited the Anza-Borrego Desert to enjoy the spring flowers.

One day in May 1995 David had gotten out of his Mazda truck and left the passenger side door open. All of a sudden his beloved dog, Misty, showed up and jumped into the seat. He was overjoyed that after six years, she returned. It was really a mystery where she had been and how she had returned. It was a joyful reunion. Shortly after we took a trip in the truck with Misty along to a campground in Lake Isabella as the wild flowers were blooming. Later we took another camping trip with her to Big Bear.

David was walking Misty in our neighborhood in August and she pulled too hard on the leash and David fell down. He tried to get up and was holding on to a drain pipe at an empty house across the street. He called to a young man passing by to knock on our door and let me know where he was. The young man carried David across the street and laid him on our couch. David did not want me to call the ambulance but I insisted and he was taken to Eisenhower Hospital where X-rays showed a fractured hip. David had been diagnosed with severe osteoporosis several years before so it came as no surprise. After having hip pinning surgery, rehabilitation and physical therapy he returned home. A few months later he had to have another operation and this time the surgeon performed a hip replacement.

Now it was my responsibility to walk Misty a couple of times a day until David recovered. As Misty was an energetic dog she was always anxious to be out and one day she dug her way out from our backyard, even though we had put large rocks around the fenced area. In January of the next year we both decided she needed a place with more freedom, so we gave her to a neighbor who seemed interested in having her. Soon after David sold his Mazda truck and we only had my car. After the surgery David at first managed with a walker, then a cane and then without any assistive device. However in May 2003 he fell while adjusting some bricks in the front yard. He did not break any bones but thought he had just injured a muscle in his right thigh. At first he used a walker and went to a chiropractor for pain in the muscle but the pain did not go away. He never had another x-ray taken. His walking was pretty limited. He was still able to get in and out of a car and could drive, but the pain persisted.

CHAPTER 30

MOTHERLESS DAUGHTERS

As a member of the Small Press Association of America (SPAN) I obtained a deeply discounted subscription to *Publisher's Weekly* which had numerous reviews of books that would soon be published. In

1995 I read previews of a book by Hope Edelman entitled *Motherless Daughters*. This piqued my curiosity so as soon as it came out I got a copy of the book from the Palm Springs Library. After reading it, I contacted an office in New York where a group was beginning to offer counseling sessions to motherless daughters. The focus was mostly on those who lost their mothers before the age of 21, which certainly fitted my needs. They gave me the name of Laurie Lucas, a counselor in Costa Mesa (Orange County) who was beginning to offer these group sessions and I signed up for them. Fortunately I had a friend, Ramona Anderson, who used to live in Ocean Beach and now was living in Laguna Niguel. (I had met Ramona on the bus going to Quartzsite where volunteers formed a connecting chain holding hands in the Walk across America to help with aid to Africa.) The sessions were being held once a week in the evening, so I stayed with her each night after the eight sessions, so managed to attend each one.

These sessions were held in a small conference room with ten persons sitting around a large table with Laurie Lucas presiding. Laurie had lost her mother at the same age as I did, so I felt she would understand. Each session had a topic or question and then we commented on it as we went around the table. We were asked not to "cross talk" or give advice but just listen. We were allowed to "pass" if the topic was too difficult. Most of the time those that passed the first round, later joined in, encouraged by what they heard. Some of the topics were: how did you find out that your mother had died; what was the reaction of your father; your siblings and friends; stepmothers or surrogate mothers; how did her death affect your relations with men; marriage and motherhood; your career decisions; gender models etc. For the first time I was able to express my inability to really grieve properly for my mother and my almost complete lack of memory for events surrounding her death and its aftermath. I also expressed my sorrow at the subsequent loss of the daily presence of my Dad, my envy of other girls who still had their mothers and my constant unconscious search for motherly qualities in women and even in some men. As soon as I met someone who could fill in that blank, I was afraid of being rejected or that they would also leave me.

In 1997 Laurie and Cami Black from the Los Angeles area helped organize the first Motherless Daughters Luncheon held on the Saturday before Mother's Day which I attended and have been going to each year ever since. Anywhere from 20 to 40 women attend these luncheon meetings at a location in Orange County. We had a special speaker chosen to inspire and encourage us. We then stood in a Circle of Remembrance holding hands and each person in turn said her name followed by her mother's name, e.g. "I am Barbara, daughter of Mary" etc. Most of us were overcome as we mentioned our mother's name out loud, possibly for the first time. Sometimes we were asked to tell little stories about our mothers, e.g. her cooking specialties, parties, sense of humor, travels and special aspects that revealed her personality. Kleenex was always available at each table and we each received a special small gift at our place. We were invited to bring photos of our mothers and other mementos of her which were placed on a table along with the photo scrapbooks compiled by one of our members. Many were so grateful that they could speak openly about their loss and be understood and completely accepted for the first time. Later Hope Edelman's colleagues published *Letters from Motherless Daughters* and *A Motherloss Workbook* that extended the support and ability to work out feelings and experiences in a healthy way. To think it took me more than 60 years to have the opportunity to grieve and mourn and come to grips with my great loss!

I tried to bring up the topic of the Motherless Daughters group at church services or at other places, but never was able to get much of a response. Eventually there was a small group of five San Diego members that met at a library each month. The group soon dwindled down to three or even two, so I stopped attending. I usually attend the Christmas Party annually in a member's home in Orange County

Letter to Mother

It occurred to me while reading what I had written above, that I would like to write a letter to my mother telling her of my journey without her:

Dear Mother, I miss you so much. You were with us in Hillside for only six years of my life. How I try so hard to remember you or what you said to me. All I have are a few images and memories of your activities in the kitchen, making custard in glass cups; of deftly separating the egg whites from the yolks; of fixing turnips with potatoes mashing them together to get us to eat them; of hanging out clothes in the backyard from a wicker laundry basket; of holding the edge of the bed pillow in your teeth as you put on the pillow slip; of sewing with the foot-operated sewing machine; of using the carpet sweeper; beating small rugs on the clothesline. Such simple memories. You were the ideal housewife and mother as I look back now. But what you said to me or if you hugged me or kissed me, I can't remember. I took so much for granted.

When you went to Bonnie Burn Sanatorium with tuberculosis we had to move to Madison to live with Dad's mother and his sisters. The move distracted me with new places and people to adjust to, so you were not always in my thoughts. One day after we had moved back to Hillside, Dad came to St. Catherine's School when I was in third grade and told Bob and me that you had died. I don't remember much more than that, or how I felt at the time. I do remember the visit to Guenther's Funeral Home to see you lying in your coffin and me wearing my First Communion dress to your funeral. I had one dream of seeing your face in the center of an oval shaped, ruffled lavender decorative pillow like one that had been on your bed. I think you might remember it. How I wish I had that pillow today, I would hug it closely to my heart.

Then in the next school year I was at Bonnie Burn Preventorium. Sometimes I would look longingly at the window nearby that had once identified your room at the Sanatorium. For our own protection the Health Department never allowed children to visit patients there, so I had not seen you since I was six. You must know that in those days we didn't know much about the process of grieving and the effects of mother loss on children. References to counseling, psychologists, therapists or the grief process were never made. Psychiatrists were strictly for persons "running down the street naked with a bloody knife in their hands." It's not even that people would say as some do now: "Well, get over it and move on." The closest they would get to some kind of indirect sympathy was when hearing of your death and my loss, they might say: "Well, you still have your father." I didn't let them know how little involvement he had. When my Aunt Marie became my guardian, they would say: "Well, you've got your aunt." They didn't know how reluctant I was about relating to her as a surrogate mother. I lied about the cause of your death as the stigma of tuberculosis was still prevalent in the culture and I felt ashamed. I would respond: "Oh, she had pneumonia or something." No one spoke about you or your death except on rare occasions by Aunt Mildred who mentioned you as being so pretty as a young woman, (with a little tinge of envy I think, as she was more plain than you, her older sister.) I also had an innate dislike of sentimental comments of pity, so I avoided speaking of you as much as possible.

During so many years it was my defense to suppress or repress thoughts of you and my loss. Even when I had a close friend in the Medical Mission Sisters, it was a big struggle for me even to tell her that you had died of tuberculosis, with no mention of how much I missed you, but in a way that I didn't recognize at the time.

It was much later in life, in the late seventies, after I left the Medical Mission Sisters that I wanted to know more about you and wrote to Bob and Mildred asking them to fill in more details. During those years the publishing of the popular book 'Roots' followed by the TV show was much discussed and caused an increased interest in genealogy and family stories. Actually, I had never read the book or watched the TV show, but it gave me the pretext to find out more about you. They both gave me a few tidbits, but Bob mostly spoke about Pop. It wasn't until about 1995 that the whole issue of mother loss came to dominate my thinking. As a result of my reading Hope Edelman's book, 'Motherless Daughters,' and my subsequent becoming a member of a support group of the same name that I came to open up a whole new way of thinking. I am eternally grateful to the group. In heaven you may be able to meet some of these mothers and be able to share your story as well—perhaps at another Circle of Remembrance where all you mothers can join hands and you can say: "I am Petronella, mother of Joan."

I hate to admit this now, but once I began thinking of mother loss, I selfishly focused on MY feelings and loss, but only after a few years of these reflections, I finally began to think more of how YOU felt. What was it like to be separated from your beloved husband, your father, your younger sister and your three young children? Were you ever angry at God because of this illness and how did you manage to keep on hoping that you might get better? You had already lost your own mother and your two brothers to the disease and you knew Pop and Mildred were also sick, so it must have felt like death was inevitable. Unfortunately, at that time the only cure or remedy was good food, fresh air and rest. What were your prayers like? Did you have to reassure Dad sometimes and console him? How did you manage your pain? Did the doctors and nurses treat you well and help you in your last days? Now that you and Dad are together in heaven, are you still able to talk about us kids and about our lives and how we have turned out? All three of us kids are now in our eighties and relatively healthy and leading satisfying productive lives.

I am full of questions now, dear Mother. How would you have told me of what I needed to know about being a woman, my changing body, about menstruation, sexuality, relationships with the opposite sex and much more? Just being with you from day to day, what would you have told me or shown me by your own behavior, regarding my appearance, my hair, use of cosmetics, clothes, good hygiene, exercise, polite behavior and good manners? How would you have taught me about household tasks, cooking and being a good wife and homemaker? What kind of encouragement would you have given me to do well in my studies? How would you have taught me the best use of money without being stingy or wasteful?

Would you have reminded me to be obedient to Dad and love him as you did? How did you feel when after you died you discovered that Dad was so overwhelmed by your death that a few years later he was not very involved in his children's lives? Was it sometimes difficult to live with Dad? What would you have told me about your own personal religious views, your way of praying and being a good Catholic? What would your reaction have been to find out that I wanted to be a missionary Sister? Or would you have hoped that I would have married a good young man and have given you grandchildren to spoil and love? Would you have remembered my birthdays with gifts that showed you understood my special likes and needs? The last birthday party I remember having was when I was five or six with gifts, "Poppers" and a cake with my friends. Would I have had at least a simple party each year or a birthday card if I had left home? A million more questions are in my mind, dear Mother, but I never got to express them.

It is finally time to thank you for so much, besides the ordinary chores of keeping a house and family. You sewed some of my clothes, including a beautiful warm chinchilla coat; you took care of me when I had measles, chicken pox, and scrapes from falls while roller skating; you took me shopping to Bamberger's in Newark where I enjoyed running up the escalator to the toy department; you taught me my night prayers and checked that I said them every night. So much more, Mother. THANK YOU!

You know that I had to leave all possessions behind when I entered the Convent in 1945. I left in 1971 and returned from the missions to the U.S. two years later. Some years after, Aunt Mildred gave me a photo of you as a young woman, and one of you about aged two, along with two child-size teacups— one blue with gold inside she said was one you had received on a birthday and the other white with flowers on it, probably part of a child's tea set. Only recently, Herb sent me a photo taken of you in 1919 with your siblings, Mildred, Frank and Edward. You were so pretty in this picture and I had it reproduced and cut out your picture and put it in a tiny pin that had been given each of us at one of the annual Mother's Day luncheons. That is all I have to remember you by now. Please watch over me and bless this life story.

Love,

Your daughter, Joan.

P.S. A few years ago I obtained a copy of a book "Fire and Flame: The Legacy of Anna Dengel," foundress of the Medical Mission Sisters. I was surprised and moved when I noticed that your pose in the photo Mildred had given me was so much like the one the photographer took of Mother Dengel as a young woman—both sitting in an elegant arm chair, both dressed in white and both holding a bouquet of artificial flowers. When I read the book, I was again surprised to find out that Mother Dengel had lost her mother at the age of nine and as she wrote: 'I attribute the compassion I had and have for the women and children of India to this great sorrow.' I never knew that Mother Dengel had lost her mother as a young girl and wish she had mentioned that in the time she was in Philadelphia, at least to me. I only found out when I read *Fire and Flame* many years later. No doubt she had similar problems when asked about the death of her mother and probably felt that others wouldn't really understand.

Letter to Dad

There is no support group for women who lost their fathers at an early age or were abandoned by their fathers, but I now feel compelled to write a letter to Dad:

Dear Dad, How much I miss you always. As a child how I loved your sense of humor and your jokes and your ability to imitate all accents and your musical talent. Remember once you told me when you were in the Army in World War I you wrote minstrel plays, produced them and acted in them. When living in Hillside how much I enjoyed trips with you to the Barnum and Bailey Circus and to Weequahic Park in Newark rowing in a canoe on the lake there. As the story goes the wind took my visor cap and I proceeded to try and retrieve it from the water and you quickly pulled me back to safety. How much fun we had going to Lake Hopatcong, to the Gingerbread Castle with the story of Hansel and Gretel; to the Jersey shore and places like Asbury Park, Bradley Beach and Point Pleasant, as I exclaimed in the car, even though still far away, "Daddy, I can smell the ocean;" to church bazaars at St. Catherine's; games of Tiddly Winks, Parcheesi, checkers, Old Maid and Michigan Rummy. Remember when we went out on Halloween and you dressed up as a hobo? Sometimes you even let me go to the meetings of the Star Wheelmen and eat pretzels while you had a beer with your friends. You seemed to enjoy these times as much as we kids did. Unfortunately, those fun times did not last, except for one time in 1939 when you took me to the New York World's Fair when you were living in Elizabeth and I had visited you.

Dad, I'm full of questions that I should have asked much earlier. How I regret not having talked to you more after mother's death. Bob wrote me years later that Mother's death left you devastated: "Dad just went to pieces after he lost Mother. She'd been his dream girl and he was never able to straighten out after she was gone. The burden was too much for him." Is that how she was for you? How did you meet her and what did she see in you? What did you see in her? Aunt Mildred told me you met at a social at St. Catherine's in Hillside and also said to me: "your mother had many beaux, but she married your father." Did you write to her from France during World War I? What was your wedding like? I've never seen pictures of it. It must have been quite traditional as I remember the set of beautiful Bavarian hand-painted white dishes with gold trim that were in the china closet. They must have been wedding gifts. Did you have to wait to get a good job before that important date? How did you get along with Pop and Mildred?

What was your reaction when you discovered that Nell (as everyone called her) had the Severynse family disease of tuberculosis and you had to send her to Bonnie Burn Sanatorium? What was it like to see her body slowly deteriorate or to watch her in pain and be unable to help? Was there anyone you could talk to about your feelings—a buddy or perhaps a priest? Were you with Mother as she was dying or near death? What were the last words you heard from her? Were you afraid that maybe us kids would come down with the dread disease, or maybe even yourself?

After Pop's death, the house was owned by Mildred, but I wonder if you would have liked to buy it but didn't have the money to pay for it. Or did you realize that Mildred needed the money from the sale to live on? You had no choice but to send us to Bonnie Burn Preventorium, but why did you and the Jolletts decide to send us three kids away to boarding school so far away? Was that your wish or grandma's and your sisters? After all, St. Vincent's had a parish school and may have charged a small tuition fee, but wouldn't a boarding school have been even more costly? I do remember the trip to boarding school when you drove us through the Catskills and then up Route 9 to the Adirondacks, past Lake Champlain to the small town of Champlain where I went to school for the next seven years. When you found out I was learning French, you sometimes wrote a few paragraphs in your letters to me in the language you had learned in France. After sixth and seventh grades I came home to Madison for Christmas and summer vacation and all was well.

I came home at Christmas in 1937 when I was in the eighth grade and found out that you had lost your job and you were living in Elizabeth working for the WPA (Works Progress Administration). At that time the WPA had a bad name among most of the public—often called 'We Putter Around' with images of men leaning on their shovels—another stigma that had to be hidden or ashamed of. Obviously you were not in a financial position to pay for my schooling at St. Mary's, but I often wonder what discussions were held about what to do with me. Bob had decided to enter the Seminary in upstate New York and Herb was already going to St. Vincent's in Madison. Why couldn't I have gone to the local public school or after to the nearby Catholic Bailey High School where Aunt Marguerite had gone? I was a truant from school for the next six months, so pretty much stayed in the house during the week. Sometime in this interval I guess Aunt Marie was made my guardian. Finally Grandma and your sisters must have pooled their resources and sent me back to St. Mary's the next September to finish eighth grade in January and in June I finished first year high school. The next two Christmases were spent in Champlain. You sent a pretty green twin sweater set, and the following year a set of hankies embroidered with purple flowers. These were the last gifts I remember from you. Later I would receive a signed Christmas card only. Then when you married Bella it was just signed "Dad and Bella." No newsy letter or other messages. This was a tough time for me, but I know it must have been hard for you too. At first you had a room with a young couple in Elizabeth and then in a small room in a boarding house with the common bathroom down the hall. You met Bella Newman there, a divorcee with children. She had a larger place with a kitchen, bath and two bedrooms. You became friends with her but stayed in your own room. I used to visit you there and found it quite friendly, during the one week each summer I stayed there. I enjoyed Bella's son, Sonny, as we played cards with you and Bella and her older daughter Mickey.

In my sophomore year in college you sent me a card saying you and Bella had been married by a Justice of the Peace and you were living in her apartment. This was very difficult for me as a fervent Catholic, where marrying outside the church was considered a big breach. I know you had been a practicing Catholic before...Knights of Columbus and the Holy Name Society and going to Mass regularly. What was it like for you to be unable to participate in your birth religion? I should have been happy for you at finding another true love, but I had reservations of getting too close to Bella, to the point of not even considering her my stepmother. Some of that feeling was a desperate loyalty to Mother. I do remember how broken up Bella was at the gravesite when you died...she really loved you very much. As you were a veteran she received the American flag from the military honor guard as they played taps. Aunt Marie drove me from the Washington house to the burial as I had missed the funeral which was held in Elizabeth. Bob, who had just been ordained a priest in June, later wrote me that in order to receive the last rites you were encouraged to promise, if you survived, to live with Bella as brother and sister. You complied and you received the Last Sacraments. That must have been tough. You died early at the age of 59 of a heart attack. The date was October 3rd 1949, at that time the feast day of St. Therese of Lisieux, the Little Flower, and patroness of missionaries, who had died of tuberculosis at the age of 24. She too had lost her mother as a small child. Now I was truly an orphan.

After I was in the convent I never saw Bella again. On my return to the U.S. in 1973 she sent me a nice short letter but I never had the opportunity of visiting her. Bob kept in touch with her when he visited Herb. Bella moved to Atlantic Highlands, New Jersey and died many years later. Her daughter Mickey had been married with children and was living in Vermont. When she heard that I had left the convent, she wrote and mailed me some of your World War I mementos and also a record you had made for Bella on Mother's Day in 1946. As it was on a scratchy 78 record, I took it to a record specialist who did his best to put it on a tape. It was much better but still some of it was lost. You sang the popular "Mother—M is for the Million Things She Gave Me." Did you ever sing it to Mother or even to Grandma, your own mother? You also sang a more comical takeoff on "Father," followed by "Mexicali Rose" which I loved. You would have been surprised that a few years ago I went with David to the city of Mexicali in connection with his art work. You also sang Sonny's favorite, "I'll Be Down to Get You in a Taxi, Honey" which was great! The rest of the tape was a folksy story of "Josh at the Museum." You certainly were good at the old-timey accent. I now treasure a photo of you as a soldier in France and your dog-tag. I play the tape once in a while and your picture is on a small stand next to the one of Mother as a young woman.

I do have to tell you that I never held much of a grudge against you for not supporting me through high school and college. I understood your circumstances, but when you got a good job at General Motors during World War II, it occurred to me that maybe you could at least have contributed some money to your mother and sisters for their expenses for me. I am quite sure you probably bought Christmas presents for Bella and her children, but nothing for me. It was only when I was on a trip to the Redwoods alone in 2002 and as I was driving through the beautiful forest, I had an imaginary conversation with you, pointing out the special sites and about how you would have enjoyed the trip. Then suddenly it came to me—you were a "Deadbeat Dad!" In my public health nursing work I encountered many of these Dads and now I was putting you in that same category. I don't know what to tell you except that you were not like most of them, but still....I know I have forgiven you in my heart, but I regret not knowing you better as a teenager and an adult.

After you lost your job and moved to Elizabeth, you never again visited your own mother and sisters in Madison or sent them a card or made a phone call to them. Was the argument about us kids so difficult and bitter that you decided to never see them again? Or were you told not to contact them again?

I miss you so much and I hope you and Mother have a chance to talk things over and love each other as you always did.

Your ever loving daughter, Joan.

CHAPTER 31

BACK AT THE RANCH

In June of 1997 I convinced David it would make a great road trip if he would show me around the places where he once had his art galleries back in the seventies and before we were married. So off we went, staying at hostels and at Sarah Ann O'Gara's house in Sacramento. We visited Santa Cruz where David once shared a gallery at the Old Sash Mill and lived out of a Volkswagon van. We passed by Boulder Creek where he had lived for a while and gave some lectures that ended up in his book *Imagination Factor*. In Santa Cruz we finally met Bishop Clinch who was living in a residential facility there. We had a lovely conversation with him. The next place was San Francisco where we stayed at the hostel at the old Presidio on the bay. David had lived several years in San Francisco so showed me most of the important sites. His gallery on Haight Street was now a Beauty Salon Supply Shop but some of the other stores he knew were still there. We visited a friend of David's who lived in San Francisco and then went to Golden Gate Park where we enjoyed a ride on the carousel. It was bitter sweet for David as he used to take his son Dan there when he was a boy. We stopped at the North Beach area and the Cliff House where we heard "The Fat Lady Sing." We drove up to Mt. Temalpais and the John Muir Redwoods where I bought a beautiful poster of the magnificent trees which I put on the back of my office door. His other gallery was in Berkeley where we also spent a little time. In Sacramento we visited the old

Victorian mansion that was now used as a hostel but didn't stay there as we stayed with my friend Sarah Ann O'Gara who ended up being a good friend of David's as well.

A week after our return David had to be hospitalized for gall bladder surgery. The year 1997 was a busy year—my *Desert Padre* book came out in July and then in October I received a copy of the *Desert Magazine Index*. We also refinanced our house to obtain a lower mortgage payment. Some time later we discussed the possibility of selling our house so consulted with my friend Bob Larson who also worked as a realtor. We wrote down all the pros and cons of moving to San Diego and were almost ready to move when David decided it was not the time to do so. I was disappointed as I had already stayed in Imperial Beach in San Diego County for a few days and thought that might be a place to live within our budget. I didn't bring the subject up again.

David and I visited the Mexican town of San Quintín on the Pacific on a Thanksgiving weekend and made several trips over the years to Dr. Mendoza, a Mexican dentist he had been seeing in Tijuana for years. Even though the trip took about 3 hours we still saved money by going to Mexico. We always stopped at the little bakery for coffee and a Mexican pastry or bought "birotes" or hard rolls fresh out of the oven at another bakery. What we didn't enjoy however, were the long waits at the border, in spite of 24 lanes at the crossing. An average wait was 45 minutes but often much longer. There was no problem getting in to Mexico, just returning to the U.S. *Since the recent "drug wars" and drug violence the wait is now often over two hours!*

Halloween of 1998 somehow had inspired David to return to his art work which he hadn't done in several years. He had painted two small portraits of an Indian man and an Indian woman for our trailer in Idyllwild but nothing since that time. His first work in paper sculpture was a monster mask, The Cheerio Man, that David wore at Halloween to greet the kids...their response instead of fear was: "cool!" After that he continued making masks, plaques, and three-dimensional figures on a variety of themes, some mythological and others replicas of some of his earlier sculpture works. He used a clay model and then covered the figure with wet paper strips and paste and when dry he removed the clay and then painted the object. He was insistent that it wasn't papier maché but paper sculpture or as the art trade calls it "mixed media." We arranged a couple of "salons" at our house for invited friends and sold a few of his works, but he was not into marketing so most of them are still around or have been given away. The "toothpaste man" he gave to his dentist, and the "Fool" on a precipice he gave to the Desert Hot Springs Library. A cookie jar that resembled a Maya head was molded over an old ice bucket that he gave to our friend Alice. Later he made one for our own kitchen. He made a paper bulldog that might help chase away the stray cats from our garden. He asked me to name it so I picked "Katrinka" after the strong lady in the Katzenjammer Kids comic strip. Later he began making imitations of Pueblo style pottery that looked so real that when people picked one up they almost dropped the object as they expected it to be heavy. We went to Mexicali, Mexico to have a local foundry cast a couple of his plaques in bronze as the work was a lot cheaper than we could find in the U.S.

My priest brother Bob visited us during the Christmas holidays in 1999 and again in 2000 as he had been offered a job as chaplain on the Carnival Cruise line whose ships embarked in San Diego and the company paid for his plane trip. Of course he did some bicycling even in the desert. This was the last time he visited us. *He is now stationed in Quebec, Canada so it's a long trip to come out West and he is very aware of his vow of poverty.*

In 1999 I joined the newly formed Desert Hot Springs Historical Society which at first had many members attending the monthly meetings. We began to think of fund-raising for the Cabot Museum. Cabot Yerxa was the colorful founding father of Desert Hot Springs and his Pueblo style home made exclusively of objects found in the desert needed some help in making it a tourist attraction. I made a trip to Blythe to do some research on Cabot's stay there after World War I where he had a general store and a post office. I spent several hours looking at old newspapers on the microfiche and at the end of the day I finally found tiny little ads for his store which proved he had been there. There was very little information on this part of his life.

Things went along quite well with the Historical Society and I was asked to help with the publicity and prizes for a fund-raising golf tournament. Research was more my interest but I did what I could by going to the local businesses, but after time I lost interest as the Society became much smaller. Also much time, money and energy had been spent on the Golf Tournament with little real revenue. I did help with the annual banquet and had invited one of my "desert" friends, Phil Brigandi, to give a talk on historical research. Some of the meetings ended up being gossip sessions and blaming others for what went wrong. There also was some confusion as to the role of the local Chamber of Commerce and the Cabot Museum volunteers who were not a part of the Historical Society. This kind of uncertainty helped me decide to finally resign from the group. I did give my research papers on Cabot's Blythe experience to be archived so I left in good graces.

In August 2000 I had my annual mammogram and a small cancer tumor was found, so I had a lumpectomy and lymph node dissection on September 18th. I jotted down some of my thoughts at learning of the diagnosis: "Is this how I will die? What about limitations? Will I be able to drive? How many more years will I live? Will I have a metastasis to another part of my body? How will David react? Whose shoulder can I cry on? What do I need to learn from this? What have I not yet done in life? Any financial implications?" David helped with my dressings very professionally and drove me where I needed to go until I got stronger. In November I started a series of radiation therapy and then put on Tamoxifen in January. I had to take this for the next five years. I had no complications. After surgery I was asked if I wanted to join a breast cancer survivor group. As with so many other difficult events in my life, I decided it was best to accept this new event, but felt it was healthier not to dwell on it and the possibility of a recurrence. I then put that thought out of my mind and moved on. However, I still get an annual mammogram.

The Medical Mission Sisters were celebrating their 75th anniversary on September 30th and I had planned on going, so I took a plane to Philadelphia ten days after my surgery, feeling a little shaky but o.k. It was wonderful to visit with old friends, hear their stories and attend the prayer services. One of the former Medical Mission Sisters, Pat Burkhardt, was also there and lived in Brooklyn. As I had no car, she offered to drive me to Brooklyn to see my brother there. His wife had died two years before and he was still having a difficult time fighting the depression that followed. This was the time we visited my Aunt Marguerite in a Nursing Home (she died shortly after this visit) and also when we visited Hillside and our parents' grave in Mt. Olivet Cemetery in Newark. It had a small military marker with his name on it. My mother was also buried there according to the records, but her name was not on the gravestone. We noticed that in full view of his grave was a large building with the sign "Budweiser" prominently displayed. Dad would have liked that.

I had been reading Carleton Sheets' books and tapes on buying property with no money down and it seemed like a feasible thing to do. So in 2001 I ended up buying a small condominium at Mission Lakes Country Club in Desert Hot Springs. All went well except that I allowed the selling agent to find a renter for it. He chose a woman whom I would not have picked myself. Things went well for a while, but as she had diabetes and was on kidney dialysis, she started having a problem paying the rent. By March of 2002 she was so far behind and the income from the rental did not earn enough to cover the expenses so I sold it after spending considerable money on repairs, new carpet etc. I was happy to have learned another lesson. I heard later that she was living at a Senior Housing complex and a few months later died of kidney failure. She was never able to pay the rent she owed me.

In the summer of 2001 David and I took a wonderful trip to visit my old friends the Langs who were now living in Santa Fe. He had never met them. Martha Lang was fascinated by his paper sculpture and he helped her plan the construction of paper lanterns to be placed in their patio for family events. We also went to visit Tina Lang O'Sullivan, one of the Langs' daughters. They had a big family get-together with Martha and Friedl and Petra Lang O'Brien's family. The children were very interested in seeing David's art work portfolio. I was very happy to have David share this friendship of mine with the Langs. He thought they were very special. Unfortunately, a few years later we received word that Martha had died of cancer of the liver. I was glad that I had visited them before she died. On this same trip we visited the Colorado town of San Luis where the residents now had a small museum and a local artist had made beautiful life-size sculptural Stations of the Cross that ended in a church at the top of a local hill. San Luis was the oldest town in Colorado and now getting on its feet as a tourist attraction. San Luis had been one of the county seats when I was Consultant for Public Health, so it was a nostalgic trip too.

September 11, 2001 we were all devastated by the news of the bombing and destruction of the World Trade Center. I realized immediately that our world would be changed forever. My worst fears that an overly militaristic reaction would embroil us for years to come were not shared by many other people in our area. It became difficult to discuss the situation with almost anyone. Only now do we realize that we went to war on false pretenses and invaded a country that had nothing to do with 9/11, nor with weapons of mass destruction, nor with Al Qaeda or Osama Bin Laden. And now we are living with the results and certainly not making friends in the rest of the world. Only recently have there been a few glimmers of hope that perhaps we made a big mistake and need to take a different direction. Amidst the numerous right-wing talk show programs there finally appeared one from the other side. Air America Radio had been slowly growing but the country was still not fully aware of what had actually happened and those that criticize our government's actions were considered unpatriotic and not supporting our troops. *Recently, one of Air America's best speakers, Al Franken, is now in the U.S. Senate.*

CHAPTER 32

IRELAND 2002

The story of this trip was entitled "Solo to Ireland: With Help from Serendipity." What follows is a shorter summary. Father John J. Crowley drew me irresistibly to his birthplace, Ireland. For eight years I had been conscious of his presence, but now I wanted to learn more about him and get a little insight into his heritage and to contrast the green of the Emerald Isle with his dry desert parish and to visit places and people that he knew and loved as an eleven year old boy. As I could not rent a car (the rental car age limit was 70) I decided to take a three-week tour of Ireland by myself in May 2002 and let serendipity work out my itinerary and activities. Aside from visits to the usual tourist attractions, I want to share with my readers some highlights of my trip. (For readers who are interested in more details of Ireland, I can send you a longer version.) Before setting out for Ireland Father Crowley's nephew's widow, Rose Crowley, gave me the name, address and phone number of one of his cousins, Peggy Lyne, who lived in Killarney. Her deceased husband, Jackie Lyne, was related to Father Crowley's mother's side of the family. He was well-known in Killarney as a star football (soccer) player.

My first stop was in Bunratty where I stayed at the Innisfree B. and B. and was talking to the owner, and as her name was Imelda McCarthy, I thought she might be related to some of Father Crowley's relatives, the McCarthys. She said that McCarthy was her husband's name and he was from Cork not Kerry. When I mentioned I was going to visit another cousin, Peggy Lyne who was a cousin by marriage to the Padre, she exclaimed: "Oh, that's my Aunt Peggy!" She was a Foley and later I visited her sister Eileen at Charlie Foley's Bar in Killarney. Imelda drove me to the bus stop and left me with a small souvenir jug of mead, like the drink I enjoyed at Bunratty Castle.

When I arrived in Killarney I stayed a couple of days at Lime Court, a B. and B. on Muckross Road run by Dom Murphy. On a little walk on Muckross Road, I met Peggy in front of her house, "Homeland," as she was weeding her garden. She invited me to stay with her a few days. She drove me to the Aghadoe Cemetery where her husband was buried and took me to see the beautiful Killarney Lakes and the surrounding mountains. Other places I visited that were part of the young John Crowley's life were the Cathedral and the Presentation Brothers School which he had attended. I was lucky to have a private tour of Killarney National Park with a guide who was active in preserving their famous red deer and even luckier to see about 15 deer casually crossing our path to the other side. Peggy drove me to the nearby town of Kenmare where I met another cousin, Nora McCarthy, who had worked as a maid in her younger years for the wealthy California oilman, Edward Doheny. Nora took us to visit her sister Philomena, a Catholic Sister who was the family historian and they both entertained us with personal stories about the Crowley family.

While in Killarney I made arrangements with the Killarney Bookstore for a book signing and sale for September of the following year. Peggy had told a reporter, Breda Joy, of the local newspaper, "Kerry's Eye," about my book on a local "native son" so she interviewed me on the phone. She sent a photographer to the home of Julie Healy Rae, another cousin, to take a photo of me and maybe a picture of the Padre. (A woman, Mary Connaire Acampora from New York who had bought my book, told me she was a relative of Julie's and had given me her address.) Unfortunately I had loaned my one copy of the book to Dom Murphy of the Lime Court B. and B. and he had loaned it to relatives in Dublin and forgot it there. Then Julie pointed to a photo on the sideboard. It was the photo of her parents (Healys) at their wedding in New York in 1918 and the priest who married them was in the picture. It was the newly ordained priest, the young Father Crowley! I had never seen this photo before but it was published in the next issue of "Kerry's Eye" along with my interview. Eventually, Dom Murphy returned my only book.

Julie took me to visit the ruins of the old Franciscan Muckross Abbey that was built in 1448 but later partially destroyed by Oliver Cromwell in 1653. Seeing it was a very moving experience for me. The young John Crowley had written a poem, "A Stone from Muckross" about it for his Holy Cross magazine in 1915. The ancient yew tree honored by the Padre was still there in the middle of the ruins. Many of the Padre's relatives' names were carved on the ancient gravestones in the adjoining cemetery. I too, picked up a small stone from Muckross.

Peggy took me one evening to the Vintage Pub owned by another cousin Tom Lyne, where he and his brother relayed to me some of the stories they had heard about the Crowleys and the Lynes—some of which had been slightly distorted in the time and telling. We had some great "craic" and a glass of Bailey's on the house along with some traditional music later.

On my Ring of Kerry trip I stopped to visit another relative, Eileen Collins in Dingle. A reader of *Desert Padre*, John Kilcoyne from Worcester, MA told me about her. His grandfather, John Lynch had been game-keeper at Muckross Estates. John Kilcoyne's father was from County Mayo and met his wife at an Ancient Order of Hibernians meeting in Worcester. As she did not have any local relatives, she went to Nora Crowley (Father Crowley's mother) for approval before she married him. One of the questions Nora asked her was: "can he sing?" That seemed to seal the deal. I had seen a brochure at O'Connor's B. and B. for Sciurd Archaeological Tours and discovered that Eileen Collins' husband Tim was the guide. Another relative was Mary Horgan and Peggy took me to visit her and found out she also was related to John Kilcoyne.

Aside from these pleasant meetings with relatives of the Lynes, I visited the old Park Place Hotel that the Crowley's had formerly owned. It was a bit run-down but still functioning. Unfortunately, the new owners or managers were unfamiliar with their story. On a later visit I was told by Superintendent Donal O'Sullivan that the Hotel was believed to be Father Crowley's birthplace. I also took a jaunting car at the Gap of Dunloe with Peggy. Here I remembered that the Crowley family had owned many of the jaunting carts and must have gone on these trips often, exploring the rocky areas and streams as well as the bridge at the Meeting of the Waters. Later this bridge was mentioned in his "Sage and Tumbleweed" columns. I stopped at Killarney Printers and got permission to copy a beautiful photo of Muckross Abbey which I later used along with the Padre's poem. On the tourist trip to the Ring of Kerry I passed by many places well known and enjoyed by the Crowley family, such as the beaches at Rossbeigh and Glenbeigh. I could have stayed forever in County Kerry to enjoy its many beauties and history, but I moved on.

My visit to County Cork was highlighted by my own private tour of the standing stones of Drombeg Stone Circle. I had been referred at the small café bookstore, Pilgrim's Rest, opposite the bus stop in Rosscarbery to Fianachta O'Calaghan who took me on a tour in his jeep. He was the perfect guide as he had assisted the archaeologist, Dr. Eddie Fahy from the University College of Cork who had conducted the excavations several years before. The site dates back to about 1000 B.C. and contains sixteen standing stones and one recumbent. At the winter solstice the rays of the setting sun fall on the flat altar stone. The burial of an adolescent contained in a pot set upright in a pit was found during the dig. The pot contained carefully placed cremated bones covered with soil. It is not known whether this was for a ritual or an ordinary burial. Nearby was a small stream with a Stone Age cooking pit. A fire is made and hot stones were thrown into a trough to heat the water. The water boiled in about 18 minutes. When the water boiled the meat was added. The whole scene, which was very simple and without signs or concessions, evoked in me a feeling of long ago and transported me to the prehistoric times and peoples who worshipped and shared ritual meals here.

I took the tour bus to see many of the other wonderful places in County Cork including the town of Cobh where many Irish left on ships after the great famine to emigrate to America, Australia and Canada. The museum there displays dioramas and interpretive descriptions which are very sad, but also evoke a feeling of admiration for the courage of the Irish people.

In County Clare I was surprised to learn that I had arrived in Ennis fortunate enough to stay at probably the last B. and B. bed available. The whole town was celebrating the Fleadh Nua (Traditional Music Festival) the weekend I arrived, so lodging was at a premium. I had not been aware of this event, but happy to hear about it. Music and dancing in the streets went on until late at night even in the rain. I watched the parade, listened to instruments new to me, such as the bodhran (drum), tin whistle and the pib uillean (hornpipe); enjoyed scary stories by Eddie Linehan, the "seanchai" (story-teller) about vengeful fairies; attended an evening concert and even took a short Irish class.

Anne McCullagh, the owner of the Ain Karem B. and B., told me about her role in having a sculpture erected in the town to honor Compassionate Friends founded for those who have lost a young child. She also had organized an annual Mass for that organization. Together we visited the limestone sculpture and she gave me a leaflet that had been used at the Mass. I shared my own story of my loss of my mother as a young child. In Ennis I took a beautiful photo of the ruins of the Franciscan Abbey with its four pinnacles which helped orient me when walking around the city. The Abbey dates from the year 1240 but like many others had been destroyed by the English. Most of the stone walls are still standing. I took a tour bus to the usual sites of the Cliffs of Moher, the Pournabron Dolmen (wedge tomb) and the Burren which are very special places in County Clare.

I was supposed to leave from Shannon Airport but Aer Lingus was on strike, so I had to take a bus from Ennis to Dublin a day early and leave Ireland from Dublin. It did give me a chance to see a little more of Ireland than I had planned and a short introduction to the city of Dublin. It had been a great trip. The following year I was back again in the month of September. *Some years later I saw a copy of an e-mail David sent to his friend Nino in Austria where he wrote: "Joan just left for Ireland…I miss her already." I was never sure if David really did miss me as he never said that to me. I think he wanted me to feel free to travel. Thank you, David.*

CHAPTER 33

IRELAND 2003

My main goal on my second trip to Ireland was for the book signing at Killarney Bookshop. I stayed for a few days at Peggy Lyne's new home on Countess Grove Road, a little further out of town than her previous home, but with a wider and more beautiful view of the countryside, with delicious wild blackberries nearby just begging to be picked. This was September and a whole different world of wild-flowers waited to be enjoyed. I first stopped at Killarney Printing where I left a copy of the 11x14 poster I had made with their photo of Muckross Abbey to which I had added Fr. Crowley's poem "A Stone From Muckross." Then I visited the library where I signed their copy of *Desert Padre* and noted that they had a flyer on my "Book Launch" as they call it. I then talked to the manager of Killarney Bookshop where we planned the setting for my upcoming book signing. It was to be on a small table set up with one tiny corner for me surrounded by numerous best sellers. The shop is very tiny.

When I returned to Peggy's home she had invited the local Radio Kerry sportscaster to interview me. My interview at Peggy's kitchen table with Richard (Weeshie) Fogarty lasted about 45 minutes. He tried to find questions that related to his interest in sports, but as he had actually read the book, he covered the rest of the story quite well. Peggy helped with answers to some of the questions. The taped interview was to be broadcast the following Sunday and he promised to send me a tape. This was my first radio interview, but of course I didn't tell him that. *Several months later back in the States, I called Peggy and she managed to get me a copy of the tape.*

At Peggy's house I received a call from a former Superintendent of Police of County Kerry, Donal O'Sullivan, who had come from his home in Tralee to meet me. I had previously told him I was in town so I met him for tea at the International Hotel. He was an author of a book about grain milling in County Cork and he gave me a signed copy. We chatted about many things, but especially about his plans to have a plaque erected in honor of Father Crowley. He said that all members of the Town Council were in favor of the proposal, especially one of the Councilors, Sean O'Grady. Mr. O'Sullivan had brought his copy with him and I autographed it for him as he regretted not being able to attend the book signing. He had visited the U.S. and had seen the monument to the Desert Padre on a visit to Death Valley, guessed that the Padre must be Irish, so later bought the book through Amazon. Later that same day I had another short interview with a reporter from *The Kerryman* newspaper. In the evening the members of the Broderick family came to visit Peggy. Rita Broderick was Peggy's husband Jackie's sister. Much talk about family affairs ensued, and they all promised to come to the book signing event.

The book signing at Killarney Bookshop went very well with many of the Padre's relatives attending. The gentleman who gave me the tour of Killarney National Park and several town officials also came. Dr. Margaret O'Connor, a classmate of Dr. Michael

Riordan (my first Irish teacher from Palm Desert, California) at the University College of Cork took the bus from her home in Cork and greeted me. We had a very nice visit. Photographers from the three local newspapers, *Kerry's Eye, The Kerryman* and *The Kingdom* all took photos that soon appeared in the local press.

Peggy had to leave early as she had been invited to County Cork for a memorial ceremony to honor her uncle Liam Lynch on the occasion of the 80th anniversary of his death in the 1921–1923 Civil War. Liam Lynch had at one time been an aide to Michael Collins, but then joined the opposition of Eamon De Valera and was killed in 1923. As it was the 80th anniversary of his death, the ruling party, Fianna Fail, headed by the Prime Minister, Brian Aherne, officiated at the event. Peggy was very proud of her uncle and shared with me some documents from one of his brothers in Australia consoling their mother on his death. Later she donated these original documents to the National Archives. That night I stayed with Julie Healy Rae. Later she drove me to her home town of Kilgarvan where her son's family now resided. In the morning she took me to the Franciscan Friary where we attended Mass.

Julie drove me to the train station where I picked up the train to Dublin. I stayed at the Harcourt Hotel near St. Stephen's Green. There were no B. and B.'s listed for the city of Dublin and those in the suburbs were too inconvenient without a car. The hotel was in the Georgian part of the city and I found out that George Bernard Shaw often stayed in room 101 (not open to the public), but a picture of the famous author hung in the lobby. In the lounge room was a quotation from him inscribed on the top of the four walls: "Ireland is like no other place under heaven and no man can touch its sod or breathe its air without becoming better or worse." (I hope I became better!) There was traditional music in the room adjoining the lounge every evening, and a full breakfast every morning.

Most of the places I wanted to visit were within walking distance such as Grafton Street, Trinity College and the National Museum. The exhibit at Trinity College Library of the Book of Kells was a highlight of this trip. I had high tea at Bewley's Café on Grafton Street and admired the stained glass windows. The National

Museum holds beautiful objects from Ireland's varied history, such as the Ardagh chalice, the Cross of Cong and the Tara brooch. A special display featured the "bog body" quite well preserved.

I took a Bus Eireann trip to the prehistoric passage grave at Newgrange, north of Dublin, with a stop at the Mellifont Abbey and another bus south to Glendalough to see the ruins of St. Kevin's monastery and the town of Avoca where I bought a beautiful woven scarf. (Much more information on these and other sites can be found in my longer version of the trip if the reader is interested.) It had been a delightful trip and made me eager to learn more about Ireland. This trip had been shorter than the one I took the previous year, and I vowed I would return again.

A sequel to my trip came shortly after. The Killarney Town Council decided in August 2002 to erect memorials to Father Crowley and to Donal Leahy, a young Killarney man who had died while serving the missions in Brazil. In March 2004 the Town Council asked for proposals for bids for an appropriate memorial. The Town Council's Arts Committee endorsed the idea and raised funds for the project. A quote in *The Kerryman* said: "this is encouraging news and proves the town council's commitment to promoting art in the town." The winning proposal came from a young married man with three young daughters with the remarkable name of "John Crowley." He was from Cork but no known relation to the Desert Padre. According to a write-up in the *Kerry's Eye* "at the core of the piece is a steel frame coated in cement. Individual pieces of Valentia (County Kerry) slate have been locked together to form a wheel using the traditional method of building stone walls." The sculptor says: "I was thinking of the idea that the caring nature of the missionaries radiated around the world. It gave me the idea of the wheel and the circle of life. They went out from Killarney—the central hub—and radiated to different parts of the world." The sculpture weighed about 1.5 tons. Shards of slate were scattered among the ferns in front of the monument to blend in further. The Council picked a site in the Fern Garden in Killarney Park and renamed the road from Inner Relief Road to Mission Road. Two identifying plaques were placed near the sculpture.

I received a flyer in the mail announcing the dedication but it arrived too late for me to attend the event. *The Kerryman* of July 22 carried a photo of the sculpture with 23 people, some family members of both of the honorees, Town Council officials and church officials. Later I received a letter with photos and clippings from Donal O'Sullivan. He told me that "tributes were paid to you for writing the book and a copy of it was shown to everybody present by Dolores Lyne who is a relative of Father Crowley." I was elated as it showed how proud the people of Killarney were of one of their own. I know that Father Crowley himself would love the thought behind the sculpture and its perfect artistic taste. I hoped to see it some day.

CHAPTER 34

ANOTHER BIG MOVE

In December of 2003 and out of the clear blue sky, David came to me and said: "I've been thinking..." He said he thought the responsibilities of owning our own house were getting a little difficult for him and the neighborhood was not improving much. We had been burglarized twice, his truck had been vandalized once and someone threw a rock in my office window. Across the street were people selling drugs and probably also selling stolen objects. I had been making plans to rent a condo in Mammoth Lakes for a month during the very hot month of August. He kind of hinted that I had paid my dues by living in the desert and maybe now it was my turn to return to my favorite San Diego area.

The time was ripe for us to sell the house as there was a housing boom in Riverside County even in less favorable neighborhoods. He said he would be glad to go along with whatever I picked if I would tend to all the details of selling the house and all that implied. What a pleasant surprise! I felt that I had made a valiant effort to bond with the desert that at first I found very unattractive. *The American Desert* magazine, *Desert Padre* and my involvement in Desert Hot Springs

Historical Society and other desert trips and activities were efforts to accomplish that bonding. The desert had taught me much but I was ready to move on. I did miss the ocean and San Diego's pleasant climate, so was very happy to be able to return there. I immediately took out books from the library e.g. *For Sale by Owner*, etc. What I had learned from Carleton Sheets also came in handy and my experience of selling my house in Alamosa and my condo in San Diego added to my needed knowledge.

David knew I would pick San Diego County for our new home so I made a special trip in February to Imperial Beach in San Diego County close to the Mexican border. We also decided that neither of us wanted the responsibility and expenses of ownership so we would be looking for a nice rental. Home prices in San Diego County were at an average of $500,000...a lot more than we could afford. As I had stayed at the local Seacoast Inn in Imperial Beach a couple of times, I decided that this was the cheapest town or area that offered closeness to the beach. One advantage of I.B. (as it was often called) was that it was an incorporated city founded in 1956 and had a hometown feeling to it. The town itself is only 2.4 square miles but the main streets are nice and wide and parking is usually easy.

In February I visited over 14 apartment complexes (ones that David found listed on the Internet.) My favorite was Mariners Point Apartments right next to the Tijuana River Estuary Reserve and three blocks from the beach. It was an 88-unit with two stories with an apartment on the ground floor and another on the second story. The owner also had a section of town houses nearby with apartments that had two-stories per unit. We decided this was not for us. The management had an office on site with several employees at all times. The complex at Mariners Point had a small swimming pool, a Jacuzzi, a small fitness room, a laundry room and our mailboxes. A contracted company took care of all the landscaping. There were several large trees, including eucalyptus and pines and some flowering pear and plum trees. Beautiful red bougainvillea adorned the fences and the dividers of the parking lot. Each residence had a numbered parking space with several unmarked ones available to the residents only. Visitors had to park on the street. Most of the residents were young people employed by the Navy, some with small children. Only a few residents were older.

We filled out an application to rent that required complete financial information including a credit report. The company required that the renters have one third of their income available for the monthly rent. With the potential sale of our house we would easily qualify. We took a look at an empty unit, but they couldn't promise any specific unit at a specific location. We would have to take whatever was available at the time we wanted to move in. There was no waiting list, so I periodically called the manager to show that we were still interested in a two-bedroom unit.

Meanwhile back in Desert Hot Springs I checked out the selling prices of similar homes by the ads in the newspapers, by information from the local title companies, and by going to "open house" events or by cruising by houses that looked similar to ours. We had to make certain repairs and some cosmetic changes before I was ready to advertise. By March I felt I had done all my homework so wrote up an ad for the newspaper. I also made an informative flyer that I put in a box attached to our mailbox that specified everything a potential buyer might want to know along with a photo of the house for those that wanted to share the flyer with someone else. The first phone call I got about the house, eventually turned out to be the best potential buyer. I set the price at what I thought was a fair price and told potential buyers that it was not negotiable. I knew my price was fair when I kept getting calls from realtors that they could sell our house for more than we were asking. "Yes, but your commission would make up the difference," I told them, so declined their assistance.

Several people came to see the house and I was fortunate that one woman with her adult son who was working at three jobs managed to get qualified for a loan. She was enchanted by the vegetable grow-box as she loved to garden and was grateful there was a central sprinkler system already installed. She agreed that we did not need to clean the carpet, (which actually was now 17 years old) as she wanted her own carpet installed. We included the washer and dryer in the garage. That was a selling point as well as the numerous shelves in the garage that David installed when he bought the house. We went to the same escrow company that we had done business with when we refinanced the house, so everything went quite smoothly. I had been making extra payments to the mortgage bank but we still owed about $30,000 on the house.

At the end of March we had a huge garage sale which helped with our expenses for the sale. Anything that did not sell went to the local thrift shops. I closed my Mesquite Press business account at the bank and made other arrangements. Moving to a smaller place with no patio and no garage meant we had to cut to the bone. The hardest part of all was dispossessing myself of some of my large book collection and files (I still have three bookcases full of books.) Packing our possessions was a big chore but it went relatively smoothly. We made tentative arrangements with Bekins moving company.

I had lived in Desert Hot Springs for 15 years, the longest time I had ever spent in the same place. Could it be that Little Jumping Joan was getting restless? I miss some of the things I loved in the area such as our comfortable enclosed patio. Here I watched the roadrunner showing off a juicy lizard to his potential mate and the antics and the perpetual motion of the hummingbirds and the aggressive mockingbird protecting her nest. What a pleasure it was to watch the garden vegetables as they sprang from the ground and then soon invited us to pick them. I would miss opening the tap to the delicious pure natural water from deep underground wells that had won several prizes in national contests for municipal water.

No longer would I attend the services at Newman Center and the friends I had made there. I would miss my Irish doctor friend who so graciously introduced me to Gaelic Irish. I also missed others related to my desert writings, especially Alice Bell, Nicolette Sundberg and Ann Japenga who now has my complete collection of the old *Desert* magazines (I have the Index so can call her if I need an article which she Xeroxes for me.) I also miss my little walks in the Big Morongo Preserve and the many canyons in the area and my meetings with the Archaeological Society. However, I do not miss the torrid summers and the very windy winters and springs that are so common especially in the Desert Hot Springs area due to its location between two very high mountains, Mt. San Gorgonio and Mt. San Jacinto. I felt I had done my best to bond with the desert but it was time to move on.

CHAPTER 35

IMPERIAL BEACH

Finally we closed escrow on April 16th, turned over the keys to the new owner, and the same day moved to Imperial Beach just a short time before Bekins arrived. They very kindly put everything in the location we had already planned on paper. Even though our apartment was small we were happy to have two bedrooms, each with its own bathroom. David generously agreed that the second bedroom would become my office, whereas David's computer and files were installed in the bedroom. David was much less of a collector than I was so I was fortunate to have this extra space.

That evening we had to eat out as we had not yet unpacked. It took us a while to find a place for everything, but eventually we squeezed everything in somehow. David and I had fun working together how to best adapt our furniture to the more limited space, for example two file cases provided a base for David's computer desk with a slab of Melmac for the top. We did the usual chores of signing up with the local electricity supplier and the telephone company. We had to find a new bank, a new church, grocery store, library and other needed services such as a new HMO for our health care. We were happy to receive a check in the mail for $79,000 from the sale of the house that enabled us to pay the rent that was much higher than our mortgage had been.

I began to explore the Tijuana River Estuary with its nearby Visitor Center and checked out the beach area. A handy tide table enabled me to know when to walk on the beach at low tide and in the Estuary at high tide in order to appreciate the special beauty of each. Later I got to know one of the Rangers at the Estuary and sometimes helped him record the native plants at the Estuary for a plant inventory. I.B.

has a wonderful Pier with the Tin Fish Restaurant at the end and a park in front of it and a couple of other small parks in the town. I joined in the fun at the beach during the Annual Sandcastle Days in July and enjoyed the music at the Symphony by the Sea event sponsored by the city in September. For a small fee the "Taste of I.B." introduced us to many of the local merchants where we also received a small gift or food. I joined the San Diego Natural History Museum in Balboa Park and went on some of their walks and other events.

I soon became a member of the Friends of the Library and later joined the I.B. Women's Club that met every month and joined a few members at weekly meetings of the craft committee. Not being very "crafty" I limited myself to making circles on old greeting cards and cutting them out to help make place mats for future craft sales. When I formerly lived in Ocean Beach, I had belonged to a group called Walkabout that does walks led by volunteers throughout San Diego County. A monthly newsletter listed the different walks that just required us to show up at a specific location at a specific time. I mostly went to ones in the South Bay area, some of the beach areas and Balboa Park.

At first I attended St. Charles Church in nearby Nestor, but later transferred to Sacred Heart Church in Coronado as I.B. did not have its own church. There I belonged to a Small Church Community that met about every two weeks to read and discuss the readings for the next Sunday Mass. They had coffee and doughnuts after Mass so I had an opportunity to get acquainted with some other parishioners. A few years later when the price of gas went up to $4.00 and the fact that a Maryknoll priest was assigned to the parish, I returned to St. Charles. He had been a missionary in Egypt and Peru and held the office of Director of the Propagation of the Faith (related to missions) for the diocese. I was very happy listening to his sermons and his efforts to improve the church, e.g. skylights which made it more bright inside. He was very popular with the congregation which consisted of many Filipinos and Hispanics, but for some reason the Bishop removed him from his position, much to everyone's sadness. The new pastor was a very well educated Filipino but I found it difficult to hear his sermons and understand them. Eventually I began attending St. Jerome's Church a few miles away with a young pastor who was a very positive person with simple practical Gospel related sermons. So for now that is my place of worship.

David had bought a used Chrysler in October and used it every week to go to the Library or shopping. He continued at first with his paper sculptures and then began attending art classes at the Senior Center. As they were teaching mostly watercolor art he decided to spend his time at his little studio at home learning the art of pastel drawing which was new to him. He made use of the kitchen table and set it up as a studio with his own home made easel with all his supplies at hand (we have another table in the living room where we can eat.) Later he constructed a cardboard easel and used his computer desk as his studio for most of his work. My contribution was to raid the recycle bins on the property for usable cardboard and occasionally making a discrete comment about what I liked about a painting.

I contacted some friends I had known in the past from work and also some of the Medical Mission Sisters living in San Diego. Some of the retired Sisters that I knew were living in an assisted living facility in the city of Orange. I went to visit some of them and in December of 2004 sadly I attended the funeral of Sister Helen Elizabeth Leary (formerly Sister De Sales) who had been in charge of the kitchen in the early Maracaibo days. At this stage of my life I keep crossing people off my Christmas list when I get word they have died. Recently after I had mailed a Christmas card to Sister Petra Berg (one of my informants for *Desert Padre*) I received a letter telling me of her death in Los Gatos…and so it goes.

In September of 2004 I saw information about Irish classes being held at the House of Ireland in Balboa Park so signed up for those which were held once a week except during the summer and Christmas holidays. Having already learned French, Spanish, Urdu and a little Latin more or less easily, I was surprised at how difficult Irish is. It was a good exercise in humility to have to struggle so much. As I am now getting older, studying Irish is a great way to keep my brain active too. The House of Ireland also offered a monthly history class that gave me more insights into the Irish people's heritage. I now have a whole shelf of books on Ireland and collecting more as time goes by. I also read the *Irish Herald*, a monthly newspaper printed in San Francisco for those Americans who are interested in all things Irish. I enjoy the bi-monthly magazine, *Ireland of the Welcomes* printed in Ireland by the Irish Tourist Board. Reading the articles only makes me feel like visiting the Emerald Isle again. In my two trips I had only visited parts of three counties...Kerry, Clare and Cork and a short time in Dublin and two day trips from that city...so many more places to explore!

I went to the University of San Diego (Catholic University) for a two week course on Irish Literature taught by a Donie O'Sullivan from Tralee. Unfortunately he showed up but the notices went out too late so not enough students signed up, and the class was canceled. I did show up however and had a chance to chat with him for a few minutes. Now I know three O'Sullivans from Tralee—Fr. Jeremiah O'Sullivan, the Pastor Emeritus at Sacred Heart Church in Coronado; the above-mentioned Donie O'Sullivan and Donal O'Sullivan whom I met in Killarney and was instrumental in sponsoring the memorial to Father Crowley in Killarney. (None of them are related.)

Imperial Beach has an excellent fitness center where I worked on some exercises with a trainer for a while. Later at the same center our HMO, Secure Horizons was offering group exercise classes called "Silver Sneakers" for their senior enrollees free so I began attending those twice a week. More recently I enrolled in the free "Stretch and Flex" classes at the Senior Center. They meet three times a week at a more convenient hour than the Silver Sneakers. I try to do a short hike or walk on the other days. Taking care of my health is a priority.

Another group I became involved in the beginning of 2005 was I.B. Beautiful. The name refers to the goal of the group which is to help keep I.B. beautiful by volunteering to weed two public gardens...one called the Triangle with red, white and blue flowers that had been set up at the time of the Bicentennial. The other was a small Serenity Garden with beautiful native plants. At Christmas time we bought many poinsettia plants and placed them in the Triangle garden for the season. Later we also offered to clean up the plants at the Sound Wall on Palm Avenue. Originally the group used to award a prize for the home whose landscaping was the best in the City or had improved the most. This had been discontinued but there is some interest in reinstating it. We met monthly at a noon potluck lunch and discussed the next work day and what needed to be done. We had to consult with the City Public Works and were able to get some funds for new plants when needed.

In November of 2002, 2003, 2004 and 2005 I attended the Old West Days in Shoshone, mostly to network with old desert friends such as Judy Palmer, a retired pediatrician from Palo Alto, and others. Judy had put a short letter in the *Inyo Register* newspaper requesting information on a nurse named May Dorville who had worked in Death Valley years ago. I did not recognize the name but I kept the clipping on my desk and many months later in September 2001 I e-mailed her with information about Dr. Riley Shrum who had also worked in Death Valley, suggesting that maybe there was some connection there. She was surprised that I had kept the clipping for so long but gave me a phone number to call when she was in Death Valley.

As I had planned a trip to Bishop we agreed to meet at her camper van at the Diamond J RV Park in October of 2001. Aside from talking about our mutual interests we both went to the old cemeteries in Bishop and the one in Independence just to check things out. Judy has kind of adopted the Shoshone Museum especially by doing research on several desert women and helping Kari Coughlin and Robin Flinchum with the exhibits there. As two lovers of desert history the two of us hit it off very well as we spent a couple of hours together exchanging information on desert stories. I introduced her to people I knew from my contacts when doing research for *American Desert* magazine and *Desert Padre*.

She once dropped in on us when I was still living in Desert Hot Springs and lately here in Imperial Beach. Since then we have corresponded by letters and e-mail. She is now helping the curator at the Death Valley National Park and every once in a while she sends me a copy of a clipping from the *Los Angeles Times* or other newspapers with items about Father Crowley. I had suggested she do some research on Dr. Riley Shrum who had been the physician during the Depression time at Death Valley Junction. As Father Crowley had mentioned him a couple of times, I though he might be a good subject for a story. She took my suggestion and gave a short paper at one of the Death Valley History Conferences which was very well received. She even found photos of him with his nurse at the clinic where he worked for Pacific Coast Borax. I filled her in on sources for information on other women she is now researching, such as Agnes Reid of Panamint Springs Resort and Louise Grantham who was a successful talc miner. Judy is a retired pediatrician who was last working at Stanford University as a researcher on cystic fibrosis and like me, enjoying retirement.

Another "desert rat" I have met there is Emmett Harder from Devore whose wife, Ruth, puts out a newsletter called *Panamint Breeze* along with other friends and Emmett has written a book about the Panamints and the southeast region of Death Valley entitled *These Canyons are Full of Ghosts*. Another friend is Cliff Walker who gave me hospitality once in Barstow and is the author of a well-researched book on California bootlegging days, entitled *One Eye Red, the Other Closed*. When I go to Shoshone I sometimes stayed at the Tecopa Hostel and then enjoyed the wonderful hot tubs at the Tecopa County Park. In February of 2004 I attended the Death Valley History Conference and again contacted people I knew from my life in the desert.

In October of 2005 I took a trip sponsored by the San Diego Natural History Museum to Chihuahua, Mexico to visit the spectacular Copper Canyon area. Our group enjoyed a week of beautiful weather and magnificent views from one of the hotels at about 7,500 feet overlooking the canyons. This is where the Tarahumara Indians live and still keep to their ancient customs and language. They are famous for being very fast runners. Part of the trip was on a railroad train that has 88 tunnels and more than 30 bridges along its 400 mile stretch. It was a pleasure to order off the menu for breakfast in the dining car. I spoke to two young Mexican geologists who were going to do reports on gold mines in the area.

At the end of the trip we stopped off at a small town of Mata Ortiz, famous for its pottery by Juan Quesada and an archaeological site called Paquime. At Casas Grandes I went to Mass and had a chance to join in on a young lady's quinceañera (when the girl is fifteen) celebration. As I left the church I was given a small wooden box with a decade Rosary in it as a souvenir of the event. As I had walked quite a distance to the church by myself, I was fortunate to get a ride back to my hotel by a couple who were driving the priest to another mission church where he was going to say Mass. Serendipity again came to the rescue.

In March of 2006 I took a trip with Elderhostel starting in Tucson to visit most of the missions of the Jesuit missionary, Father Francisco Kino. We stayed the whole week in the town of Magdalena in the Mexican State of Sonora where he is now buried. From the motel we set out each day to visit other missions, some in ruins, some in restoration, but all with beautiful surroundings and fascinating histories. In Arizona I stopped by to visit two friends, Willma Gore in Sedona and the other in Fountain Hills. Sedona is a really spectacular place of Arizona with red rocks everywhere.

In July of 2006 a Trinity College classmate, Julie Wood and her husband Bill, stopped by for a short visit. She lives in Long Island but has a son who lives in San Diego so she was able to drop by and share some updating. Unfortunately Trinity College in Burlington had to close because of financial problems. I still keep in touch with Julie, my college roommate Gennie, who lives in Vermont and Peggy Magner Kopeski from Rhode Island. As this was an election year, Gennie and I talked on the phone about politics especially as she was knowledgeable about the former governor of Vermont, Howard Dean, whom she recommended as head of the Democratic Party. Other visitors were Roxie Rauch Wotring, Lee Oldham, Judy Palmer, and Laurie Gibson whom I had met at the San Diego Publishers Alliance and was moving to Pacific Grove.

CHAPTER 36

IRELAND AGAIN

In August of 2006 I made my third trip to Ireland, this time with Elderhostel. Some excerpts from my journal of the trip called "Discovering the West of Ireland" follow. When we arrived in Dublin we heard about the terrorist threat on London using some type of gel explosive and the order came out to prohibit all liquids and gels in carry-on luggage. The Irish solved this problem very neatly by allowing us to have our carry-on luggage put in the baggage compartment in the cargo hold. As I was only going on the short trip to Shannon, this was not a big inconvenience for me. I was met by an Elderhostel staff member from Kinsale and then taken in a van to Killarney via Limerick. We stayed at the International Hotel in the heart of downtown Killarney.

Earlier I had left a message for Dr. Margaret O'Connor (whom I had met at the Killarney Book Shop for my book signing) to call me from Cork. It was quite late when she phoned back. She was unable to visit me in Killarney as she was baby-sitting a grandchild and I couldn't take a trip to Cork. She talked a long while especially about her interest in the efforts to beatify Mother Anna Dengel who had been a student of the University of Cork's Medical School and worked as a lab assistant to her mother who was also a doctor. It was difficult to end the conversation and I was dead tired, but I didn't have the heart to tell her. I finally got to bed at about 10:30 p.m.

Our first lecture at the Great Southern Hotel was by Batt Burns, a wonderful Seanachie or story-teller who had been brought up by his grandfather, Sigisford Clifford, a seanachie in the town of Sneem. He told us some very good old time Irish stories. I bought two of his CD's. A bronze bust of his grandfather is at the Bog Village on the Ring of Kerry. In the evening a couple from California and Sister Margretta and I were invited to Clare and Paddy Lynch's home in Tralee for supper. Their adult daughter Lorraine was also there. Later I found out that Sister Margretta was from the same Franciscan Oldenberg community in Indiana as my friend from Bishop, Mary Franke, who had formerly belonged to that same order. They knew each other quite well as I later found out. SERENDIPITY is still following me around! Elderhostel had contacted various families in Tralee and other nearby towns so that we could enjoy meeting some Irish families in their own homes. We had a simple home-cooked meal and talked on various topics including where we had all come from and how our families had emigrated to America. The couple had a son and a grandson in Connecticut so were familiar with American culture.

Our bus driver, Martin Thomas, was from Brea in County Wicklow and stayed with us for the whole trip. We visited the Dingle Peninsula and toured the Blasket Island Visitor Center (unfortunately not the actual Island.) Here I bought Peig Sayers' book, "An Old Woman's Reflections." It had been written in Irish but translated by her son. Our guide for the trip was an archaeologist who pointed out the various sites, including the Dunbeg Stone Fort, and the Gallarus Oratory with its abundant fuchsia bushes nearby. At the Great Southern Hotel in Killarney we enjoyed a wonderful demonstration of Irish instruments and were given a tin whistle to practice on for a while (what a terrible noise!) We learned about how the Irish drum (the bodhran) is played and the hornpipe (the pib uillean) an instrument similar to the Scotch bagpipe but not quite as loud.

We took a jaunting cart to Ross Castle. No one seemed to want to sit in the front seat with the jarvey (driver) so I sat next to Charlie. When he was asked to be photographed with some of the group, he turned over the reins to me. Jessica was a docile and obedient horse and I felt honored. At Ross Castle we had a tour of Lake Leane on the tour boat, the Lily of Killarney. Unfortunately we could only see the overgrown woods of the island of Innisfallen. That evening I was invited by Father Crowley's relatives, Peggy Lyne, her daughter Dolores Lyne and Julie Healy Rae to have dinner with them at the Hotel Europe on the shores of Lake Leane. Dolores gave me her phone number so I could call her when I got to Galway where she lives. The next day we took a bus to the Iveragh Peninsula on the Ring of Kerry with comments by Michael Courtney, a former mayor of Killarney. He was especially knowledgeable about Daniel O'Connell, the Irish Liberator.

I had been told by Dolores to see the lady at O'Leary's Antique Shop next to the Killarney Book Shop. It was not open but I knocked on the door and an older lady met me. She had no information on the Crowley family (which I had hoped to obtain) but she gave me five old postcard photos of the ruins of the monastery on Innisfallen. I gave some away and kept one for myself.

One reason I wanted to visit Killarney again was that I found out that the memorial to Father Crowley had been erected a short while before. It was on the newly named Mission Road. It had been previously named the Inner Relief Road so if nothing else this was a great improvement! It is just a few steps from the International Hotel and across the street from Killarney National Park. It is located in the former Fern Garden with two plaques, one in honor of Father Crowley and one honoring a young lay missionary, Donal Leahy, who had died in the missions of Brazil. The memorial is a huge wheel-like monument made from slate from the quarry at Valentia Island at the tip of the Iveragh Peninsula. Father Crowley would have been pleased that they used local material and a very simple but elegant design.

After a fairly long bus trip we arrived in Galway city where we stayed at the Flannery Hotel in the outskirts of Galway on the Dublin Road. It was quieter than the International Hotel but without the class and the convenience of being so close to everything in the downtown area. Almost all the waitresses, maids and janitors were Polish (so much for my thinking I could practice my Irish on the Irish country girls.) There were many Polish immigrants in Ireland as well as many tourists from all over Europe.

We listened to various speakers...Peadar O'Dowd on the history and present state of Galway; Dr. Lionel Pilkington on the theatre in Ireland and on Yeats and Lady Gregory. In the afternoon we visited Coole Park, once the home of Lady Gregory and later on to Kilmacduagh with the ruins of several monastic buildings and a leaning Round Tower. Donal Taheny who stayed on our bus gave us the history and archaeology of the area.

In the evening we had dinner at Pierre's on Quay St. in downtown Galway. Dolores Lyne and her husband James Herrold met me at a nearby pub. We then drove to the home of Dolores' artist friend, Leonie King. Her home was an ancient Norman castle called Oranmore Castle that was built in the 14th Century as a fortress type castle that guarded the approach to Galway from the south. It fell into ruin and was purchased by Leonie's mother, Anita Leslie King who also wrote "Jennie," the story of Winston Churchhill's American mother, Jennie Randolph Churchill. Anita's grandmother was Leonie Leslie, a sister of Jennie's. I met Leonie's 96-year old father Commodore King who had been a submarine commander in

World War II. Leonie and her husband were restoring the castle so we could only see the furnishings in the Great Hall. We all enjoyed some wine and cookies in the ancient kitchen. Leonie gave me three pictures of the castle, one an engraving dated 1792; another was a photo taken in 1900 with the surrounding buildings still intact; the last photo was from 1940 when only the main castle building was still standing but in very poor condition. She did not have any more recent photos available and it was too dark to take a photo. They are still working very hard on bringing the castle to its former glory.

Another great trip was the 45-minute ferry ride to the town of Kilronan on the Aran Island of Inishmore. A small minibus took us to Dun Aengus with its ruins and the walls of the fort on the sheer cliffs overlooking the sea. The Fort or Dun (meaning "Fort" in Irish) is thought to date from about 1000 B.C. Later we had a lecture by a former priest, Dara Molloy, who was now a self-styled Celtic priest. He is beginning to organize a project on Celtic spirituality and living a simple life style. We also had a lecture by Paul Gosling on the role of the Celts in Ireland. Celts are not a political identity but a people and culture. He gave a brief summary of Irish mythology, especially the story of Cuchulain (most of us learned of this hero from Frank McCourt's *Angela's Ashes*.) Other topics were the fairies and fairy forts that are found all over Ireland.

I had been told by friends in our Irish class to visit Charlie Byrne's Bookshop, so I spent my free afternoon taking a bus from the hotel to visit the store and bought some Galway history books and a roomy tote bag. In another shop, Ensoms, I purchased Irish language books. I walked around the downtown area and returned to the hotel on the bus. It was very crowded with many university students but one of them kindly gave me his seat.

We were treated that evening to a Siamsa Tire Seisiun, a musical group of three young girls and their parents. They presented a touching dramatization of St. Bridget healing a young crippled girl. Other groups performed traditional singing and dancing.

We then took the long ride from Galway to Donegal. On the way we stopped at the popular shrine to the Virgin Mary at Knock. Many visitors come from Europe and America to present their petitions there. In the town of Gurteen we had a wonderful bowl of Irish stew at the Teach Murray pub. The Coleman Heritage Center has exhibits of the South Sligo traditional music and dance. We watched a slide show featuring the different instruments.

Our last stop was at the Tara Hotel in the harbor of Killibegs. Killibegs is mostly a fishing town, but in a talk by a local fisherman we learned about the limits placed on their catches because of trade restrictions from the European Union, so some efforts have been made to invest in the tourist industry. In the town of Glencolumcille a local expert narrated the story of Father McDyer who developed a small community center or Folk Art Village that we toured. It is also the site of a Gaelic cultural center where classes are held on Irish language and culture. We later took a group photo at the seacoast at the Strand with a magnificent view on all sides. Another historic spot was St. Columba's church and cemetery. Here were buried both Protestants and Catholics and a mass grave for famine victims. We could see the Ben Bulben Mountains in the distance.

One of the most surprising parts of the Elderhostel trip was learning more about the Protestant Orange Order. As most parts of Donegal are adjacent to parts of Northern Ireland, there are many towns with Protestant populations. Rossnowlagh is the only town that hosts the July 12th Orange Parade in the Irish Republic. We visited one Protestant church and had an interesting presentation there by a young Methodist minister. He was a committed member of the Orange Order and gave its history, its goals and precepts and demonstrated the uniforms they use for their annual Parade, along with banners and other regalia they used when they marched. The minister's young daughter performed a simple dance that is used during the parades. He did acknowledge "The Troubles" but emphasized the Order's tolerance and respect, although the precepts do mention being against anything Roman Catholic. He never mentioned Ian Paisley.

Later in the bus Martin talked about Paisley's blocking the Good Friday Agreement but is hopeful that one day Northern Ireland will join the Republic, possibly after Paisley's death. The strong economy of the Irish Republic and the increasing majority of Roman

Catholics in Northern Ireland may be factors that change the dynamics. However, Northern Ireland would have to give up some pensions, a lower tax rate and higher savings interest rates they now receive as members of the United Kingdom. After the presentation the ladies of the church served us a simple meal in the parish hall. Martin's opinion was that reconciliation would probably not be in his lifetime. *I now wonder how he felt when he later saw photos of Ian Paisley shaking hands with the Sinn Fein leader, Gerry Adams!*

In the city of Donegal we had a tour of the Donegal Castle with its three eras: the early O'Donnells (later the castle was burned by Red Hugh O'Donnell in the "Flight of the Earls;") then an Englishman named Sir Basil Brooke owned it and is now restored as a tourist attraction The guide showed us the "garderobe" room that was used as a toilet with the waste falling through a hole in the floor to the bottom of the castle. One part of the castle was still in ruins without a roof. We had our farewell supper with free drinks and traditional music played by a couple with accordion, fiddle and tin whistle. At my request they played "She Passed through the Fair" and "The Sally Gardens."

On the return to Shannon we stopped at Drumcliffe, a historic tower with ties to St. Columba and also the poet Yeats. A Church of Ireland minister showed a video on both in the small stone church. A Celtic cross in the cemetery contains engravings of Adam and Eve, Cain and Abel and other scriptural references. We paid homage to Yeats at his tombstone where we read the epitaph he had planned for himself: "Cast a cold eye on life, on death. Horseman, pass by." We had lunch at the Yeats Country Inn. We spent our last night in Ennis, County Clare before boarding our flights from Shannon Airport and my trip to Los Angeles. Another great serendipitous trip!

CHAPTER 37

BACK HOME

In September of 2006 David had visited an electronic store and had car trouble. An employee, Arthur Holt who had waited on him, offered to drive David home. David decided he had enough of problems with the car so gave the Buick to Arthur. After that I was the only driver with my Honda.

In October 2006 I heard about a seven-day cruise on the Holland-American line to Baja and that some of the members of Walkabout were getting special rates. Although I had never been particularly interested in a cruise, I decided to try it out. David was not interested in going on the trip. Everything went well except that on the second day out one of the ship's engines (there were two) was disabled so we went only to Cabo San Lucas and Mazatlan but had to skip Puerta Vallarta as the ship lost a lot of time. One activity I enjoyed was the piano bar where the pianist had us make requests for our favorite tunes and we sang along. It was an enjoyable trip but I was disappointed. They did give us a small discount on our ship bill and a discount on future trips. However, I felt I had my experience with cruises and declined to accept the future trips.

In November I attended the Shoshone Old West Days and early in the morning on my return home I was driving on highway 127 on a part with a very narrow shoulder. As I was looking at a side road I got a little too close to the shoulder so I had to correct the car in the other direction and on returning to my lane I drove off the fairly steep shoulder and the car landed on the four wheels in a flat area. I remember going over the edge and then waking up looking at what appeared similar to a blue jacket I used to own. It was the blue airbag. I heard myself crying out: "Help me!" I looked around for my purse so I could use my cell phone to call for help, only to read "out of service" when I called 911. My glasses had bounced off my face and nowhere to be found, but I remembered I had my pair of prescription sunglasses and found them on the floor so that helped me see. I had severe pain in my right ankle but was able to get out of the car, happy that the door actually opened. I limped but stood up, holding on to my purse. The trunk of the car couldn't be opened so unable to take anything from there. I waited anxiously until a pickup truck drove by on the road above me and I was able to wave and cry out "help me!" Fortunately a young man came down the slope and helped me limp to his truck. I did get his name and address which he wrote on a small scrap of paper. *When I got home and was better, I sent him a thank you note for his acting as a Good Samaritan. He had attended a friend's wedding at Furnace Creek Inn and was on his way back home to the Coast.*

I asked him to drive me back to Shoshone and told him that Judy Palmer was in room 26 at the motel. He knocked on the door but no answer. Then I remembered she was going to clean up at the museum, so he knocked there and no answer. Shortly after Judy came back from her morning run and he told her about me. Judy took over as the practical person she is and helped me negotiate various tasks. She got in touch with Susan Sorrells, the town owner, who contacted the sheriff or highway patrol to see about my poor destroyed Honda. She then drove me to the town of Pahrump, across the border into Nevada where we went to the local hospital. They took an X-ray of my right ankle and a chest X-ray. I had a broken ankle on the inside of my foot and a sprained ankle on the outside. They put a temporary splint on my right foot and I left with a pair of crutches. The chest x-ray did not show any broken ribs although I had bruises there and a gash on my right knee which was bandaged. *A couple of years later I had an MRI for an illness and it showed "old rib fractures on the right side."* My right hip was also pretty sore.

At one point Judy left the emergency room and came back with my regular eyeglasses. Apparently, my friend Emmett Harder had gone to the site of the accident and looked around. He found my glasses in the dirt so he drove to Pahrump to deliver them to Judy. I now had my regular glasses, which was helpful as it started getting too dark for sunglasses. After leaving the hospital Judy found out, after calling Susan Sorrells, that the Highway Patrol had towed my car to Auto Works in Pahrump where we saw the car which had been totaled. They had to use a crow bar to open the trunk and retrieve my suitcase and other belongings and put them in Judy's van. I was given some Vicodin pills so the pain was minimal. I also think it gave me a slight "high" as Judy and I had some great conversations on the road with lots of laughs. I showed her how to take the back roads to Imperial Beach as Highway 15 is always crowded from the returning crowd from Las Vegas on Sundays.

She let me use her satellite cell phone to try to call David. He hardly can hear the phone when it rings, so I called my neighbor across the street, Katrinka Sieber, who knocked on his window to tell him I would be calling him. I told him I had a car accident but was o.k. "with 'only' a broken ankle" and would be arriving about midnight with Judy. Judy and I stopped before leaving Pahrump to have a bite to eat and some coffee as I had left Shoshone expecting to eat on the road. I walked down the three steps to our apartment using my crutches. David was relieved to see me and fixed a nice hot meal for me and Judy. She stayed that night and also all day Monday. She spent the time as my nurse, doctor, helper and friend. She called the insurance company for me and Coronado Hospital. On Tuesday she first dropped me off at the voting place as it was Election Day.

Then she drove me to Coronado Hospital where they decided to admit me instead to the Coronado Villas, an adjacent nursing home also used for rehabilitation services. My first night after having a pain pill, and just getting off to sleep about 10:30 p.m., I was awakened by the nurse's aide asking me "what is your height?!" Unfortunately it was about five days before the orthopedic surgeon arrived to evaluate my injury and put on a cast. So I started Physical Therapy quite late. I spent a total of eleven days in the three-bed unit with two other patients. One was a 103 year old lady who was living in memories of the past, which was o.k. in the daytime, but she became more aggressive at night, demanding that a particular relative take her out of the hospital, and shouting at her young children to behave, etc. She was shouting a lot so I couldn't sleep. The other patient was more confused at night also and tried to jump over the bedrails. This action would probably have caused an injury, so I was left to use the call bell to ask for the nurse. She always came to me first but I had to tell her the problems were with my roommates. The physical therapist helped me use my crutches and a walker.

Before discharge the staff held a case management meeting. I had invited my neighbor, Jan Daniels who is also a nurse, to attend as she might be the best person to interpret everything to David. They agreed that I would be having a Visiting Nurse, a P.T. and a home health aide to help with personal care for at least three days to check how I could adapt to my disability. As I was discharged on a Saturday I wasn't surprised that I received no call from a Home Health Agency on Sunday. I never did receive any calls even though I had called a number that Judy had given me to check on my home care. They said they would look into it, but I never heard from them again.

I did receive a rented wheelchair, a 3-in-one commode with toilet riser, a walker and a special shoe I could use over my cast. I had to manage until I finally had the cast removed on December 27th. I went to Coronado Hospital for P.T. to help me with leg exercises. I was reimbursed by my insurance agency for these expenses and also for the value of my totaled car.

During my convalescence some of the ladies from the I.B. Womens' Club kindly brought me some home-cooked meals and one did my laundry, Robin Fuller came to give me a massage and Cece helped me with housework. As David was not fond of turkey, I celebrated Thanksgiving the best way I knew how with a home delivered Thanksgiving meal from Meals on Wheels. Meanwhile David had gone to Fuller Honda and with money from his Ameritrade funds paid for a new 2007 Honda Accord just like my old one only new! It wasn't until January 12th that I was able to take my first drive in the new car. Later I reimbursed David for this expense as it was my car and the insurance agency had paid for the old one. At least I was kept busy during the holiday season by sending out my usual Christmas cards. Later I received a package from Emmett Harder with my old tan cardigan which had been found in the dirt near the site of my accident and also my St. Christopher's clip that hung on the car window visor!

In the beginning of 2007 David had begun to have bouts of depression with panic attacks. I finally convinced him to see Dr. Gordon. He wanted me to be present during the office visit. She offered a referral to a psychiatrist which he refused. He did take the pills which later had to be changed to another medication as he was getting aural hallucinations which disturbed him very much. I had a difficult time trying to get him to eat so I made easy puddings and other simple meals so he would get the needed nourishment. I could tell he was still not well emotionally and occasionally mentioned suicide as a possible solution to his depression. He improved slowly with the new medication and his appetite was a little better.

I resigned from my membership in I.B. Beautiful as their focus changed considerably with more emphasis on starting a Farmer's Market and also efforts to have a "play place" for dogs. However I was not without something to do. I signed up for something more close to my heart—Docent training at the Tijuana River Estuary. It was a class of 28 hours. When finished I decided on offering to do a Nature Walk with emphasis on plant life of the Estuary. I still do that every second Saturday of the month. The walk is just around the Visitor Center and I really enjoy it. After the walk I give the participants a plant list and a little laminated card that I thought might be a good souvenir. The poem is one from the English mystic poet, William Blake: "To see a world in a grain of sand/ and a heaven in a wildflower: Hold infinity in the palm of your hand/ and eternity in an hour." I keep a copy of it on the wall near my desk window.

In March I attended a Celtic Spirituality conference at St. Charles Church and found it very helpful. The Sister who helped organize the event was Sister Paula Smith who lives in San Ysidro. Later I contacted her and found out she was a Medical Missionary of Mary who lives nearby in San Ysidro.

My prayer life is pretty limited now with weekly attendance at Mass and some spiritual reading, such as the Celtic spirituality book, "Anam Cara," by John O'Donohue. He has a chapter entitled: "Aging: The Beauty of the Inner Harvest" which I have found most helpful in writing these thoughts and reflecting on my present stage of life. Sister Miriam Therese's "Paradoxology" makes Teilhard de Chardin's works on the Christian view of evolution come to life with the newest scientific findings in quantum physics. She manages to move quantum theology to a more poetic yet practical place. My early Baltimore Catechism book said: "God is everywhere," especially in people, but now I see more clearly that God is literally everywhere, in the farthest star and the tiniest microbe and even in the chaos of everyday life. So much to think about!

A sign that I must be praying is when I find my eyes and nose tingling with unshed tears when some word in the sermon or some action of the congregation makes me full of longing in my search for God. These unshed tears may also be a form of self-pity, but so be it. Sometimes my longing is for a mother, a father, a real family, and a need to belong. I find myself saying to myself "Stop the world, I want to get <u>on</u>" when I feel that my background is so different from others I meet and I missed out on so many things that others take for granted. From the Scriptures my favorite prayers are: "Lord, that I may see;" "Lord, I believe, help my unbelief." In my episodes of doubt I ask: "Lord, to whom shall we go?" For consolation I remember the words of the Apocalypse that "God will wipe every tear from their eyes." A prayer which comes easy and often is: "Thank you, Lord."

CHAPTER 38

A SAD TIME

My friend Sarah Ann O'Gara visited a couple of days around Memorial Day weekend. As David enjoyed her company, I asked her to spend time with him in the hope of distracting him from his depression. At the end of June 2007 I attended the three-day Lone Pine Reunion which is held every three years. I had just returned home on the 25th and was on the phone with Sarah Ann telling her of my trip when I heard David shout out in a loud voice "Joan!" I left the phone off the hook and ran to the kitchen. He had dropped his fork as he prepared his supper and fell as he bent to pick it up. As he was in severe pain and could not even sit up, I called my neighbors upstairs and Bob and Jan Daniel helped me and called 911.

The ambulance drove him to Coronado Hospital Emergency Room. I was in the front seat and the Medic watched David in the back. When he discovered she was from Chicago they had a pretty upbeat conversation on all things Chicago. They had given him a pain shot so he was trying to be brave. Bob and Jan followed in their car and we all waited a couple of hours before he was seen and hospitalized.

X-rays showed a fracture in his left leg and a fracture in his right hip (the same one that had a hip replacement due to a previous fracture.) Bob and Jan drove me back home. *I wondered later what would have happened to David if I had not been at home when he fell, but thanked God that I was there to help and also that Bob and Jan were available.*

The left leg fracture was operated on at Coronado, but the doctors felt they needed a higher level of services for the right hip fracture, so he was admitted to Sharp Hospital in Kearny Mesa, about a 45-mile round-trip away. He endured several complications, including jaundice caused by a gallstone that had to be removed by laparoscopy (a procedure that only requires a small incision into the abdomen.) The surgery on his right hip was difficult and long. He lost a lot of blood during the surgery and began having heart and lung problems. The doctors planned on doing a thoracentesis (a procedure that punctures the pleural space to drain the fluid in the pleural cavity,) but were unable to put him in the proper position for that procedure.

At one point the doctors discussed with me his Advanced Directives for Health Care which stated he did not want to be resuscitated. They and I agreed on Palliative Care with the possibility of moving to a Hospice Care facility. His respiratory and heart condition deteriorated so much that soon he did not respond. I do remember some words he did say before that: "You have no idea...I don't know how to find the words..." He was referring to his love for me. That was his last verbal contact with me. My last words to him, (whether he heard or not) were: "Thank you for loving me so much..." He died on July 11th, seventeen days after his fall. He died of pulmonary and heart failure although his death certificate read: "complications of leg and hip fracture" with contributing factors of "osteoporosis and ischemic heart disease." David was 87 years old. He had a full life and I was privileged that he shared it with me.

His death was not unexpected, but the finality of it came to me as I was alone to make arrangements for his funeral, leaving me with little time to grieve and consider the effect of his death on me. Fortunately we had paid for cremation arrangements with Humphrey

Mortuary a few years before. The customer service representative, Jill Gibson, was very helpful as I slowly made plans for his cremation and a memorial service. Pam Langston, a member of Friends of the I.B. Library, worked on weekends at the Mortuary and helped me with arrangements for the service.

I invited several friends and people who knew David or me. It was more a celebration of his life especially as an artist. I told everyone who came that they could pick one of his pastel paintings to take home (there were a lot to choose from.) A friend, Sr. Jeanette, offered a beautiful opening prayer. I gave a short summary of his life. Several people came to the lectern to say a few words about how he touched their life. One was a daughter of a public health nurse friend who was in a wheelchair as she had multiple sclerosis. David had met her mother once and suggested that maybe her daughter could try her hand at pastel painting as a distraction and a source of pleasure and accomplishment. The daughter mentioned how much this had helped her. Bob Daniel gave a biblical tribute and honored David's memory as did several others. I asked the staff to play a C.D. that featured Louis Armstrong's songs, e.g. "What a Wonderful World" and at the exit "When the Saints Go Marching In." These were some of David's favorites. During the time when people were choosing their painting, we heard the New Orleans "Jazz Funeral," a piece we had both loved. We had a bulletin board that our neighbors, the Daniels, had helped fix up with photos of David at different periods of his life. Another board listed some of David's favorite things. A bucket of individual yellow roses (David's favorites) was placed at the center of the room. Each attendee was given a rose to take home. I had asked people not to send flowers but if they wished, to make donations to the Art Classes that were held at the Senior Center for them to purchase needed art supplies. People were very generous and the local senior artists and the teacher were very pleased with the gift. Others who could not attend also had their choice of a painting later.

A couple of weeks later I went with Jill Gibson when his cremated remains were placed in a niche in the beautiful military cemetery at Fort Rosecrans in Point Loma, San Diego County. I was given a folded American flag. He is gone but not forgotten. I visit the site on his birthday and his day of death and leave a few yellow roses. This is where my ashes will also be placed and where I now make my new Meditation on Death.

CHAPTER 39

ALONE AGAIN

In time I began to realize that I would no longer have David's magic healing hands to comfort me when needed; that he would not be home to welcome me after a trip with a soft voice of relief: "you're home;" that I would have no one to tell about all the wonders I had seen and adventures I experienced; I would no longer hear his loud: "wow" when out to see the California poppies and be amazed at their spectacular beauty. There are so many times when I would think: "I have to tell David about this" and remember that he is no longer here. I remember some of his "Buddhist" advise, e.g. "Ah so" when things do not go as planned. I try to take his mantra from his alternative health practice: "listen to your body" and stay healthy. I have reminders of him by some of his art work such as the paper-sculptured dog "Katrinka" that guards the apartment; by the sculpture of his logo, a falcon with a fish still hanging from its claws over his old computer desk; by the pastel he did of my Teddy bears sitting in the rocking chair; of one of his early-days acrylic paintings of an abstract Tree of Jesse (although he would never say what the painting meant to him or if it had that name—"what does it mean to you?")

I'm still finding some of his favorite brown rice in the fridge and I've learned to get my chocolate fix from a jar of chocolate chips he handily used to keep them there. He put them in the lid and ate them one by one, whereas I pour a handful into my fist and eat them all at once. I can't enumerate all that I have learned from David, but little bits of his wisdom and insight come to mind every once in a while. But most of all, I miss his steadfast and unconditional love.

I decided to stay in the same two-bedroom apartment with minor changes in my life style. I had one unfortunate episode in March of 2008 that frightened me. I found out later from Robin about the details. I had an E. Coli blood infection which resulted in a severe electrolyte imbalance and caused me to be unable to remember anything about the episode. My friend, Robin, my massage therapist whom I had called to help me, came and called 911. She accompanied me in a very agitated state in the ambulance to UCSD Hospital where after several tests I was diagnosed and treated. I was there only one day as I recovered easily with fluid and antibiotics. What a wake-up call for me! Subsequently I purchased an ADT medical alert system which would ensure that if I had an accident or were unable to get to a phone for help, then 911 would be notified. I have been in good health, but when one is living alone, it's helpful to know there is a system to come to the rescue if needed.

My last Elderhostel trip to Ireland was in 2008 and was entitled "Walking Irish History," using the Kerry Way and later the Western Way in the Connemara area and visits to other interesting places. In the evening we went over little historical incidents related to the places we had seen. While in Killarney I visited Peggy Lyne and we took a trip on a small boat she hired to visit the ruins of the old monastery on Innisfallen Island, just opposite Ross Castle. It was beautiful, and for Peggy, it proved to be a nostalgic and romantic trip as Innisfallen reminded her that it was where her husband Jackie Lyne took her when he was first dating her.

When near Galway I met Dolores Lyne, Peggy's daughter, at the restaurant in Moycullen. I had given her my itinerary and this was the most convenient place to meet her. As she is an artist she gave me a print of a water color painting of hers. It was a beautiful rendition of the rocky countryside of Connemara. She had brought along extra copies so each member of our group also received one. My fourth and probably my last trip to Ireland made me consider a trip closer to home.

I had been waiting for my younger brother Herb to come out West to visit me, but my hopes were stymied when I received news from his friend Rose, that he had an episode of carotid artery blockage and had to go in for surgery. After that he was even more reluctant to travel. I hadn't seen him or Bob since 2000 when I flew east to visit him and also to attend the Medical Mission Sisters 75ᵗʰ anniversary. So I decided after trying unsuccessfully to find a companion to share the driving, that I would go on my own. Flying did not appeal to me as an option as I had so many places to visit and the "friendly skies" were less friendly than in the past.

It ended up being a twenty-seven day trip from May 9ᵗʰ to June 5ᵗʰ, 2010 so I got to see much of the United States. A couple of touristy spots were on the legendary Route 66 especially in California and Arizona. I now have my own coffee cup hanging on the #1 hook above the counter in the soon-to be opened Iron Hog Café (mostly for motorcyclists) on Route 66. I had my picture taken at the Bagdad Café. In Oatman, Arizona I met two couples in the Olive Oatman Restaurant and Ice Cream Parlor, and started a little small talk. When they mentioned they were from Rhode Island, I took a chance and asked them if they might know Kay Selke, a member of our I. B. Women's Club. One of the women was Kay's sister, and one of the men was her brother!

The weather was great and I carefully followed the Weather Channel to avoid tornados and heavy rainstorms along the way. In Wichita I stopped off to visit Father Colin Boor, my friend from the old days in Maracaibo. He later thanked me by writing: "There aren't many left from our era who can remember the locha (the 0.125 coin) and Lake Maracaibo derricks." The rest of the journey took me across many rivers and states, each welcoming spring into summer with an abundance of beautiful scenes and then headed straight through towering green trees and colorful flowers until I reached Red Bank, New Jersey where my brother Herb lived.

Herb appeared a little apprehensive about his medical condition but able to take me around the grounds of a lovely gated community where he and Rose are renting a condo. As we walked around the lake it was the first time I was able to discuss some events of our early lives. He admitted that our Aunt Marie had "bugged" him a lot about becoming a priest, which he did not appreciate, nor her strict concerns about his dating etc. That may be one reason why he joined the Navy. He also shared with me the fact that Dad had once driven him (when he was in the Navy and had no car) to visit the Jolletts in Madison. He said Dad stayed in the car a few blocks away while he visited them. That confirmed my impression that Dad broke off with his family, and that relations never were mended by either side. A sad situation. However, Herb did add that after his own wife Anna had died, he understood Dad's behavior after Mother's death in an entirely new way.

As my priest brother Bob, was stationed in Quebec, we arranged to meet in the city of Plattsburg in upstate New York. He was able to take the train from Quebec and then we stayed at the Day's Inn for a visit. From Bob I learned that Dad had been fired from the Jersey Central Railroad even before the company had financial problems. According to Bob, Dad's work performance had definitely declined after Mother's death. I had always been told that the loss of his job was due to a bankruptcy, not to poor work performance—another sad situation. Bob is still as conservative as ever, but we managed to have a friendly visit and both of us realized that this was probably our last visit. Herb had also made that same conclusion as we parted. Still, I am happy that I took the trouble to visit both of them. I have appointed Herb as the executor of my estate, with Sarah Ann O'Gara as the successor executor.

From upstate New York I drove through the Adirondacks on Route 9, across the ferry at Crown Point, through rural Vermont, Massachusetts and Connecticut to Chepachet, Rhode Island to visit a college classmate, Peggy Magner Kopeski. She had recently suffered a stroke and was being cared for very lovingly by her husband Mike. She was so happy to see me, but a real fun conversation was difficult as she had some residual speech impairment. Gennie, my former college roommate, had asked me not to visit her in Vermont as her husband was suffering from Alzheimers, and new people and changes upset him. We had a nice conversation on the phone, but I did as she wished. It was a big disappointment for me. I try to call her frequently just to keep her spirits up. On my return from my visits in the Northeast, I stopped for another short visit with Herb in Red Bank.

I stayed with the Medical Mission Sisters in Philadelphia for a couple of days and visited several old friends and met new ones. I accompanied the Sister-nurse to a nursing care facility to visit my special friend, Sr. Mary Louise Lynch, but here too, conversation was limited. I went with an associate to visit other elderly and sick Sisters and was pleased to see how well they are being cared for. They all left me inspired by their realistic approach to their limitations. I walked to the cemetery on the grounds and read every gravestone (so many more than when I had entered as a postulant and only Sister Hildegarde was buried there.) I had known personally many of them and the others' names were familiar to me. So much has changed since my early days in Fox Chase that the whole visit was bitter/sweet.

I stopped by in Sandy Spring, Maryland to visit my friend, Jane Blewett and her husband, Lou Niznik, in their home in a Quaker retirement facility. Both are Medical Mission Associates and find plenty to do in a friendly environment. Both are active in eco-spirituality issues and we had a pleasant visit.

On my return I stayed overnight in Mark Twain's home town of Hannibal, Missouri on the Mississippi River. I joined a short tour of houses and buildings that held memories of one of my favorite authors. In Colorado I drove over the Rocky Mountain Trail Ridge Road at over 12,000 feet. My plan to take a short hike was cancelled as I could hardly walk in the parking lot because of the high altitude. However the scenery was spectacular with 20-foot snow banks on the sides of the road that reminded me of Colorado winters.

Another pleasant day was spent in the Mojave Desert National Preserve where I stayed at the old Nipton Hotel in the Clara Bow Room and visited in Goffs with Dennis Casebier. He told me that the new publisher of the *Desert Magazine Index*, Neal Samson, had just been visiting about a half hour before my arrival. I had only spoken to him on the phone, so was sorry I missed him.

There was much road construction and repairs all across the U.S. even on county roads and turnpikes. One highway sign, among the many, caught my eye. It was a regular official sign that read: "Squeeze to the right." I squeezed. Other signs varied according to the area:

"watch out for tortoises," "eagles on the road," "watch out for burros," "watch out for moose," "deer crossing," and even one that included them all: "watch out for animals." This seemed to be quite necessary as I saw many dead animals on the sides of the roads. The view of about six young antelope running in a meadow near the highway tempted me to join them. The whole trip made the song "America the Beautiful" come alive as I drove from "sea to shining sea" and I was reminded of what a tremendous country we have. I arrived home tired but inspired and happy that I had made a personal contact with my two brothers.

I got an extra boost to write these memoirs when Ofelia Gastelum, the program chairperson for the I.B. Woman's Club asked me to speak at one of the meetings. The scheduled speaker was unable to show up so she asked me to fill in and tell my life story as an introduction to the members of the club. She had contacted me previously about this possibility so I was not completely unprepared. Everyone listened attentively and thought I had an "interesting" life. This comment has helped me continue this story when I wondered if anyone would want to read it. If they don't, so be it. At least it has helped me put my life into some kind of perspective to understand my life better. I have also received encouragement from Karen Kenyon who began a small Writer's Group that now meets regularly in Solana Beach to critique each others' writings and also from memoir professionals, Peggy Lang and Bob Goodman. I write not only for myself, but also to share with many of my friends who only know bits and pieces of my life. God has been very good to me and I am grateful for my many friends. I have to stop writing here or the book will never see the light of day.

EPILOGUE

To return to my question in the Prologue—I have found a partial answer. Now I can say: "Here am I, Little Jumping Joan, when nobody's with me, yet now I'm *not* alone." My lifelong search for a home, family and love is coming to an end. I don't have one family but many—here in Imperial Beach—those whom I meet at the Senior Center, the I. B. Women's Club, the staff and volunteers at the Tijuana Estuary, the staff at my apartment at Mariner's Point and those I meet in casual encounters in the "Classic Beach Town" of Imperial Beach. In San Diego County I am blessed by being a member of the Walkabout group and members of the Solana Beach Writer's Group who have helped me in critiquing this story. I remember fondly those I worked with at the San Diego County Public Health Department and the Area Agency on Aging.

Among the families a little further away are those friendly "desert rats" and friends that I meet in Shoshone, Death Valley, and the Coachella Valley. Another family belongs to my *American Desert Magazine* and *Desert Index* days while living in Desert Hot Springs. Another is made up of the many I have met as a result of my biography of Father Crowley, both in the U.S. and in Ireland. The people I have met in Lone Pine and the Eastern Sierra hold a special place in my heart. I still have some contact with Trinity College friends, a few from my Maracaibo, Venezuela days, those I met at Dayton when I taught "Health for Missionaries," the Diaspora of Boulder,

Colorado and the San Luis Valley. The Medical Mission Sisters and former members are also part of my "extended family" and I think of them often. I find a special love for all my "Sisters at Heart" in the Motherless Daughters group who have helped me in so many ways to learn how to grieve.

The friends and family I have may not always be near, but they are in my heart and give me comfort. My favorite prayer and most frequent is: "Thank you, Lord" for all you have given me and bless all my "families."

The days ahead may be long or short, but that is in God's hands. I know He has cared for me through many ups and downs and will continue to do so.

As I used to write on the *Desert Padre* books that I signed, I do so here: "Enjoy!"

For information about Joan Brook's book, *Desert Padre*, contact Community Printing and Publishing, 187 West Line St., Bishop, California 93514 (760-873-3049)